The
small
wild goose
pagoda

~

Also by Irwin Allan Sealy:

Red: An Alphabet (2006)
The Brainfever Bird: An Illusion (2003)
The Everest Hotel: A Calendar (1998)
From Yukon to Yucatan: A Western Journey (1994)
Hero: A Fable (1991)
The Trotter-Nama: A Chronicle (1988)

The small wild goose pagoda

{an almanack}

IRWIN ALLAN SEALY

ALEPH

ALEPH

ALEPH BOOK COMPANY
An independent publishing firm
promoted by *Rupa Publications India*

First published in India in 2014 by
Aleph Book Company
7/16 Ansari Road, Daryaganj
New Delhi 110002

Copyright © Irwin Allan Sealy 2014
Illustrations from the Author's China sketchbook

All rights reserved.

No part of this publication may be reproduced,
transmitted, or stored in a retrieval system, in
any form or by any means, without permission
in writing from Aleph Book Company.

ISBN: 978-93-83064-48-9

1 3 5 7 9 10 8 6 4 2

Printed and bound in India by Replika Press Pvt. Ltd.

This book is sold subject to the condition that it
shall not, by way of trade or otherwise, be lent,
resold, hired out, or otherwise circulated without
the publisher's prior consent in any form of
binding or cover other than that in which it is
published.

*To
the 433 square yards*

When the house is built, Death comes.
~Turkish proverb

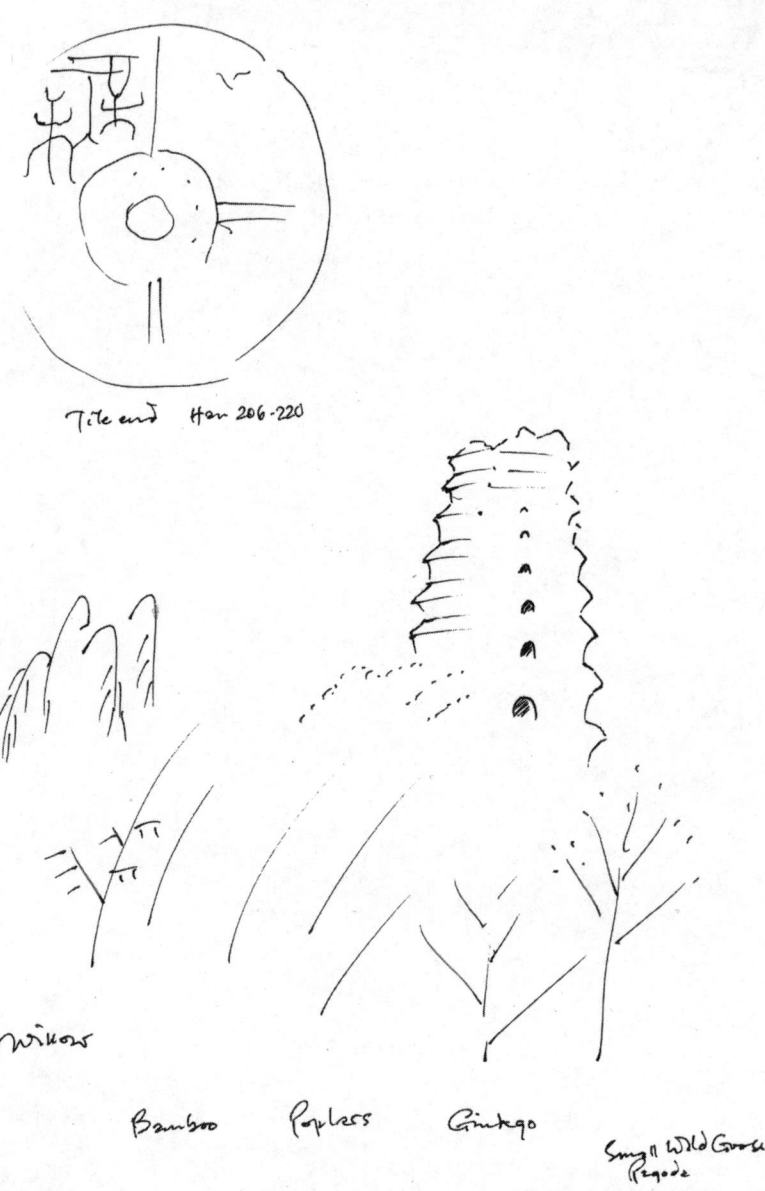

Tile end   Han 206-220

willow

Bamboo   Poplars   Ginkgo

Small Wild Goose Pagoda
rainy afternoon

contents

March / 12
April / 31
May / 57
June / 76
July / 95
August / 108
September / 127
October / 158
November / 173
December / 188
January / 203
February / 211
March / 223
April / 232
May / 240
June / 252
July / 270

A little past midnight a man comes to the gate of the house hidden by trees and, finding it locked, glances each way, gets a grip on the top of the boundary wall, and hauls himself up in the shadows of the sodium streetlight. His right foot scrabbles on the flat of the wall, finds no hold and pushes in hard, so there's a moment when he's hanging out into nothing over the storm-water drain. A stick figure, all bent arms and legs. It's done in two or three seconds. This spider, now balanced on the top of the wall.

Now not there.

He lands in a flower bed, on something stalky, his cheek brushed by the cobweb he fell through, a hand patting his back so he turns sharply into the angle of the wall, just a frond, then stumbles backward through a thorn bush out onto grass.

The house is in darkness. He crosses the lawn and climbs three steps up into the verandah. Cautiously tries the mesh door. It opens, sticking a little. Unbolted means they're away. Feels for the padlock and yes it's there, heavy, bevel-edged, squarish in the hand, brass, not new, not old. Draws out the crowbar that hangs down the inside of his jeans leg, a sword he sometimes thinks, sticks the business end in behind the hasp, and begins to force. The hasp buckles but doesn't give. He wastes no more time on it. Puts down the crowbar and takes out the small tools of his trade. Time he has. In twenty minutes the lock is laid open, its tines scattered on the floor. He lifts the bent staple and slides back the bolt. Pushes open the door. Pulls it to behind him.

In.

Stands a moment while his eyes adjust. Always this first survey in the dark, his gaze sweeping a notional horizon. The terrain. Never less than knowable, so open to violation he sometimes walks down the street looking at women and thinking: *my, you're a nice house.*

It starts with a gate, though you could say it started with a wall.
First Habilis showed me how you raise a wall, then he taught me how to lay a beam. Peace, not security, was what I was after: that, and a certain effect. Traffic on the road outside had increased, and a high sheer face would, I felt, throw street noise back. And, I wanted a gateway rather than a gate.

Together we raised the old gateposts to above head height. Next he sent me to an iron merchant who makes beam skeletons; meanwhile he built a scaffolding of eucalyptus poles and planks to take the concrete pour. I returned with the gate's beam backbone, a hunched dinosaur skeleton flagged and swinging thirteen-foot-long on the roof rack of the old Fiat, and in two weeks we had turned the gate into an entranceway. Bricked into a parapet, plastered and painted white, the blank length of the lintel was relieved with a row of small square navy blue tiles. With its crisp white line below and a hat of white bougainvillea above, the hanging beam promised nothing less than a modernist mews within. Corbusier looking on and smiling.

After that one thing led to another. The iron gate was raised to close the gap under the new beam: panels were welded along its top edge and the old upright bars of it clad in sheet iron. The new panels were an opportunity. We filled them with a wrought iron frieze depicting the six seasons of Sanskrit poetry: the same stylized tree in bud, in new leaf, and in full leaf on the left panel; and on the right in fruit-time, in leaf fall, and at first frost. A single iron leaf falls from the tree in autumn; in winter that leaf beneath the bare tree, a breve.

It's an ancient motif in modern dress, and so is the pagoda beyond.

The idea for the pagoda came from a recent journey but its origin lay in some childhood afternoon spent poring over a willow pattern plate. Was that my first sight of China, that cold English fantasy in blue and white? Had I just asked my mother why we called the crockery we ate off *china*? Or did the two words come together in my mind as I hung over the strange foreign scene? It was, but how was I to know, the best-known pattern of its time, product of a vogue for things Chinese that seized Europe in the eighteenth century. And the tragic story it told could hardly fail to make an impression on a child.

The willow pattern shows a mandarin's lakeside house and garden with three figures crossing a bridge. According to legend the two figures in front are young lovers caught eloping; the one coming behind, brandishing what appears to be a whip, is the enraged father who drives them into the little pavilion on the other side and sets fire to it. A majestic tree of heaven towers over the ornate pillars and pagoda roof of the rich man's house. In the sky above, appear two turtle doves facing each other, the released souls of the lovers billing while the willow of the pattern weeps gently below on the bank of the lake, leaning over the bridge to caress the ill-fated pair in life. Some image like this would have been at the heart of my very notion *pagoda*.

Our pagoda is at the end of the old drive, on the former portico. Stand back from the gate of the seasons and you can see it from the main road. It rises from the hidden and long-absorbed portico, its outline visible above the gate beam through the weeping branches of a rosewood tree. The eye is led up a series of crossbeams (the hanging gate beam, the beam over the sunporch beyond, and a further beam on the portico itself) as up a giant flight of white steps to the open deck of the pagoda's uppermost storey where a glass chimney stands over the skywell. Hints and references apart—the skywell is one—it's not a conventional pagoda. Its lines are modern. It tops the rosewood tree and the taffrail on the study roof, and rising up through a pair of slim black pillars (echoing the pillars on the mandarin's house) ends in a silver arch, taut and humming, like a kite against the sky.

It's not, as I say, a traditional pagoda, with scalloped eaves and diminishing storeys. But it has, in its climax, and in its functionless presence, a severe and alluring beauty, and it does have an odd number of floors, three. Functionless, that is, in its top floor, since the two floors below are a kitchen at the ground level and a study midway. The arch crowns the open deck of the third floor, a sheet of tensile aluminium fitted to an iron frame whose half-moon curve gives the pagoda its air of benign finality. The two black pillars, enamelled iron—in the age of the willow pattern they would have been of granite—anchor the arch in front, and two squared-off brick pillars secure it behind. It has to be well trussed or like the kite it is it could fly away in a gale. A brick lattice links the two rear pillars and makes a lace backdrop to the glass chimney.

The glass chimney stands at the centre of the pagoda's top floor, and in a way at the very heart of the pagoda itself. This miniature tower does have a function: its four walls shield the skywell of the study below from monsoon spray. Centred in the whole (its axis the wind chime suspended above it) a kind of crystal inner pagoda, its square is set, like the skywell, to point forward, and by a fortunate chance you see the transparent geometry of that prow as you step onto the brick path from the lesser gate.

Because of course we now needed a new gate to enter by. The old one had turned gateway (and garage to the ancient Fiat) and that entailed a wicket alongside. The wicket is a smaller, matching gateway with a lesser and lower beam and its own set of navy blue tiles (just two) above a gate whose bars echo the old, but without the iron cladding and the decorative panel.

The thief came in over the wall, that much was plain from the scuff marks on the whitewash where his foot looked for purchase. He was not a child or he might have been tempted to try the gap between the smaller gate and its beam. This wicket gate has an outer bolt that slides home into a hole in the old gatepost, but it's never locked on the outside. Behind the lock-plate are a second bolt and bolthole, and it's on the inner clasp that old Dhani hangs a padlock when required, so the world is not notified that we're away. To reach in through the bars and turn the key in a lock hung backwards must have tried the patience of an old man, but he's got the hang of it now.

The thief guessed all the same, and perhaps tested the lock old Dhani hung there, before climbing the wall.

Old Dhani

Every morning a riderless bicycle emerges from a gate three houses along from us, turns onto the main road, and slowly makes its way along the dusty verge till it reaches the pollard willow at the gate of the six seasons. There its owner becomes visible. He's a bent man, so doubled up his head travels at saddle height, and he must crane his neck to look ahead.

Old Dhani, leaning on his Atlas. The bike we renovated together, changing the decrepit saddle, the pedal cleats worn down to smooth black wafers, the carrier, the creaky stand, the tyres and tubes, the grips, until nothing was left of the old bike except the idea of it. He didn't want the frame painted, though we had a painter on hand in Habilis, and in fact painting in progress from a tin of black paint. Perhaps he liked the look of the original decals that still read—if Dhani could read, if Habilis could read—*ATLAS*.

The lettering, in scrappy red on a yellow ground, simply a kind of decoration. Writing.

Dhani is his Atlas. He looks odd, a little lost, without it. There are those who remember him riding it—I can, if I try—but nowadays he pushes, half leaning, half steering, wobbling a little, slowing down at times without actually stopping for a breather, unless nobody's looking. The truth is he dodders, and I'm told he fell the other day, but old words like *steadfast* belong with old Dhani. Wheeling his bike, and only ever wheeling it, he overturns the wisdom that bikes are for riding. (There are valid maps of the world that show the South Pole at the top.) Bent double, his head dipping sometimes below the level of the crossbar, so the high point in him is not his red headscarf but a spur on his vertebral arch, once the column of an upright man, he balances the world.

He shambles in, pulls the bike onto its stand and turns to latch the gate of a house he's come to every working day for thirty years. The bolting should be a simple matter, but the gate has drooped so the bolt is now a fraction lower than the hole in the old gatepost. Before going away I greased the bolthole, but the bolt still takes a little persuasion.

He relocks the padlock on the clasp and works the bolt in, fanning the hasp. He hasn't forgotten how years ago his bike, this same bike, was snatched at this very gate. Something alerted him back then: he shouted, others gave chase, and the thief was caught and cuffed about a bit, he says. So he takes no chances.

He lifts the catch on the carrier and draws out the heavier of two khurpis, leaving the slender poke weeder for another day, and turns and walks up the brick path that Habilis and I laid ten years ago. Brushing against the privet at the harp seat, mumbling a harmless curse at my choice of that narrow neck for a thorny shrub, he fetches out his broom and wicker basket from behind the garage door. Back on the path, he straightens up and stares at the house.

The front door is standing open.

It shouldn't be. We're away.

There's something wrong. He edges up the stairs, steps over the scattered tines of the padlock: *someone has broken in!*

He creeps into the house, open-mouthed, going as far as the bedroom door. The wardrobes have been emptied, there's stuff lying all over the floor.

26th January

Robinson Bay. Once more I hear the oystercatchers' cry, inhale the groiny stink of the sea. Ten years on, I sleep in the bed with the oak headboard, the one Maeve was born in, use the old Kelvinator fridge, and the concrete-floor bathroom. Turn driftwood logs in the fireplace, pick horse mushrooms in the paddocks under the yellow hills. Cross the wooden bridge over the Buxton with its bulrushes and froth of algae on brown water, and climb the white limestone knoll beyond the creek to visit the cabin I once coveted. It's gone! The Council have removed it, and its dunny, that sentrybox of a loo that stood outdoors backed up against a windbreak of old macrocarpa pines like a condemned man looking out to sea one last time.

This late evening we're expecting another sight on the horizon, towards Shag Rock. Maeve sees it first, pointing to a lump of ice in the pink haze. A full moon rising. We watch it shake off the weight of the cold Pacific. The hillock around us has returned to wilderness, the steep drive is overgrown with chest-high grass. Apples redden in the jungly overhang, lupins and wild geraniums throng the native bush. The chalk path is bordered with white sprays of fennel and the wheat grass of summer that waves gold and welcoming from the treacherous edge of the gully.

30th

On the last night but one we walk at midnight to Tweedy's corner. Robinson

Bay is asleep. The moon is a diminished thing, with a slice taken off the wrong side (down here), but its glittering gangway lumens the night. A dark patch of sky overhead poised like a candle snuffer. Some force in abeyance is waiting to overwhelm the one streetlight on Moody Street. The bay lies spread out between the hills and the headland, lit by the sad black light of the waning moon. The rumoured ocean is a pond. Halfhearted breakers roll in and crash on a wide beach that glows like a lighthouse every time a wave slops over wet sand. We walk a little way along the road—across the white letters of the word BRIDGE elongated for the motorist at the wheel—to put a tree between us and the streetlight, and the sky comes up luminous again. Our moon shadows lie across the road, faint as the lettering that warns of the one-lane bridge ahead.

31st

Went twice into the sea today, once before Maeve awoke, the morning so warm and still. The last can of fish for dinner. Our week's rations have lasted well, filled out with damper and sea lettuce and green-lip mussels. Tomorrow the trek out, seven kilometres with lightened packs.

We've lit fires every night, and sat well back. Supper is the last two fruit mince pies with coffee. After Maeve goes to bed, I read at the fireplace where she read out aloud nightly thirty years ago. At bedtime I place the old fireguard round the embers, respecting the fears she instilled in me in this land of wooden houses. (Today a curl of cloud over the hills had her imagining a bush fire.) I try to imagine a house built of wood in our valley; it would perish in three monsoons, eaten by mould and white ants.

1st February

A strange layer of cloud out to sea at sunrise, squatting there like a shelf of Antarctic ice. Later it proves a sea fog that moves inland and shelters us from the sun as we walk. Still later we learn the fog cost two lives.

On one of these nights, in the other hemisphere, the thief.

Dhani takes the break in personally. It's not as if he was deputed watchman, like Habilis the time before. As mali, his job was to go on gardening as usual; the only addition to his duties was to come by at nightfall and turn on the verandah light and put the lock on the gate. But he feels compromised all the same.

'Never once in all these years,' he mutters over and over again when I get back.

Not that the thief got much. An old 35 mm camera, Terry's Russian binoculars, some money. He spent the night fossicking in the bedrooms, the old study, the pantry. The missing bottle of Scotch I don't mind, but I resent his finger in the jar of almonds that I find open. I blanch the almonds but still can't bring myself to eat them. And we lose our garbage collection. Garbage collectors are the first to know when you're away and I suspect there's a network of informers. I terminate the service and take to walking the rubbish down to the bin by Police Lines after dinner.

'Did you inform the police?' my father asks, a retired cop.

'No.'

'Good.'

Dad knows I wouldn't; he's just checking, long distance. Old cop habit.

The 433 square yards

We live in a small brick house in Dehradun, in the foothills of the Himalayas. One and a half bedrooms, two and a half gardens, front, back, and side (three if you count a piece of public land outside the front boundary, fenced in and planted with trees), an old Fiat, an internet link with the world, and a terrace roof for walking on under the sky.

Thirty paces down the length of the roof, roughly a tennis court up there. The house is rectangular, the plot of land a larger rectangle that measures off at something under four thousand square feet. We have 433 square yards of India.

Here is the natural and social history of that plot.

The 433 square yards are bound ('and abutted,' says the deed) to the north by two plots with houses, all but ghost houses, the owners living elsewhere, so there are two absent neighbours, one on either side of a midpoint in our back boundary wall. With the Himalayas floating above them in the distance they could be our Tibet and Afghanistan. As if to complete the political map, the remaining boundaries east and west, separate us from our Bangladesh and Pakistan, with corresponding cordialities. The southern boundary faces the street, our Indian Ocean, whose tarmac widens at this point to accommodate an island, call it Sri Lanka, that conducts traffic along a lesser road heading south towards Antarctica. *Here be seamonsters*, an old map might caution; mostly, here be collisions that bring the residents of the Threenecks to their gates.

Along the chief road a cavalcade races past our gate once a year on Uttarakhand Day, when the Lady Chief of Police escorts the Lady Governor of the state to the nearby Police Lines to unfurl the national flag. The cavalcade runs an old race, for the road, Racecourse Road, an oval some two kilometres around, actually follows the course of a former racecourse, running where the horses ran. On a moonless night you can hear the thunder of hooves, and when the Chief Minister's helicopter hovers over the unpaved Police Lines helipad you can taste the dust they once raised.

Racecourse, the suburb, is known for its wide verges. Our verge, some thirty feet from road to boundary wall—the wall the thief came over—serves with its trees as a greenbelt between us and the present race. The three-way junction, our Threenecks, can be noisy twice a day, but it ensures that a space two plots wide will remain forever free across the street from us. During the coldest months the winter sun tracks across our southern prospect unobstructed from sunrise to sunset, the sky there insured in perpetuity.

House plots with us are of two kinds, lion-mouthed (shermukhi) and cow-mouthed (gaumukhi). Cow-mouthed plots, narrow in front and widening as you go back, are preferred for security purposes (assuming your rear is covered). Ours is lion-mouthed, wider in front. The burglar had a wider range of options, though he reasonably took a handhold right beside the wicket gate. The stormwater drain that forms a kind of moat outside is bridged for access there. Jags of broken glass—blue, green, brown, clear—now top the wall where he came over and there's a Natal plum below now too, with vicious thorns, but lightning doesn't strike in the same place twice. There's nothing to say he won't try a little further along next time, say where the thornless coffee tree is.

'And stop for a cappuccino,' Filo puts in, our daughter.

So, really, lion lies down with cow in this matter of security.

It's a shoebox of a house, with add-ons. The garden makes amends for the box, and over the years Habilis and I have chipped away at the architect's pure rectangle. The front verandah was a Mayan altar served on one side by a steep set of blocky steps rising directly off the drive. When the drive was abolished and the garage shifted to the front gate, a brick walk from the new wicket gate scuttled the Mayan steps, skirted a little lawn, and came to a halt at a greystone sunporch fronting the old portico. Both lawn and sunporch are legacies of the old drive. To reach the verandah you now mount a flight of wide low steps that give onto the front lawn and hardly notice the brick walk. If you came in over the wall, you might take this for a welcome and proceed regally up them. But then landscape and security are often at loggerheads, and thieves offer fresh perspectives on architecture nightly. The fact is a man who wants to get in gets in.

The taming of the 433 square yards, long before Habilis arrived on the scene, was the work of Old Dhani, working under my mother. There's a photo of them together in the garden, my mother in her dressing gown, Dhani spry in a tight sweater; neither has a single grey hair. Twenty-five years on, Dhani looks his age, whatever that is. He's no help there. He can count, but in his book seventy or eighty is splitting hairs: you get old, bas. I've asked my father (though it was my mother's garden that Dhani and I turned around; she would have been his paymistress) and he can't tell either. Dhani is probably the younger man there but not by much. He may have worked for my parents at the previous house too, a house they rented one gate along from here, so it's over thirty years he's served this family. That other garden is now derelict since the owner sold to an investor who's let it all run down. Our present house was built from that secure base, with the intervening plot (now Pak) used to store materials: foundation stones were offloaded there, huge river boulders gathered from the mountain wash; bricks were stacked and gravel dumped, and lengths of iron roof-rod cut and fabricated on that ground. When this house was ready my parents moved straight in and Dhani started from scratch here on soil unturned for a hundred years or more.

March

2 March
'Mali stopped coming?' a young man called over the fence to me yesterday, a mali himself and eager to step into Dhani's shoes. An easterner too, who says 'goeth' for goes. He was watering the neighbours' lawn. 'Haven't seen him lately.'

Everybody knows Dhani's past it; he should be hanging up his khurpi now, going home to die.

'Maliji? He was here a minute ago,' I called back lightly. 'Up that mango tree.'

'*Really!*'

'Really.'

It's years since Dhani climbed a tree but I wasn't going to stand for poaching.

Dhani's caste marks him as an immigrant, and when he speaks of his country, his *des*, it is with the accent of a foreigner. A foreigner in the old sense, from a far district, another part of the cowbelt. He is an easterner come to stay, like so many of his kind who left a village where there was family but no work. Gardeners are typically from those parts (it's professionally important that they keep the accent) and a new generation of malis still takes the road Dhani took forty years ago.

Yesterday I overpaid him, forgetting he'd taken an advance. He didn't mind, and I remembered too late. (It was a day of shelling out anyway: a car mechanic, a computer engineer.) Dhani's wage mounts twice yearly to keep up with inflation, up a hundred rupees every January and June. In a class society overpayment is notional anyway. How much do I owe this man who lives in a garage? How much does he owe me? So what's 500 rupees?

To get home, though there's nothing for him there now, he would have to take a train to Lucknow, fare 290 rupees unreserved second class (out of the 2,000 rupees I hand over each month for an hour-and-a-half's work every morning five days a week), then a bus to Faizabad, then a three-wheel tempo to his village, then a short walk to the house, tile-roof, he assured me once, where he was born. He grew up in a large family of share-croppers growing potatoes and rice, sold from the field, a plot of two bighas, some four times the size of this compound of ours, tiny for farming. So the journey he made as a young man, as he may have guessed when making it, was for good.

'This was all jungle when I first came here,' he waves an almost feminine hand. The fingers are slender and muddied, the undernails black. 'In those days ten rupees could fill your stomach.'

I detect a veiled allusion to the overpayment, to inflation, to seniority, to long service, and nod noncommittally.

A scrolled photograph long as an arm and narrow as a hand has travelled back from New Zealand with me. It was left in Maeve's Christchurch house by a tenant doing a thesis on a well-known local business whose life had neatly spanned the twentieth century. The photo shows the entire Essex Bakery establishment in the late 1930s or early forties, assembled on the sidewalk outside the factory, some fifty or sixty people, with the owners seated in the middle, the office staff on either side, and the other workers shading off by rank to the drudges at the ends. Horse-drawn delivery carriages and one or two shiny new motor vans are parked alongside, with grooms and drivers in attendance. On the ground sit delivery boys in shorts, smirking. The company was a corner bakery made good, and the trophies—*Best Risen Loaf in Canterbury*, say—are on a table at the centre. I have spent enough hours with this photograph to know every individual in it down to the soles of his shoes. The clothes are diagnostic: once you learn their language every class and station of life in the dominion is immediately apparent, from the waistcoated fob-watched toffs in the middle, through managerial and then clerical types to workers at the various stages of the loaf. At the far left is a duff fellow in a fuzzy serge coat and shapeless pants creeping as far from the camera as he possibly can but regarding it too with sovereign contempt. I started when I first saw him. For there at the edge of the known world was Dhani! Bearded, true, after the manner of his class and race and time but wearing a familiar look of fogged amusement at the fuss. A groundsman, a cottager, someone who wouldn't tug the forelock but might still tip his hat at the boss.

'*All* jungle,' groundsman Dhani waves a conjuring hand.

I've heard the claim before. Dhani would have made it when I first met him thirty years ago and we were planting out the front lawn. In those days the boundary wall was so low you could watch people go by on the raised road. (The old level still shows as a plaster ridge in the wall Habilis raised.) You'd have seen the blur of horses' hooves if they were still running, but back then they were already thirty years dead.

I look out at the old racecourse, cleared and cleared again in the past century and know what Dhani saw when he first came here was bush, not virgin forest. Forested for aeons with a tall straight hardwood—the sal or *Shorea robusta*, in cream spring blossom as I write—this valley at the foot of the Himalayas was farmed in patches across the centuries when raiders from other parts permitted. In 1813 the English arrived to stake their claim; by the end of a siege at whose fag end Gurkha women were rolling great rocks down at them from a redoubt near here, they had won a loyal ally and a fertile valley. With the British peace a colonial town sprang up alongside the old trading centre and this end of the outskirts became a racecourse, once the most picturesque of the Raj. In its heyday, the 1890s, jockeys crowding the rail would have found no relief in the gradient at our point on the course, the bottom end, but at the top, a mile to the north, on the downhill home stretch, their parti-coloured silks would have looked fine bobbing against a background of snow-capped Himalaya.

It didn't last. By the forties, the decade before Independence, everybody would have been too jittery to think of racing, and this sparsely wooded tract at the edge of town where leopards prowled and jackals slunk had returned to scrub. Once, during the War, American GIs got it going and raced mules and chariots and dhobi's donkeys, but that was a blip. After Partition it was cleared and allotted to refugees, Sikhs and Hindus, who'd lost land in Pakistan; a generation later, overgrown again, it was re-cleared and sold on in plots to buyers like ourselves. One last time we cleared it of its thickets of lantana and hemp and the weed called 'shameless'.

Our lion-mouth was bought with foreign money, following an emigration bid to Australia that lasted one year. When my parents returned to India, they had to start afresh. Our furniture of many years had been dispersed before they left, my mother's piano going to a local school, so the new sofa set was a wicker one. (It's still in place.) We pooled our money—my sister, who stayed on to become an Australian, was never without a second job; I found one in a Sydney shoe factory, cleaning machines already old—and bought the land. These 433 square yards. The land registered, my father began to build, and the next year they moved into a house where the ironwork had not got beyond a coat of primer. For a long time I took this red oxide of the door and window frames, and the gate as well, to be their chosen colour. I had come back with a building works of my own, a first novel half-written, to a house still new, before making my way to the city in the plains where it was set, Lucknow. (I'd gone to boarding school there for seven years, next door to Dhani's village.) On my first visit to the new house that summer I broke the ground in the front yard with a pickaxe; Dhani came behind me, beating down the sod, planting out tufts of spiky grass that joined up in one monsoon to form the lawn of today. He would have gossiped about my intervention.

It was a different, and young, garden. My mother preferred flowers, annuals and flowering shrubs. She had plans to open a little kindergarten in the house, but was overtaken by a vicious form of arthritis called lupus. Four years later she was dead, from an attempted cure. She was a year older than I am now. Dhani was shaken; he still mentions her.

'This rose,' he will say, or 'that lemon tree, is from her time.'

I don't know when 'my time' began. From Dhani's perspective it was when I began to pay him. As for when I began to think of this valley as my home, that's a harder question. I had spent the decade of my twenties abroad; a lucky scholarship had come my way. In my early thirties Maeve and I were in Lucknow, and then when the house fell vacant we moved in. It has been home these twenty years, but as for the valley, the thought of a place in the world that was mine, a city to which I belonged and gave myself so it returned the favour, that came slowly.

All through my childhood home was further east—we were as eastern as Dhani—in the succession of small towns of my father's postings as an officer of the Uttar Pradesh police. The houses we occupied in these places (Allahabad, Hamirpur, Fatehpur, Fatehgarh, Varanasi, Jhansi, Mirzapur, Bareilly, Moradabad, Saharanpur, Muzaffarnagar, showing a westward drift, as if Dehradun, the last posting, on the very edge of Punjab, were fated) came with the job, often with large compounds that a boy could lose himself in, but they were left behind every two years when my father was transferred. We got accustomed to moving on; for a child there was excitement in the actual move, and perhaps even my long-suffering mother would have found some pleasure in the novelty of yet another house. I remember the ritual of packing, over which my father presided, every tumbler and piece of china, every willow pattern plate, wrapped in layers of newspaper, the cups with a crumpled wad in the hollow and a special twist at the handle, the crates then lined with straw and cardboard dunnage; the steel trunks with linen and glass ornaments interleaved; the packing case of *Reader's Digest* back numbers strip banded; the furniture sewn up in gunny sacking; lamps and gramophone and valve radio swaddled like babies. And always, from small town to small town, my mother's piano on its squeaky castors, grumbling as it was heaved onto the back of a Tata truck whose brow wore, like some sinister caste mark, the invariable legend, till my mother would have come to dread the very words: *PUBLIC CARRIER*.

So she would have taken this house to heart. I imagine her bolting the front door at night and repeating in astonishment, '*my house! my door!*' after a lifetime of furnishing strange houses, of taking up curtain hems, only to let them back down two years later. This last unpacking on the 433, of chattels simply brought over from the rented house next door, must have been sweet. She never travelled from the house again. 'Feet first!' I imagine her saying. She was laid out in the living room and her coffin rested briefly, I'm told, on the dining table. After her death my father returned to Australia, remarried and moved to England.

The house had one long empty spell when Dhani camped in the chief room (turning it into a garage), the one my mother intended for her schoolroom, the room the thief would have stepped into when he swung open the front door. All the other rooms open off it. (Once during a power cut I placed a candle on the dining table and found its rays penetrated every room in the house: spare bedroom, spare bathroom—for the 'students'—kitchen, store, master bedroom.) Small, single-storeyed, just over a thousand square feet, the house is modest by Racecourse standards. Cramped, my mother told me I declared on first inspection, and over the few years of her pleasure in it she twice reminded me of this careless judgment.

It *is* a small house, and Habilis and I have expanded its simple rectangle, pushing out windows, adding covered bays. The portico itself was an afterthought, an early one, added by my father during construction: it appears on the blueprint, although its square footage does not seem to be included in the stated covered area, perhaps because it had no walls. Some time after we moved in I felt its concrete roof was wasted on a car. The Fiat came to be parked further and further out, as first a kitchen and then an adjoining mesh room took its place. It was the start, but I didn't know it, of the pagoda.

The garden occupies three times the space of the house on the 433. It is the equal of the house, and seems to understand its worth; with its distinctive rooms under the sky it has always held its own against the interior. The prize goes to neither: the prize is the roof. *All night the cisterns whisper in the roof,* goes Geoffrey Hill's haunting line. It's not that kind of roof: there's no *in*. There are water tanks up there, but they're *on* the roof, a slab roof, a flat concrete terrace. That terrace is our lungs, even (counting the cloister) our heart. Screened, yet open to the sky, it's a refuge where you walk among the treetops morning and night, or sit and watch the progress of the clouds, the egrets, and the wheeling stars.

The opera box

A few years ago, a second storey came up to the west, on the Pakistan side. Next we knew, there was a rental apartment whose balcony hung right on the boundary: a succession of tenants looked straight into our yard. The washing line on that balcony projected into our space and rained clothes and pegs. I made an attempt at privacy by building a little room on our portico directly under the offending balcony. The rain room, as such rooftop rooms are called in these parts, had a high arched roof intended as a blind. It proved an imperfect one; it screened you if you stood directly alongside it, but left the ends of the roof terrace exposed, and it let in the rain. It did nothing about the rain of lost properties either. These littered the iron staircase leading up to the rain room. One family shed soiled nappies on our side of the wall. We began to call that space 'Away.' The current tenant had taken to peeing down one of our tall mast trees on the boundary on nights that he was up late, a patter in the small hours that I was hard put to identify. He may have been emptying a hot-water bottle. I growled at him one night from the shadows and that particular rain stopped.

Pegs, even piss, I can take; it was the loss of privacy that irked. I wasn't even sure of its legality. No windows on boundaries: that law of the land is generally obeyed, the way driving happens mostly on the left. But a balcony? This one caused heartburn every time you climbed the stairway to the roof. Our roof stair hangs on the eastern side of the house, the Bangla side; one year Habilis screened that whole side of the roof from end to end, with a doorway in the middle. Now every time you stepped through that curtain of brick lace, there in the west hung the offending balcony, like a box at the opera. Our roof had been a refuge; now it was a stage. We were the spectacle.

Natural history
Land is no plot, simply earth. Stand on this ground and ponder its past and you sort by glacial degrees through shales and upheaved Gondwana seabed to the stony soil Dhani and I still work. The first range of the Himalayas looms to the north; two rivers, the Ganga and the Jamuna, pierce that range to east and west of us, as well as a dozen lesser streams with their wash of river sand and boulders. The entire valley, lying crosswise between the two rivers, drains south, with a watershed down the middle, and a water table that favours those who live up against the southern hills. (Here, in Racecourse you must bore a long way down for water; a few kilometres to the

south you have only to scratch the surface.) It's limey soil. Water in this valley leaves a trace of white scale where it dries. Fortunes were made mining and slaking limestone until a court order in the seventies put an end to the quarrying that had begun to disfigure the hillsides. Today the limekilns are cold little Martello towers with a past; in another country they would be snapped up and gentrified. They dot a poor district called simply Limekiln, Habilis's current home, where not long ago the air was thick with smoke and dust. It's all geology, history simply a trick of light.

So these 433 square yards are a legal figment. The racecourse is too, its civil society a kind of pretence. On any given day a sparrow hawk can swoop down on a garden lizard, tear it to pieces, and eat it down to its tail in a minute. Civet cats bivouac under our outdoor staircase, among my sacks of harvested coir, and a stray tom camps on the verandah. Last autumn a rogue monkey looked in, just scouting. The present population of the 433 is partly a matter of scale: life-and-death battles rage just out of sight, bees clump and vanish, algae infiltrate the garden hose. Snail shells, spent housing, wash up on the lawn in the monsoon. Waves of white ants sweep under the house, wasps build in the cooler, and every leaf hides a beetle or feeds a worm. Count fruit flies, and your census is committed to microbes. The soil at racecourses, Maeve tells me, teems with tetanus organisms for centuries after the horses are gone to the knacker's yard.

There may have been a farmer's straw brake on this patch in its rice paddy past (before the hundred-and-fifty-year-old racecourse, whose stables survive as a human warren halfway up the oval and behind the ring of middle-class houses), but among householders residing in engineered dwellings our predecessor was likely a tailorbird. Noisiest bird in the garden (prime target of that medieval pope who had the songbirds silenced because they disturbed his siesta) he stakes a relentless claim. A pert olive green and white bird, he builds in broad-leafed shrubs, such as this yellow hibiscus; his nest is a smock sewn up one side with any available thread, say the green nylon binding twine off a cement sack. He calls with the half-second monotony of a silicon chip and his encyclicals can go for an hour without stopping; the needle in his tail—idle in stitchery—a metronome marking time.

Worked into the call is the percussion of a beak-click more fearsome than a heretic's tooth-grinding. It would have echoed right around the papal garden, and besides his rufous pontiff's cap is clear provocation. He is barely two inches tall.

The brush cleared, his house swept away, the 433 lay bare for human habitation.

The album of our house-build starts with a photo of yellow winter grass. Actually it's the plot next door, with cattle grazing on it and a small boy with a stick. The boy is half naked, in the way of the rural poor, a reminder that Racecourse was still at the edge of town. The photograph was the first of several rolls we meant to take; that plan, as much as the album, reveals our excitement at the build, amounting to awe that the ones building should be ourselves. All through my childhood, only the rich built: businessmen mostly, and doctors and lawyers. We would watch their mansions come up with a kind of innocent pleasure, as at a circus or sports ground, applauding the athlete or acrobat for a feat well beyond our talents.

18 March
Dhani returns from the spring holiday to sweep up leaves.

The wrought iron tree on the gate sheds a single leaf. Not so the bauhinia, whose leaves threaten to choke the stormwater drain. Their deeply cloven form gives the tree its common name, 'camel-hoof'. Its orchid-like flower makes it our most elegant tree, even counting the coral, but Mohan the welder, marvelling at the pattern falling into place under his torch, knew he'd gone one better.

'It'll be the rage in gates!'

The standard Racecourse gate is still a cake stand. Patiala Marzipan is among its kinder names, and its signature, under a row of tin fleurs-de-lys, is a sewing machine flywheel you turn to lift the latch.

The last leaf still hissing under a stream of water from the two-litre cola bottle, my drawings gone black from handling, Habilis and I loaded the panels onto the luggage rack of the Fiat and drove them slowly home.

The frieze gave me a name for the house: *Ritusamhara,* the title of Kalidasa's poem of the seasons. I thought to have it carved in granite and set in the gatepost, and I had a motive. If ever a Christian were to assassinate a beloved Prime Minister, it would serve to reassure the mob: they might just pass us by when they saw Sanskrit on the gate. Such thoughts flit through a man's head when he reads the papers on certain days. (On such days I plan a cubby hole behind a hinged mirror.) The granite plaque is still to come but we do have a tin version: it can cover the alien name SEALY in an emergency. It troubles me that I should feel this way in a nation state that remains resolutely impartial. But in everyday life you deal with the folk, not the state.

The design has a basic flaw: fall comes *after* winter here, alongside and during spring. Born at the junction the two rivers, and bred in the heartland between them, I knew this at the back of my head, but was overruled by a Western rhetoric: *spring, summer, autumn, winter.*

The four stages

Four stages marked the ideal life in classical times.

1. First the **student**, poring over signs on birch bark scrolls, keeping himself pure.
2. Next the **householder**, marrying, making his way in the world, watering pot-herbs, offering rice to crows.

    —*God! I left the hose on the spinach seedlings. Go see, Good Student. They'll be swamped.*

3. The **forest dweller**. At sixty a man began paring away his qualities, preparing to be nobody. Striving, ambition, the pomade jar, these things were put away. He did not disburse his wealth but when he acquired a cardigan he gave away a sweater. He dwelt at the edge of the forest if not further in, alone, or with his wife.
4. Lastly, at eighty, he turned **ascetic**. His wife was careful to precede him into death; no fate like that of a widow. The cardigan fell away, its last button parting with a sigh. He ceased to comb his hair and took to wandering the face of the earth.

I was a young man when I dug out that lawn with Dhani. The student in me was well buried by then, unless it was his grave I was digging. Two years later I was married, to a flightless biped. Maeve's Indian visa was running out. The P&O liners no longer automatically stopped at Bombay, and there were no cargo ships on the horizon that summer. A true kiwi, she did not fly: it was marriage to a citizen, or jail. So on a June afternoon we were wed under the ceiling fans of St Francis Church by the Parade Ground, and the next day I returned to typing my novel. We had already lived in Gore Bay, a lonely hamlet on the shores of the Pacific (population nine), and Lucknow (population one million). That autumn, when I took the novel to London to look for a publisher, Maeve travelled overland alone; with my Indian passport I wouldn't have got further than the Pak border. Presently there was a daughter, reared in both countries and often schooled at home, a gypsy who one summer invented a long-arm fruit-picker that may have been more symbol than tool.

Tochter

Philomena. Also Filo, Millefeuille, Milly-fooey, but chiefly **Tochter**—daughter—from her childhood weakness for a Germanic version of the Beatles' song, 'She loves you'.

'*She* **laughs** *you*,' Dr Strangelove reports, through clenched teeth, '*yeah, yeah, yeah.*'

It's habit forming. Nobody in this house says *love* any more. I laugh cheese, she laughs Björk.

One evening when Tochter was five a man turned up at the old gate and put his watch in my hands.

'I painted this house for your father,' he said.

He needed money urgently.

I handed the watch back and gave him the loan; there was a fifty-fifty chance I'd see him again. Two weeks later he reappeared with the money.

Now I needed help. The plot next door had been sold and the boundary wall wanted raising right away.

'Not to worry,' he said. 'Actually I'm a bricklayer as *well* as a painter.'

Next day he arrived with a cartload of bricks. They were pale yellow and crumbled in the hand. The buffalo snorted, the hare-lipped carter looked away.

'Seconds,' Habilis admitted.

He never tried that again. The whole Pak length of wall was raised, with proper bricks, along that side of the 433 later called Away, where the Fiat still stood squarely in the portico. A few months later I found we needed another screen, in the back yard. This wholly new wall—a swung dash with an arch in it—was the product of many drawings. Habilis took the intricate brick patterning in his stride. I bought myself a trowel and learnt the use of a plumbline. Next I had a hard look at the portico; it seemed wasted on a car, the space surely better given to—what—a study? Habilis couldn't agree more.

I didn't know it but I had turned Householder. And the portico, ten years before I went to China, was turning pagoda. Using a third of the portico for a roof, Habilis built me a monk's carrel separated from the house by a passage. When the carrel proved impracticable we abolished the passage and amalgamated it with the house: the enlarged room made a perfect kitchen, and the old kitchen, always far too big, turned Filo's bedroom. The reshaping of the house had begun, with Habilis as preferred builder. I never went in search of him but I didn't think of looking for another mason again.

He'd turn up when he was ready. He's done all the rebuilding this house has seen: bricklaying, stonemasonry, concreting, plastering, painting, even cowboy plumbing. Tempter and instructor, teaching me his arts, laying mysteries bare.

The works have never really ceased. Am I haunted by the Turkish proverb? *When the house is built, Death comes.* Perhaps that is what I want to inscribe in granite.

—*Still here, Forest Dweller sir?*

—*Some small delay, Good Student. And you, why do you tarry? Get you a wife and make just the one child, for India's sake. Build a house, tight and true. But shun the Racecourse gate, will you?*

—*And when do you depart for the forest, sir?*

—*Do as I say, boy, not as I do. And suppose I bring the forest to the house?*

The greenbelt
This fenced-off plot beyond the boundary was annexed some twenty years ago, making me two enemies. One was the buffalo herder accustomed to grazing his milch herd on the verge. He's still out there on other folk's verges, this urban villager, in lungi and vest, his skin gone buffalo black, his hair gone white as milk. The other was our municipal sweeper, a giantess who looked over my newly planted trees and said in her deep voice: 'You're giving me a lot of leaves to sweep up.'

'Every leaf,' I assured her, 'I will pick up myself.' And went on planting.

For twenty years she has swept the neighbours' frontage to either side and left ours severely alone. She lights little rubbish fires up against our hedge.

There are other nuisances. A sick dog will sneak in to die, and the municipal workers must be paid 'for the kerosene' before they act. Pigs will break in and kill a frangipani just as it's putting out its first deep red flowers; they scratch their sides against the slender trunk and bring it down. Usually it's the piglets that get in and set up a squealing when they can't get out as mother and child face each other through the baffling wire mesh.

—*Oh, I have been tempted by suckling pig, boy.*

Mortality runs high in public planting, but today the survivors on the verge, can stand for a group portrait:

Front row (nearest the street), left to right: Night jasmine (the harsingar), Chinese camphor, Weeping fig (*Ficus benjamina*), Mexican silk cotton, Bullet wood (*Mimusop elengi*, the maulsari), Flame of the Forest, Weeping willow.

Middle row: Persian rose, Golden shower (Koelreuteria), Red Frangipani (RIP, Death to Pigs), White Frangipani, Elephant apple (*Dillennia*), Chinese box (*Murraya*).

Back row (nearest the house): Violet oil nut (Pongamia), Coral (*Erythrina crista-galli*), Rain tree (Tochter's 'shuttlecock tree'), Purple camel-hoof (Bauhinia).

Seated on the ground: golden privet, crown of thorns, rambling rose, cape gooseberry, assorted hibiscus: mauve, red, lacy orange.

Corkscrew blur at fence: suckling pig.

These trees are flowerers (fruiting trees are kept within the boundary, *on* the 433). The dense evergreens face the road, our hoplite phalanx, while the flowering trees look inward.

The leaves swept up, Dhani squats in the way when I nose the Fiat in at the willow. He doesn't move, assuming with a Martian's innocence that the car can go round him. I back up, thinking: *hornbill!* He has the hornbill's unworldly manner—the hornbill is essentially a pterodactyl—and something of its air of a baby grown old, a fledgling blueness to the skin behind his antique ears.

But a cricket's cough, *er-hu, er-hu.*

GARDEN WORK FOR SPRING

Harrow soil: I go ahead of Dhani here, breaking up the soil, driving straight down with the axle shaft to make clods that he then knocks down to a manageable grain. I dig a foot deep then lever this way and that all round. The axle shaft is the handiest tool in the garden and may be one of a kind. Bought from the cannibals by the cemetery (the car cannibals) and taken to the gypsy blacksmiths of Dharampur who beat out an edge over a charcoal fire. The gypsy camp has vanished but the edge holds. Habilis uses this tool too, as a cold chisel, for breaching a nine-inch wall, and will borrow it for months at a time, holding up garden work. As a crowbar it has no equal in the tool room. When I go away I bring it indoors. It's already a replacement, the last one stolen by three gypsy girls with sacks on their backs. I confronted them but pointed at the wrong sack. They laughed and ran off.

Weed trefoil: Dhani loves this job, battling a weed that is his equal, squatting for hours on the lawn with his lance khurpi, pulling up each plant by its thread-like roots, inching along with a stubbornness the weed will match when it returns next year.

Compost: The pit is under the coral tree, the hornbills' favourite perch when they're not on the TV cable. The cable loop ordinarily goes from roof to roof. I refused the installers entry, they bypassed the house, and we get the one channel: Hornbill.

Victor's been. My preferred labourer, but also a part-time waiter who comes when he pleases. His small neat form battling the tangle of brushwood at the compost heap today, his faint hunch helping the rake he wields like a third arm as he drags a year's mulch to the edge of the pit. I'm hoeing in the grainy undersoil, digging out wads of caked leaf mould that form a lid on the true compost, light and moist and friable, when the pit throws up a surprise. Handwriting—my *own*! It's a moment before I realize what it is: a manuscript page ragged and mouldy. *The Everest Hotel* was the last book I wrote by hand. A nature book, this one manuscript was spared the flames last year; composted, it has entered the garden it drew on. I thought it would have broken down to soil by now, so I dust off and preserve this stubborn fragment.

21 March
Dhani sweeping up the last of the camel-hoof leaves.

When leaving, he claps his hands *one-two*, dusting off, but also letting you know he's off.

22 March
Today when I saw the Atlas approaching in the distance I set his broom out, went from room to room covering beds and bookshelves, chopping boards and computers, inverting the dining table chairs onto the dining table. His job includes sweeping and swabbing the house. In my mother's time this happened every day. With us it was twice a week, then as he grew older, once. Today the house was in a special mess.

But the Atlas passed the gate—and kept going!
Ah, *Saturday*.

Last year I gave him Saturdays off. He grumbled at first. It would upset his whole routine, he said. Now he finds an extra Sunday no bad thing.

30 March

Parrots swoop down on the camel-hoof, intent on villainy. Each year they descend on the tree, dangle upside down and nip every flower in the bud. I fire off volleys from my birthday present, a catapult Maeve bought off a Granada gypsy. A pebble rips through a leaf just shy of an astonished red beak. It works on pigs too. Storm Petrel, my mother, called me.

She was no turtledove. Her birthday fell on the summer solstice, longest and hottest day of the year. A fancy dress pageant had to mark her special day when she was a child, and all nine sibs had to endure furs and astrakhans or pay a terrible price. (A photo from the 1930s shows the ice fairy's wand raised up above a sweaty armpit.) My temper was blamed on Mars, the equinox a time of hailstones that wreck a garden in minutes. Two Marches back the verandah filled with six inches of scattershot hail and the racecourse was carpeted in white. People crept out with cameras. The olive tree trunk still bears the scars.

A China file

For years I kept a Russia file. It began quite naturally with the great Russian novelists and progressed from there to poetry. I went to Russia, hopping off a cheap Aeroflot flight, my head full of 'the Four', that group of poets whose last survivor was Anna Akhmatova. A Petersburg-Old Delhi novel came of that, *The Brainfever Bird*, a story of poetry and biological warfare. It was a time of footloose Russian scientists and for a year I inhabited one in love with a young Indian puppeteer.

Now, suddenly, a China file. It began with talks. Last year a group of Chinese writers came to Delhi. I put the gate key in Dhani's hand and went to meet them. Talks by day, evening readings, and, late at night, in someone's room, songs over unsteady tumblers of red wine. After the conference we took the writers—Ouyang Jianghe,

Xi Chuan, Zhai Yongming, Ge Fei, Li Tuo, and Bei Dao—to Agra and Fatehpur Sikri, to the redstone palace of the Great Mughal. On the way our bus broke down in Krishna's town, Vrindavan, where a monkey stole my glasses. It was cleanly done: a single swipe from behind. I felt nothing, simply a loss of vision.

the china poets

    the china poets have come to do you homage madgesty
    and wee of hindoostan wyth them

    two rivers run in ouyang jianghe's name
    he wept before your grandson's taj mahal
    see river-river's cupped hands brim

    with marble tears now hear our erhu
    the night cricket accompany falsetto xi chuan
    whose fisher song unites yamuna and yangtze

    watch zhai yong ming unseam
    from this lump of Szechuan coal
    chrysanthemum

    beer bottles judder and converse as ge fei's fist
    expounds table
    feel him reinvent the microblog

    old li tuo puddled concrete for the chairman in '66
    skimming off that flinty broth reflections
    which today could profit china (or highness us)

    bei dao spreads before you a leather jerkin from
    that moment after
    tiananmen when poets were rockstars

    these trifles and their whole art they offer with clean hands emperor

    yet no hand clean as the monkey's that snatched the glasses
    off his nose who looks some days like
    me (but at five so like the helmsman i was called mousy
    tung) and lately sadly shrek

attend king to our project
let it run monkey-fleet from roof to
roof as we watch helpless from our line of rickshaws the string of boys in
cottage industry pursuit of promissory notes a hundred times the price of
one banana

the bait worked highness though i
never thought to see a face full clear again much less
yours in sikri

as now with painful clarity before
your absent throne eyes lightly shut against the present

an inch between me and the redstone floor

Now the Chinese have invited us to China, in May.

30 March, evening.
At midnight I turn sixty, turn Forest Dweller.
The police gong strikes the hour amid firecrackers and motorcycle horns and hoarse cries of victory. The nation celebrates my birthday, I point out to Maeve, but she pretends they're cricket fans celebrating our victory over Pakistan. At each explosion she winces, she and every dog and cat and bird. I see my father wandering about this very house repeating: 'Sixty. I'm *sixty*!'

—*Forest Dweller sir, what is sixty?*
—*It is when a closet door creaks and you no longer expect a woman to step out.*
—*And sleep, what is that?*
—*Leave that poor girl alone, Young Husband. Go fetch a shovel.*

GARDEN CHORE
Manure: bargain with the cow manure carter, a great rogue. He drops the price, then drops off uncured dung.

The Small Wild Goose Pagoda

Scholar Lu in his garden

April

One sharp spring morning in the year AD 644 the Chinese pilgrim Xuan Zang stood on the banks of the Indus River picking his teeth as he watched a black thunderhead rise up out of nowhere and set his boats rocking. Only the frogs, waking out of long sleep, enjoyed the storm that fell swift and savage upon the traveller. *Gangsta, gangnam-style*, they shrilled for the next forty minutes while Xuan Zang held his head in his hands, and wept. Great waves sprang up and capsized two of seven boats loaded with gold-washed manuscripts, one hundred and eight pot plants (including two sweet tamarind saplings), countless seeds, and an eye-tooth relic. It is said the fishes helped rescue many of the holy manuscripts, recognizing the virtue in them, but in the confusion the chief relic went missing. Past midnight the last of the wet scrolls was spread carefully by rushlight on the riverbank awaiting the sun that shone bright and clear next day. Surveying the wreckage Xuan Zang took stock and recalled the soothsayer's warning: no green leaf must leave Hindustan. The sweet tamarinds remained anchored to the bottom of the river in their terracotta pots, swaying like dervishes, the Buddha eye-tooth was gone, bobbing away in its camphorwood case to be netted by a fisherman who would sell it for the price of a toddy, and suddenly the Chinese capital looked very far away.

Zoom out, reader. He'll get home all right. The Silk Route has been tramped a thousand years before this latest pilgrim. Glory with its leaden trappings awaits him in Chang-an, distinction will weigh him down, blunt his prose, do him no good. He has simply to find the old broad way, put one foot before the next, and his Indic karma (he has spent sixteen years here) will see him through. A great tower will be built in his honour, thousands of tons of rammed earth, the Great Wild Goose Pagoda. And with every passing year his heart will grow colder within him, though he soldiers on with his translation of the Buddhist texts he panniered back. He spent his youth abroad.

How much better, he sometimes thinks, now he is sixty and the hair on his forearms going grey, looking out from the top storey of the pagoda, if he had died in a blaze of swordplay at the hands of those brigands on the Yanqi Road than live to grind his teeth so! He can still be free, he knows, and no, not by throwing himself from this balcony. Simply by turning his back on the clutter of time and circumstance, by climbing down this spiral stair and reaching the gate and continuing to walk in any direction the first wind chime declares.

2 April
Dhani is planting out the second sweet tamarind sapling, after the first one succumbed to winter. A little grumpy as he dredges leaf-mould. I leave the actual planting (and the sowing) of things to him and he appreciates that, but today he's preoccupied.

'Who's going to take me in?'

Turns out the doctor's widow would like her garage back. Just when I'm trying to focus on China—*what do I read, what do I say?*—reality.

(Is writing unreal? Is China?)

We come back in. The flowerbed at the front verandah is a jungle of cottage-garden blooms: cornflower, larkspur, with beet greens and tomatoes pushing through. This is a tree garden: flowers qua flowers are admitted on sufferance, but this one bed is free; anything's permitted in it, the wilder the better. A great drift of snowy petunias has fallen across the grass, blocking the way to the lawn. Dhani'd love to neaten it all up.

'Put her off,' I say.

He nods. But he wheels his bike off in the opposite direction to the widow. He has to check on the dentist's garage. It's never let, but you never know.

I slip back to China. I could talk about miniature painting and the decorative urge in Indian writing. I could talk about their exiles in the West and our malingerers. I could improvise, leave it to chance. (Anyway, when it's my turn to speak I'm back at boarding school, in the stocks.)

Or I could play monkey king, tell them of my own journey.

The call comes from the quadrant you know least. And always you are first led astray. Canada, cold, immense, desolate, with its lumberjacks and gold-panners, haunted my boyhood in a way Canadians, huddled against the US border would find odd, even amusing. I can still shut my eyes and see a blurred black-and-white photo of a logjam on the Fraser river. Even after I went there as a student, to the only English literature programme in the world that looked beyond the North Atlantic (Plato to NATO ruled elsewhere), I left without seeing the far north of my dreams. Not till I returned ten years later, and travelled to the top edge of the continent, to the Eskimo island of Tuktoyaktuk, at the start of a land journey that ended on the shores of the gulf of Mexico, was my appetite for vastness satisfied. The book that came of the journey, *From Yukon to Yucatan*, marked the limit of that push: mileage, scale, magnitude, the West. It was subtitled *A Western Journey*, a play as much on the Occident as on the cowboy frontier that I followed on my journey down to the bottom of Mexico.

I was doing a kind of Xuan Zang in reverse, trying if not to empty myself of the West (as if that were possible) to view it through Eastern eyes, with something of the blithe security of those countless Westerners who have travelled through Asia. My travelling companion on that journey was the poet Basho (in a book picked simply for its title in the English translation *The Narrow Road to the Deep North*) and perhaps he set me right. It was not vastness calling at all; it was something much nearer. I found it in my next book, *The Everest Hotel*, set in one square mile of my hometown.

For the longest time I thought Basho would get to the tip of Hokkaido (he doesn't; he travels to northern Honshu, far enough in his day) and up on that Arctic pebble beach I stood with my back to the North Pole and cheered him on. I had just flown, close to tears, across a totem from my boyhood, so precious I would repeat its name as I fell asleep, the Great Bear Lake. Only later, with the exhilaration of the journey behind me, did I come to dwell on the crucial part of Basho's title: the *narrow* road.

Stricture, the needle's eye, saves you from the numbness of a quest whose fascinating details can multiply endlessly. (Chekhov, another pointillist, returning from a three-month journey across Siberia, realizes this. He has already written 'The Steppe', an almost perfect account of a long wagon journey seen through the eyes of a child; how could a fact-finding mission hope to match that?) Basho has no programme, though he would like to watch the harvest moon come up over Mount Obasute; sadly that night the sky is clouded over. It is a gentleman's journey though, his Grand Tour of Japan; you'd never guess from his first person singular that there was a muleteer tagging along. One too many there, not excluding himself. He must wind all the way down to nothing to hear the single plip of a frog in a well.

Xuan Zang's itinerary is drawn up by faith; geography too, but mostly he follows his Buddhist mission. Zeal is a fearsome thing: it can keep you married forever to duty, in or out of the robe, your monkishness a cloak for a certain sort of deafness.

So. I must carry a blank slate to China, my sketchbook. It's good my camera was stolen.

—*How goes the honeymoon, Young Householder?*
—*Sweet in parts, Forest Dweller sir.*
—*Be grateful. Now build that house.*
—*We could house-sit for you, Forest Dweller sir, while you're in China.*
—*So the camel ousts the Bedouin from his tent. Go build.*
—*It says here Xuan Zang died at 62, sir. Make haste.*
—*You tempt fate, boy. Fetch the machete.*

GARDEN WORK FOR APRIL

- Lop the mulberry. (*More lip and you lop the jacaranda.*)
- Harvest drumsticks

The shingle is littered with creamy flowers fallen from the Drumstick tree *(Moringa oleifera)*. A russet bee goes among them making drunken love to each unresisting corpse. Overnight the tendrils on this drooping branch have turned drumsticks that tap Dhani's bent back as he sweeps. They're tender just now and can be harvested as beans; chopped and sunned with bruised mustard seed, they make a rare pickle.

—*Ready to eat when you return from China, sir.*
—*Why, the new bride!*
—*A Home Science graduate, Forest Dweller sir.*
—*Homely and beautiful! For that undeserving boy? Ah well. Welcome to the 433, girl.*

3 April

A three-storey block of flats has come up behind us in the past year, blocking off our view of the hills. The balconies in it threaten our backyard, though nothing like the opera box, and I plant a silver oak and a second tea tree at the top right corner, our northeast. (Yunnan would be just beyond.) The tea tree, with narrow yellow leaves that freshen to an astringent lemon in the rains, goes in at the swing seat, beside a pomegranate now in scarlet flower. There's a tea tree already at Tibet just misting over in white catkins that dust the leaves with snow in hottest May. The tea tree's a favourite: its minute leaves vanish into the grass and a drop of its resin will disinfect a cut; Maeve is never without a little bottle of tea tree oil.

Just the one empty plot of land remains in our neck of Racecourse—across the street, beside the jewellers. Five stories, permitted by the newest building code, could come up there. But there are things still worse than a five-storey building.

When I was a boy the comic book of H.G. Wells' *The War of the Worlds* (Classics Illustrated, no. 71) had a steely allure: the giant robots that strode across its countryside atomising men and buildings in their path could freeze your blood. When one hove up behind an English cottage (the cottage itself a thing of wonder) you cringed, hardly daring to peep into the next frame. For sheer fright only *Frankenstein* (Classics Illustrated, no. 52) came close. It was Wells' genius to cram the fears of the machine age into a story whose classical symmetry found the actual Martians to be at last—mere slime. But the creatures that slithered out of the space capsule, mortally afflicted, could only disappoint a boy of the fifties; I always regarded those towering robots as the true Martians (rather as the monster, not the doctor, proved the true Frankenstein) and they pursued me into my dreams.

How was I to know they'd invade my suburb one day?

It's almost hidden by the avocado now, but when the cell phone tower came up I was ready to leave. For days there had been this nameless clanking in the air, but the foundations were in someone's backyard and no one at the Threenecks guessed until the tower topped the owners' double-storey house. With cell phone towers the mechanical engineering is primitive, unchanged for a hundred years: the scary part is—almost disappointingly—invisible, emanating from those sinister drums mounted on top. Over the next week my responses covered the whole range of emotions associated with a death.

1. It can't be.
2. It is.
3. I won't have it.
4. I'm getting out of here. What's moveable? The olive (maybe, just), Stoneman, the harp seat. Take them and run.
5. Run where? And who's to say one won't come up *there*?
6. Look, it's not *that* close. The avocado'll hide it. And you're half dead anyway.
7. [*Hammering from that direction*] Go for it, bastards. We'll fortify that corner.

And we did.

One corner of the house pointed that way, mother naked; the rest was shielded by the house next door (as if the rays don't pass through bricks). Habilis and I pushed out the corner window and built on a walk-in closet, double-wythe brick wall. It's now the tool room, lined with racks of tools, tackle, sheet iron, grilles, and aluminium board.

Metal is thought to confuse the creatures.

The War of the Worlds drags on. The invisible used to be a blessed sphere: angels might be active there. Today everybody I know has a cell phone and claims life is impossible without one. (How did they manage before?) The skull count still to come. A pair of hawks has made a nest at the very top of the tower, but they're careful to keep to that height. You won't find them at microwave level.

A weary cynicism possesses me. The flame tree has put out fresh leaves. I've been months waiting on them, but when I go to the gate

I see a buffalo with its head angled above the tree guard, placidly munching on a fuzzy new stalk. Normally I would reach for the gypsy slingshot; today I simply turn away.

House tax to pay before I leave for China.

The house file

A file exists on the original house-build, my father's. Its pale green covers came apart years ago from the bulking of that wad of instamatic photos that began with the bare plot next door. The rest of the series shows this house at stages in its progress: trenches, foundations, walls, roof, portico. A mason—not Habilis—with an Elvis puff, certain labourers, easterners all, reappear in many shots; in one my mother sits in summer cottons, a sort of housecoat, with her newspaper folded on the edge of the verandah-to-be, chatting with her favourite labourer. (An Allahabadi herself.) In another my father in winter woollies, gloves in a fist behind his back, disputes a point with the contractor, standing on the roof directly above the study where I sit thirty years on. There's one of Uncle Terry, pipe in hand (a pukka gentleman who rented to the end of his days, until his money ran out and the nuns of the Little Flower convent took him in) come by in the Fiat to see how property might look.

The severed halves of the file were fastened with a length of pink cotton tape glued to the underside of its cardboard backing. Some time after my father passed HOUSE-BUILDING/HOUSE TAX on to me, along with files marked ELECTRICITY and WATER and GAS and TELEPHONE, I realized I had been inducted into a long line of file-keepers stretching back to the seventeenth century, when Anglo-Indians first became clerks to rulers with a bottomless appetite for records. Writers, they were called then, generations of them, and a famous building in Calcutta, the Writers' Building, exists to this day, its function unchanged though the Anglo-Indians are gone from it to the far corners of the world. Some remained from that diaspora, but not as clerks. A handful of schoolteachers, some railwaymen, cops like my father. Callings that did not require you to stick out in independent India, though stick out you did if your skin was light. In the earliest days soldiery called the hardy, and surveying, and ship-building, but someone of my temperament would have turned to book-keeping, writing. When I came to aspire to another kind of writing it seemed almost presumptuous in me.

A blueprint in the house file shows a plan and two elevations for a house set on a plot of land 433 yards square, or three thousand nine hundred and seven square feet. For years these figures rattled in and out of my head. Whenever someone asked me I was foxed. I would go to the file and the numbers would leap out. Ah yes! *433 square yards.* And then I would go and forget again. Lately the 433 has taken on a runic quality, lodged in my brain, if not yet the 3907 square feet.

Sometimes I feel these four hundred and thirty-three square yards are all I can ever truly know of my country. If that is so I should know them well. With the zeal of a reformed wanderer, I suspect I do.

7 April
Dhani weeding in the sun in his dark cherry shirt, with a salt and pepper houndstooth scarf tied about his neck though summer is here. He's like that. Summer begins when he's ready.

8 April
He's swept and swabbed and gone. His signature is on the counterpane: every time he sweeps in the bedroom there's a neck where, reversing the broom, he'll leave a scroll of lint on the bedspread. His mark is on the terrazzo too. One by one the white and yellow marble chips in it come on like city lights till the whole floor glows.

9 April
Four giant Chinese palmyra fans, fit for an emperor, swung down to the fireplace by the compost heap where Dhani waits with a box of matches. One by one, ceremonially, I lower the fans onto the flames. Their webbing turns brown and ignites, the pennants fluttering. The vicious shark-toothed stems simply char. Once, Dhani specialized in huge brush fires that withered whole branches overhead. He loved stoking those, would stand back with a grim smile like the Devil's assistant, as the hair on his forearms frizzled. Age has becalmed him.

I bake three potatoes in the ashes.

5:00 PM Power comes back on. Sitting naked all afternoon, sweating at the soles of the feet. May and June are the killers. This year I'll be spared.

14 April
On the train to Delhi to get my Chinese visa I look out the window. Night black as a ticket collector's jacket, so I study the back of the snack tray in front of me.
    1. Hold the snack tray. 2. Lift and flush it with the seatback rest. 3. Pull and rotate the knob to lock the snack tray. Do not put your hand between snack tray and seat back to avoid injury to yourself.

    I expect Chinese English signs to perplex—*Do not dash water on the fender*, says the label on our China oven-toaster-grill—but will they share this pompous innocence?

16 April
Going to bolt the wicket gate just now, I spring back. Old man Dhani's dark cherry shirt is there, bent over, leaking yellow: he's pissing in the drain! Well, it is a sullage drain. Habilis, who squats at the same drain, Mussalman fashion, uses the far end, by the fireplace, but is never seen to. Short of a revolution, neither would use our bathroom.

    When I was a student the walls of Delhi University were covered with slogans painted at night by fugitives from the middle-class. CHINA'S CHAIRMAN IS OUR CHAIRMAN! We heard the Cambridge Marxist Joan Robinson had given her house to a porter and taken up residence in the garden lodge.

    A month from departure, I'm worrying. Will my voice shake? Shall I read 'the china poets', for fun? Impossible, with its reference to Mao.

17 April
No power all day. A house full of dust after last night's storm—right after Dhani swept. Sweep, dust, swab, all over again, lop the damaged mango, mend a broom, put up a stew.

18 April
Picking the first peaches. Their colour is up and the birds are sticking their beaks in. Bounty! Even the windfalls are sweet. In the green ones you can taste clear back to the blossom.

THREENECKS
A streetpole banner: the nation's new saviour calls for a day of protest against corruption. He is said to be squeaky clean, but a man with a raised finger is already halfway to hell.
  Other calls echo nearer by: *'Rita! Rita!'*
  Herald of spring, the Rita ice-cream man has a more hopeful call. At his station opposite our gate, his cart newly illuminated with ice-blue battery-powered long-life bulbs. In the dark old days he once asked my father why we passed him by.
  'I cut a sorry figure,' my father insists he said, in English, 'just standing here.' A drunk, Maeve reckons.
  Today three tipper trucks, a grader, two road rollers, and a team of men in gumboots cramp his style as they pave Racecourse Road. I gawp at the machines, so new, so unlikely; buses, cars, scooters, pedestrians, wriggle around the work. Maeve watches the knots form and unform: no flags, no barriers, no policemen, just the usual give and take. Things sort themselves out, she reckons. By evening rush hour it's all over, autobahn smooth, and quiet returns by nine.
  Twenty years ago the racecourse was a narrow potholed track. A gurkha nightwatchman would stump along with his whistle and ironshod stave, pounding the road like a nightjar. Tucked up in bed Tochter would hear the mournful call—*whoooo-wood-of-thunk-thunk-thunk*—and shiver.
  'The chowkidar bird!' I'd whisper.
  Maeve actually did think it a bird the first time.

Dog-walker
They walk the course, each with his thoroughbred, sniffed at by the libertarian mongrel pack. Invariably young men, in disguised unemployment. When I met their kin in *The Good Soldier Schweik* I was amazed: World War I Austria! In technology we are now just

two years behind the West, in social relations exactly one hundred. Our dog-walkers wear the teenage son's castoff Nikes and work the leash brutally. In our dealings with captive species we remain medieval.

White-haired Dhani was the exception among dog-walkers. He walked the widow's dog at four in the morning. Writing *Red,* a novel about two painters, Matisse and a thief of the local Blackshorts Gang, I wrote all night till the muezzin's call; colours were clearer then. For a span of half-an-hour Dhani and I (and the mullah) were the only ones up, he at the start of his day I at the end of mine. The first of the winter walkers, the mystery throat-clearer for example, didn't start till half past four and by then Dhani and the Pomeranian were already on their way home. The rich stride washed and dressed down the middle of the empty road; Dhani took his uncombed head of hair along the soft shoulder, now leading his charge, now being led. Afternoons at four he brought her back to the Threenecks to watch the world go by. She'd sit beside him, embarrassed after all these years, pretending interest in fleas, looking away at the traffic, gazing adoringly when he hung his head, pricking up her ears at the *bung* of a howitzer, the peacetime army claiming the horizon.

But now she's gone and the widow wants her garage back.

Until last year Dhani worked six houses, and a few years before that he was doing eight or nine. It was sometimes hard to know why. He was not married and had no dependents. But he seemed to have debts or obligations. He had a nephew who got mentioned around the first of the month, and there was a young woman who came to the gate to ask for him every other month. They'd go into a huddle under the camel-hoof tree and the next day Dhani would cough, *erhu,* and ask for an advance. He's not innumerate; he keeps track, not just of money. He once shook off a tightwad employer and turned to me with a smile that said, *you get what's coming to you.*

Then there are the mysteries. The time a woman, not young, not old, grabbed his bike from behind and would not let go. Seasoned dog-walker, Dhani hauled bike and woman forward (he wouldn't win such a match today).

Dhani: Let go, or I'll show you what!
Woman: *You're not getting away with this.*
Dhani: Woman, you'll get the thrashing of your life!
Woman: *Big talker.*
Dhani: You'll get *such* a smack!
Woman: *You wouldn't dare.*
Dhani: Just try me.

I ducked right down as they went by.

19 April
Dhani squats with the axle shaft where the original pear tree used to be, the one my father had him cut down, bringing a curse on the garden. Another pear tree has died there and digging out the stump is a sit-down job. When he digs he folds into himself so his knees tuck under his ears and his arms wrap around his legs at the ankle to allow him to poke between his feet. Today I'm putting in yet another pear tree, a piece of folly he won't even comment on.

Victor larks in, looking for work so I have him dig too, only his job is to locate our mains pipe. Someone's stealing our water at supply. (My father was convinced there was a join.)

The two holes are ticklishly close together.

'You're too far out,' Dhani says, 'the water mains pipe runs *this* way.'

I cave in and combine the two holes: Victor gets the axle shaft, Dhani grunts and returns to weeding. Then Victor goes and cuts a toe and poultices it with mud.

Toes
It took a long time for me to learn to bare my feet. It took a long time for me to even use the word *foot*. It was not that my feet were deformed. I was simply the victim of a prejudice: to a man Anglo-Indians hid their feet. In a country that has never understood the closed-in shoe, my folk took their values in the whole cloth from the British side. The colonizers despised Indian footwear, and I must have got this intolerance with my mother's milk, for in my childhood

the sight of a man's feet in sandals (the poor were curiously exempt) was enough to make me ill. The word *foot* was bad enough; *toes* was simply taboo. Painful circumlocution got me around the things; when the word was unavoidable I fell silent. It took years of unlearning to suppress the shudder built into these ten common nouns. My use of the word here could be bravado.

Dhani's toes are just disorderly, after the manner of old age. They stick out like pointers at a crossroads in a book of nursery rhymes: *He found a crooked sixpence upon a crooked style.* Victor's feet come misshapen, the two middle toes on each foot hardly there at all. But between them, Victor and Dhani may have cured me of an old malady.

Tochter's Anatomy

At the age of fourteen Tochter made a detailed plan of the 433. I recall that plan, made to scale, something like those anatomical charts you find framed in a butchery, the cuts made on a carcass:

The new gate: (Habilis) The gate of seasons with its adjoining wicket.

The harp seat: (Habilis/Dhani) The harp seat faces the old lawn. It came about in this way. Ten years ago the city fathers decided to bury one of the beauties of our city, a savage act, as harsh as any of those prehistoric ceremonies that sacrificed a bright child for the good of the many.

The East Canal was one of Dehradun's landmarks, a channel of fresh water down from the mountains; it fed the town's waterworks and watered its gardens emptying out into the croplands to the south. It was being constantly fouled in our usual way so they sent it underground. Its sandstone walls were dismantled and for weeks blocks of valley limestone lay in heaps by the side of the road, bedrock for the widened road. One night I felt moved to take a souvenir: a single ashlar block. I had after all spent afternoons beside the canal as a boy. The next night I came back for another block, and the habit was formed. One by one I carried off, on the scooter footboard, enough blocks to build a memorial: a stone crescent with diminishing iron bands for a seat. On the keystone I carved in old gothic letters

𝔍𝔐
𝔈𝔆

In Memoriam East Canal.

Stoneman lawn: (Dhani/Habilis) Four stones were left over from the haul. Stood one upon the other they made a figure. A hatchet headstone upon a wide cheststone upon a long torsostone upon a blocky base. Brutish and short (but not nasty and Hobbesian), Stoneman owes his craggy good looks to the anonymous stonecutter who dressed the original blocks. He broods over a handkerchief of lawn that dropped from the sky. When we tore up the old drive, its concrete gave way to grass. Stoneman lawn is fringed with mast trees and a magnolia (whose roots run like varicose veins just under the grass) and a brick walk from the small gate.

The sunporch: (Habilis) Abutting the new lawn at the portico, this greystone patio is a winter refuge. It's also the workplace for wood and iron work.

The portico: (Habilis) That was. Now a mesh room fore and a kitchen aft.

The shadeporch: (Habilis) A redstone patio behind the portico.

Away: (Pak) A Japanese environmentalist declares an end to 'away,' that happy elsewhere for disposables; he might have asked us first. Biros, key chains, nappies, and opera tickets rain from above along this stretch of western boundary, things fallen and things thrown *away*.

The Venturi tunnel: (Habilis) The alley down the western or Pak side of the house, a narrow passage to the backyard—until the iron stair went in. So called from the funnelling effect where the boundary angles in to create a draught.

Workside: (Anon) A set of buttress bays under the external stair to the roof make up the works end of the house, its seamy side. Paints, poisons, brooms, and ladders live here, and a crowded terrazzo workbench transported from the old kitchen. The alley down this eastern or Bengal side of the 433 is now the only outer way to the backyard, endstopped with a blind gate that hides the cloister.

The cloister: (Habilis/Dhani/Me) Our walled garden. Essentially the backyard, it deserves a section to itself.

The walled garden

The backyard was very different in my mother's day, given over to vegetables and a few flowering shrubs. The wall was low, privacy not a felt need; my mother would wave to acquaintances across the empty lots. In those days the sight of a neighbour pegging out washing was not a scandal; inner garments on the line were not connected with the body parts they covered. Eating al fresco was no crime, to be seen with your hair down no infamy; Eden was nearer then.

At some point we fell from that innocence. I felt the pressure of even so mild a presence as the gentle physicist at our back. Iron in silk, he refused to let us raise the Tibet boundary. It would cost him winter sunshine, he said, and anyway the bricks were his. Checked, I took a twig and drew a great capital S in the dust on our side of the boundary. The next day I sent for a load of bricks. We would build a wall of our own and it would be not just a wall but a feature.

Form and function went hand in hand. A free-standing wall, I reasoned, would stand more securely in an S-shape, and cut a figure besides. True, the S is more an old-style *f* whose top end just touches the back wall, while its bottom end sweeps away from it to curve around the mulberry, but our serpentine wall has, additionally, midway, an arch in it. And because a gap remained at the top right corner of the 433, across from Yunnan, we filled it with a swing seat set in a horseshoe-shaped recess bowered with star jasmine. Habilis gave me my first lesson in bricklaying here. The cloister was underway.

Top left a lily bank rises steeply to Afghanistan. A jacaranda my mother planted in the very corner survives festooned with red bougainvillea; it has grown feeble from the mounding up of earth and rubble around its trunk, and an elfin staircase of wood-ear mushroom rings the bark, but lately new growth has stemmed the rot. Midway along the Afghan boundary and set into the wall is the red ledge of a stone seat, projecting over grass and flanked by the yellow tea tree and a strapping young jackfruit with its sombre canopy of leaves.

An outsider would enter the cloister by the blind gate on the Bangla border. (We go in by the back verandah.) Pushing through the iron door he would find himself on a gravel walk lined with ferns leading along the eastern boundary up to the swing seat in the arbour; brick pillars, with stone benches in between, turn the walk into an arcade. A grape vine inclined to straggle has been trained to cover the walk. Dhani has installed a trellis of honeysuckle to back a bench. Lime and lemon trees remained where my mother had put them, on either side now of the brick arch. Orange and pomegranate have since joined the company, and the tea tree towers over the group like a blond giant. Bay leaf and cinnamon guard the blind gate; fig and apricot keep the opposite boundary. The litchi, first tree planted on the 433, and the new drumstick, both fine fruiters, bookend the back verandah. And one new defiant pear.

It's an irregular square, not quite the Alhambra. The back verandah was a covered stage jutting out from the house: its arcade of iron pillars forms a right angle with the brick pillars of the gravel walk, and these are all the pillars the cloister has (the two remaining walls of the square are of exposed brick, stanchioned but not pillared). A set of greystone steps leads off the verandah onto grass.

The back lawn: (Dhani) is an oval garth at the heart of the garden.

A few years ago I travelled Italy and France with a private fixation. Invited to the Paris Book Fair, I stayed on, sleeping cheap, eating little and hunting out medieval cloisters, from the simple sandstone one in Tulle to the elaborate majolica-tiled Chiostro di Santa Chiara in Naples. I sketched many a cloister, but the one that haunts me is one I missed. Boarding the train after a fruitless day in Sorrento, I opened my Michelin guide and found I had walked *right past* the gate of the Church of San Francisco on my way to the station. The church has a twelfth-century cloister attached.

—*STOP THE TRAIN, Young Householder!*
—*Sir?*
—*It says here the chiostro pillars have* vegetable-*motif capitals. Stop the train! Tell the guard!*

—*The platform's gone, sir.*
—*Ah, boy, it had pillars in the twelfth-century Arabic style!*

Returning home I made no changes to the garden. The pillars here are of common brick and make their point in short order. They have no vegetable capitals but a simple twist at the top, the bricks of the last-but-one course set by Habilis at forty-five degrees so each pillar face has a point. No artichoke, but it'll have to do.

It does. The lemons on this crooked tree are a pale version of the vivid citrons of Calabria, but there they are.

MORAL: *Good Householder, read the guide book* before *the journey.*

Broadband

Into this pastorale—broadband internet!

It transforms my life: the first day I learn what a podcast is, listen to four poets read their work, watch a Bollywood trailer (and wish I hadn't: my luscious Bips can't act) check my mail, clicking between functions at the speed of light.

Back from the quack, pick up lunch at the steamroller surdy (so-called by Filo for his tandoor tied to an abandoned roadworks machine). Mixed ECG result: one wild card heartbeat.

Exhausted, I think: *stay fit for China.* Put out the banana bed in the redstone patio just outside the kitchen door because cool air trickles down through the sieve of the house too in a Venturi way. Gian Battista Venturi was an eighteenth century scientist who worked out a theorem for choked flows in air and water. Wind speeds up in canyons, as every Chicagoan knows. On still summer days we sit in the redstone patio (at the narrow end of the funnel) to catch induced breezes.

20 April

Woke at three this morning, went up to the roof. Air chill, sky indigo, Plough dug deep into the horizon. I grew up calling this constellation the Great Bear, but a plough it is, this way down. Generations of farmers gave it that plain unvarnished name. Except for Orion with his club and girdle I can never see the classical figures in the sky.

Today the daredevil who brought down our fishtail palm ten years ago rattled the gate-latch, looking for more trees to fell.

'That useless broad there with the big bottom,' he pointed at the Mexican silk cotton in the greenbelt.

'That useless broad is about to put out new leaves, my friend.'

He looks at me. The last time he drove a hard bargain (more likely I drove a soft one).

'And after that come the most *outlandish* flowers.'

'On the planet,' I'm about to add, 'in shocking pink and yellow.' When I see the very colours on his embroidered cap.

Forest-dwellers, Gujjars know their trees. Would not harm a silk cotton except for money. They could be a caste of woodcutters—tree malis—but they keep buffaloes and sell the milk for a living. Muslims, yet vegetarian, nomads yet dwelling in fixed huts with wonderfully plaited roofs. If a Gujjar doesn't know a silk cotton he doesn't know his clean hand from his unclean. True, this one's hips have a baobabish swell.

'Ah well.' He gave up with a melancholy smile, and wandered off. No bulge in his clothing betraying the machete that could sever your head with one stroke.

Evening. The city's been gassing mosquitoes (smell the spray?) but they're back. They bite, let it be said for them, at fixed hours, morning and evening.

I leave off pretending at the laptop and spring up. Go inspect the old almirah Victor and I brought round to the sunporch for restoration a month ago.

Almirah

Nice Arabic word. Ten years it stood under the Bengal staircase minus its mirror, a catchall wardrobe in solid teak. (Well, quondam solid.) Now I want it indoors, for Tochter, who comes this winter. Three areas need work:

1) the back, which broke in delivery when the rickshaw man from the rag and bone market rode like a crazed jockey down the racecourse.

2) the bottom, rotted away from ten monsoons.
3) the mirror door, askew from the weight of the long-gone mirror.

I need some timber oddments.

—*Quiet today, Good Householder.*
—*The solar eclipse, sir,* and *a Tuesday.*
—*Ah,* Banesday! *Make the most of it, boy! Go wander.*

Tuesday almanack

Almanak. Another nice Arabic word. Dog Spanish actually.

In a country soon to be the most populous in the world you need to secure your privacy, jink a bit. Feast when the world fasts, drink when it says stay dry. My almanack is in debt, but inversely, to the orthodox calendar (see Chaturvedi's *Universal Ritual Guide,* Deep-Fryers Lane, Varanasi).

—*Forest Dweller sir, you would not stand the great Chaturvedi on his head!*
—*I find him standing on his head, girl, and set him back on his feet. Observe.*

Banesday, 3 PM (AM *or* PM, three is a good lean hour.) I jump into the Fiat, go fill petrol at the one honest pump in town, hang a right at the Treasury, get a wave through from the cop at the Prince Hotel crossing (mid-afternoon siesta, traffic lights not working). Busiest part of town on an ordinary day. The timber market is just beyond the railway station in a hollow where sawmills and lumberyards slumber. I park in the shade of a banyan tree, no other cars. A young man sits dozing at his desk among offcuts stacked to a plan he alone knows. Sawdust has settled on every surface in the shop softening all outlines to a blur. The air is full of gold. The chief miller has a bandana tied around his nose, his wiry hair gone blond. I pick a wide piece that could serve as a baseboard, a rail, and some short slats, and tie the lot to the roof rack. No traffic when I nose out onto the main road. An hour's work on any other day. Tuesday afternoon, twenty minutes flat. Luck?

—*Find the gap, Fair Home Science Student.*
—*Mind* the *gap, they say on the Delhi Metro, sir.*
—*Aping London, girl. Leave that to our metropolitans.*
—*Write us a new almanack, Forest Dweller sir.*
—*The Chinese got a new one with every king. The Americans put their king away with one. Mine hands you the crown. Very well, herewith a recipe for godsent contingencies.*

RECIPE: **Happenchance soup**

—*Six waters go into this swill, girl. And where is the Young Householder?*
—*Out paying bills, Forest Dweller sir.*
—*Water bill for no water, phone bill for a dead phone! He'll be a good long time. Put the brown rice on to boil, and come sit beside an old Forest Dweller. Here is an old stamp album. Come closer.*

INGREDIENTS
1. Rice starch. *Forget Home Science. In godsent contingencies the Good Housewife will neglect the scum off the head.*
2. Tamarind swill (*rice starch poured hot into an emptied tetrapak of tamarind paste and shaken*)
3. Bouquet garni from steamroller radishes and onions (*never eaten raw, girl, for the E. coli, not the spunky aroma*)
4. Cess from steaming green pumpkin
5. Sago whey from the breakfast porridge pot, for thickening
6. Half a cup of cold black tea, for colour
7. Ginger wine dregs, two years in the decanter, perchance for flavour
8. Mint off a postage stamp
9. Turmeric off a damp spoon, a last stab at colour

Let simmer gently an hour, ignoring the froth, the scum. Savour the stamp collection, the musky aroma. Sieve out all solids. Salt to taste.
Salt further.
Salt still further.
Leave to cool.
Taste.

Pour out all at the roots of the litchi tree, girl. Lick the starch off your fingers. Serve the Young Husband instant noodles. He will never know the difference.

21 April

A woman comes to the boundary wall, to the peach tree where Dhani is sweeping up leaves, to report her neuralgia. She complains softly from the centre of her suffering and he listens, says a few words, and turns away. She returns to say more, which he listens to with his head down. Adds a word and turns away again. He will not be deflected from his work.

It occurs to me Dhani could be a witch doctor. In folk medicine the line between herbs and spirits is thinly drawn. Something in the way people face him suggests other powers in the man, but he would never reveal them to a likely doubter. Habilis I know will spill chicken blood. Dhani I think stops at the dark red china rose. I *think*. Dhani jiggling tail feathers, rolling his eyes? I rule nothing out.

When he's leaving he stumbles—I *jump*—but rights himself in time. Now if Habilis tripped I'd laugh, rub it in. No love lost there, just equal parts of admiration, mutual need, and hostility. Affection would embarrass both of us.

22 April

The sound of water trickling into some hidden pool.

Twice I stop in my tracks. Then it dawns like a smile: it's the hose puddling in a jungle of petunia, spent poppies, and withered mint. An ancient reflex, this wish for a fountain, it grows stronger as the summer comes on. The odd thing is that the trickle comes at noon, and from the mains supply that normally shuts off at eight. Six to eight is our morning ration, and then two hours in the evening, six to eight again. I'm thought a fool not to have a suction pump hooked up to the mains supply: everybody has one. At times like this you simply suck water into your tank and leave the neighbour's tank dry. As for this fountain business it's proof of how far removed you can get from reality.

Saffron glow at the redstone patio, dulls to litmus pink by the afternoon. Orange tree putting out crumpled baby fists that open in a day into perfect ovals; new leaves on the cinnamon, nail polish red. The juvenile pear shimmers in silk; it's heard all about the seven generations that went before it and smiles with the serenity of the young who know they will never die.

24 April
Mayfly trapped between the mesh door and the wooden door all morning. Back from the market I release him at lunchtime. His one day on earth and he spends three hours in prison, ten-year term for a man.

25 April
The red pantry Mother-Hubbard bare. What do I bring back from China? Hundred-year-old eggs, bird's nest soup, black-lingerie mushrooms?

Sun hidden at 9:30 in the morning. Power went off at nine, leaving the washing machine stranded between wash and rinse cycles. Water too is rationed now. Grey water drains anyway to the hollyhocks. I stick a finger in the discharge pipe, winkle out the wadded mango blossom, withered to a light muesli.

Dark at midday. A leaf drags across the verandah, the scraping bodes rain. Sky yellow as an old dog's teeth.

Laptop battery in the red: with power gone this too must be hoarded.

Today I miss good risen bread. If you want a plausible loaf you must bake it yourself.

RECIPE: **Powercut Bread**
The Almanack solicits your close attention. Attend. Daily power cuts from nine to twelve mean your baking must be carefully scheduled to allow for rise, knock down, second rise, and baking. The proving of bread, the knocking down of it, all the theory of breadmaking, I learnt from the diary of Mr Hawker of Stacey and Hawker of Christchurch, the gentlemen in the long photograph. The practice of breadmaking has come out of an oven the size of a small TV. The

bakery is Filo's room. A bedroom, as in old China, only here you don't sleep on the oven.

This Sunday morning, Fair Home Science student, your almanackist is running late. Nine o'clock is fifteen minutes away and the loaf has just gone in the oven. A half-baked loaf awaits the Forest Dweller. He curses God and government. Then, a wild notion: *two loaves cook faster than one.* With a small oven you lose heat right away if you open the door, but what can you do, girl? *Yank open the oven door, cut the lump of dough in half, and slam the door shut.* Sit out the next fifteen minutes, waiting on the oven timer, table-rapping the ghost in the loaf. Switch on the desk lamp so you know when the power does go off.

The oven times out exactly as the desk lamp dies. Ping. The loaves come out joined at the spine like Siamese twins.

The skewer comes out—clean!

Libations, girl. Brew good Arabica, pour olive oil, mine the mother lode of garlic (Chinese garlic, more shapely, has less bite than our runty knobs), serve with Sikkim gouda. Almanackists of the world unite! Poor Robin, cheese-parer, would demur. Ben Franklin would straightway patent 'Powercut Bread'.

MORAL: *Inspiration, Fair Home Science student, is the daughter of Desperation. Kiss me!*

26 April
Gibbous-moon shadows, deep black. Uncle Full Moon casts a feebler light, genial all night long, still there with his fixed smile just before dawn. The gibbous moon tells its dark stories and is gone before you tire of them.

28 April
You want the air without the dust. Hence the whole rigmarole of opening and shutting doors and windows at either end of a storm. Edging nearer is the storm everybody's been waiting for.

Like China, so near.

April 29
Most days Dhani's silent. In the early years, finding a sombre spirit in me, he was happy to do his job and leave. Pleasantries are not his style, but I think also I was on probation. I found him taciturn but never disobliging, merely inclined to do things in his own time. In his old age he can simply turn in on himself and look ancient and unforthcoming. When there's nothing to say there's nothing to say (or else a mouthful of tobacco juice). He speaks when spoken to but will sometimes offer a remark. (Yesterday he was curious about the almirah. A gift for Tochter, I tell him. 'Ah, so when is she coming back?' He doesn't say: *a gift should be new*.) When he needs money he becomes voluble, but this necessity, which must be painful to him, is distressing for me too. I rush for the wallet I once hid from him ('Lead us not into temptation,' my mother always said, quoting *her* mother) while he hems and haws.

30 April
Peachfest. The glee with which birds wipe their beaks on the branch after feasting! Even the timid white-eye of the tinny rasp, more cricket than bird. The purple sunbird is all pipette: peachflesh purees down that long curved catheter of his, dulcifies in that streamlined body that jets about the garden at half the speed of sound. Oral hygiene (beak-keeping) is necessarily a longueur with him.

The hornbill doesn't bother with soft fruit. The hard date of the China fan palm is his treat, slow-ripening to suit his glacial approach. Antediluvian, ungainly, he's a Model T at the F1. Will tilt his head with infinite solicitude to inspect the branch above; meanwhile the sunbird has looked left, looked right, had a piss, done jail time, and been to a brothel in Barcelona.

 —*Unheard of abundance from a three-year-old tree, Good Householder.*
 —*Why bother with windfall, sir?*
 —*Ah, but you do. Besides, the Almanack declares the next fruiting of this order will occur in 2031.*
 —*You will be eighty, and ready for Forest Dwelling, surely?*

APRIL CHORE

 —*Dig till you find the join in the pipe, boy.*

Almirah (2)
Start with the rotten base. Strip away unsound wood, screw in the fresh baseboard. Keep your mind off China.
 For the footing, a set of cut-off chair legs, laid flat.
 A high chair was made for my mother when she was unable to bend her knees from arthritis. Years later, it became the swing seat in the arbour, its legs sawn off. The heavier forelegs from that chair now go under the front of the almirah, so it leans slightly back.

 —*The first principle of freestanding cupboardry, boy?*
 —*That the cupboard not tip forwards onto you, sir.*
 —*Ream down half an inch, then drill, so your screws lodge tight.*

 I've just put away my tools for the day when Habilis comes by, rings the cowbell.

Xuan Zang crossing the Himalaya

May

This cowbell. It dates from the summer (it was May) of 1995, before helmets. Filo was five years old. Here she is on the saddle of the old warhorse from the Bajaj stable, the 150 cc Chetak, stepney rear-mounted. The spare wheel was good for hanging an extra piece of luggage, but also a kind of seat-back for the pillion rider, Maeve. Our daughter sits sandwiched between us on the long seat of the Chetak (see Todd's *Annals of Rajasthan*, for Rana Pratap, knight, and Chetak, his horse), a heavy Lambretta-style scooter. We are riding on the back roads of the Himalayas, twenty days on two wheels, while forest fires burn out of control on the hillsides and the distant snows flicker through a haze of smoke. An hour into the hills on day one Filo begins to whimper. Bred in the plains by nuns, and then two years in our valley, she has never seen a mountain before. She has learnt to trust us, but these plunging gorges she has not seen the like of before. We pull over, rest among pines. I check the luggage, three lumpy bags slung about the vehicle, while Maeve explains about mountains and bikes and balance. A single squirrel's chatter fills the glen. Filo dries her tears. We remount and go on our way through the piny air. By midday she has forgotten her fear, is leaning recklessly out into the void. Her mother tucks her back into the pouch like a kangaroo. Every day we set out at dawn, travel an empty road past slate-roof hamlets and paddy terraces and deep woods of mountain oak and rhododendron for two or three hours till we find a likely town, look for a room, lunch, and spend the rest of the day wandering. The plains are scorching, we're not in any hurry to get home. We're in heaven. One of our stops is the market town of Gwaldam. It's there, in the steep bazaar, I find the cowbell.

Habilis

Habilis will sometimes forget to shave but he never comes to the gate downright scruffy. He favours a business shirt worn hanging out (I've never seen him in a tee), slacks and sandals, though in winter he has a line in jackets that ratchet up his class dramatically. A labourer he is not. Countless labourers go by the gate on their way to building sites, mostly younger, shabbier men, often village boys, drawstring pyjama pants under their shirts, a rustic towel on the shoulder, lunch box in hand. Habilis would sooner starve than carry his lunch. Masons have a more dignified bearing, altogether less rag-tag than that trudging file of labouring men. Habilis is a whole half-cycle ahead of Dhani: not quite industrial man to Dhani's peasant, but an urban bricklayer from the time of Gilgamesh. A citified tradesman you would say at once, speaking with a chaste tongue, while Dhani's never lost its burr.

He is handsome, hairy (a wolf in a shirt), strong, well-built but not in a baroque way, combative, yet civil, even charming: the alpha male, but mellowed from that dread golem to a creature of individual worth. Professionally he's skilled, resourceful, painstaking, the builder, if not of ziggurats, of tight roofs, and damp-proof floors, and many miles of protective wall.

Homo habilis, home-maker.

He's come to borrow the hacksaw. It's a visit, I know, a prospecting too, and a real need. Habilis values all tools, equally and indifferently, as only a jack of all trades can, the way a rake loves women. And he knows where to come. Over the years he's built up a catalogue of my tools, down to a knowledge of each one's flaws, to which he'll add a new one of his own. 'Not the small wire-cutters,' he'll say, 'the *big* ones, with the missing grip.' They'll come back with both grips missing. A stream of tools issues from this gate, not just the standard builder's three: pick, shovel, and pan. A trowel he will not borrow; every good mason has his own, and his own plumbline. Nor have I ever needed to keep a tally. A good workman has a code with tools, I've found over and over again. Habilis has, at least I think he does. He will not snaffle your hacksaw, though he may hang onto it longer than you'd like.

'When do I get it back?'
'Tomorrow evening.'
Why did I bother. It's always tomorrow evening.
He looks over the peach tree while I fetch the saw. I bring out

a polythene bag too.

'Help yourself,' I say. 'There's plenty, as you can see, even for the birds.'

When the bag is full (Habilis has a family, two sons, two daughters, and 'Her') he lays it gently in the dicky of the old scooter. Shafts of solicitude can flash from him, but with tools, as with men, with labourers, he's merciless.

'And the roof?' he says, coming back.

'Soon.'

If it weren't for China I'd be tempted. Lately he's been hard to get. But let the design mature.

'Give me the contract.'

'There will be no contract.' He knows very well I distrust his dealings but not his skills. 'Day wages, as before.'

For the past year or two he has been on the verge of contractorhood. There was even an interval, on the heels of a lucrative contract, when he bought a car and handed me a business card. It said **Mohd. Sheikh, Building Contractor, All Kind of Constructions, Quotation On Demand**. I still have it, with his mobile number in shaky ballpoint on the back. The car lasted a month, in and out of garages, an anonymous rode-hard white Maruti 800. One day he parked it in the drive here and came to the gate all but spinning the key on his index finger.

'Now you must get a proper car,' he said. He meant it was time to stop running around in an old Fiat. Nobody did that any more, much less a sahib.

'How's yours?'

'Not bad. Takes a bit of maintenance.' He used the English 'maintenance'.

Habilis speaks a vivid Hindi and has a range of English words, though not sentences, the learnt vocabulary of his trade. 'Shut-ring,' he will say, for shuttering or formwork, 'karnis' for cornice, 'tepar' for taper, and, alarmingly, 'garotte,' for grout. 'Pal-ain,' (plain) means level, while 'level' is not a quality but a thing, a spirit-level, like a tape measure, an 'inchitape.' An 'architek' is something Filo is studying to become so she can hire him for large projects. Habilis was a painter first, I sometimes forget, a man who mystified me with paint names, until I saw that 'Sam-o-sam' was Snowcem, and 'A'pace', Apex. I follow suit when speaking Hindi: 'holepass,' for holdfast, 'single,' for shingle (the larger gravels are naturally 'double') though my tongue refuses 'lintar' for 'lintel,' meaning not lintel but roof.

Dhani never bothers with English, though he surprised me once with 'man-hole,' split into its compound parts and given all the gravity of a spondee. On the other hand if you add in his knowledge of flower names, he might run Habilis a close race: lark-ispar, petoonia, pinji, ispaidar, soot-illiam, Ali-Haq.

GARDEN WORK FOR MAY
- Lop the mulberry before China
- Lop the mulberry before China
- Lop the mulberry before China

1 May

Power gone early today. By some miracle a trickle of water into the tanks.

Evening stormlight. Pink quisqualis blossom against an iron sky that refuses to rain. The watering kettle chosen by the strange martian light, all its aluminium skin glowing, the half-Turkish pickelhaube on its lid picked out. Half the sky is gold, half black. I sprint up the staircase. An eight-year-old would be shouting with joy. Eight is the last time you are happy. Later come pleasures, not happiness, unless in love.

3 May

The last of the peaches picked in by early morning light, parrots leering from the camel-hoof. A perfect specimen merits a separate trip down the ladder and into the house. You set it down gently apart from the crowd that await sorting on the dining table. Later you put off eating it again and again.

Almirah (3)

Can I finish it before China? Now hurrying with what was meant to fill in time.

The last two sawn-off chair legs go on at floor level. I spread a cloth and work lying down. But the screws are long screws and the last one won't budge. It's dark and I'm tired and tempted to defect to local practice.

Bash it in, sir. With local carpenters a screw is simply a funny sort of nail. I consider the time, the position, but haven't the courage. Principles can hang a man. Then a reprieve:

—*Forest Dweller sir, try this little heel of white hand soap.*
—*The job is not yet done, Sweet Home Science student.*
—*Oh no, just stroke it on the screw threads.*

The screw slides home.

—*Wax will do too, Forest Dweller sir. Save your candle stubs.*
—*And maybe a shorter screw, sir?*
—*You keep out of this, boy. I hear you banging away in the almirah like a bad carpenter.*

CHORE FOR MAY
Slake lime for the peach tree.

The way lime clods seethe in the bucket! Antarctic bluffs in spring. Glow of the hidden rose in them, like cracks in living flesh.

—*Ah, her ivory heels that far-off summer, boy!*
—*Forest Dweller sir, the chore.*

THREENECKS

Lunched, I wash up and go to the gate to 'eat the air'. Step out, and there's a breeze. The after-school rush almost done; stragglers, a hosiery vendor, a radish seller. The bright mad boy striding along, waving his swagger stick, beaming. I realize I haven't seen the half-naked woman lately, with matted hair and angelic smile. Some days her eyes cloud over and she howls at passing cars and beats the telephone pole with a rock.

5 May
BRAKES FAIL! On Haridwar Road. Fortunately the traffic kept moving. Dodged the bus ahead of me and veered left, steering wildly—*Jesus, Jesus, Jesus*—one panicked hand searching for something—what, what, what? To switch off the ignition, of course. The gear teeth bit and I rolled to a stop on the side of the road. Sat there, sweating. Then went and got Inam, who drove very slowly to his garage.
    An old nightmare. And now it comes true.

6 May
Inam delivers the old Fiat to the gate, has me drive it. I go very slow at first, my faith shaken.

7 May
Yellow sky and swaying treetops, classic storm signals. Then rain in earnest, but without the storm, which goes somewhere else.
    Up the iron stair to the rain room on the portico. Some day this will make a fine study. The rosewood tree has grown, its young branches hanging right down to the floor of the little forecourt so you stand festooned in green.
    Coming down I see an upturned motorcycle helmet on the ground at Away. Sick of this grisly rain from the opera box. But how to build a wall in midair?

A summer palace
Ever since I saw a picture of the summer palace in Beijing the Wemmick in me has been ruminating. A summer palace! I'm halfway *there* with the rain room. This small-man's dreaming, caught so well in Dickens' lawyer's clerk whose snug hideaway comes complete with a drawbridge that snaps shut directly off the public lane (and, one can imagine, a vile drain), is both comical and sad. It marks my origins and my discontents. Lower middle class, daydreams looking to assuage restlessness, small satisfactions gnawed at by guilt, gestures towards wholeness, my life a series of notices served to caution. Sixty is high time. If not for quitting the domus then at least being free of this beaverish house-build. Yet, this morning I drew an imaginary hexagon

in the dust on the floor up there, stepped into it like a necromancer, and conjured up my xanadu—even to the glass skylights in it.

Days like this I question my sanity, so strong this current of happiness. The grey morning light brings it on again, the cool damp air sucking me out into the garden to sit or do until the hobbled heart quietens.

I laugh You, I laugh You.
This objectless fervour. Laugh *Who* or What?
The potted oakleaf hydrangea from Scotland has flowered. Again ecstasy, again Wemmickish anxiety: *put it in the ground right away.* I set about it, stop once for bread and honey. An hour later it's done, though two pear trees died here (the curse). Victor helped me raise this bed and fill it with leaf mould, so I get a start when he walks in the gate now. Tousled and unshaven and looking for a loan. He too looks sideways at the peach tree—Habilis will have told him—so I fill a bag for him from the fridge. If ever a man needed a drawbridge it's Victor. Liquor pursues him home and empties his pockets every night. Habilis says he actually owned a room once, his patrimony, but sold it for drink.

I stand before him full of unspoken advice. He smiles his small unshaven smile.

8 May
Ticket to delhi booked. *Note*: delhi does not autocapitalize but Beijing does—now there's an index of our standing in the world.
(PS. rome doesn't autocap either.)

10 May
Dhani placidly weeding the stormwater drain, a job he once disdained, till I did it for him. In all else he teaches me.

Router
Two gods have entered my life in the same month, both with the same name, *router*. Jealous gods, but one is downright savage. The first the wireless router installed with broadband. The other router routs wood, and if you're not careful, flesh.

I bought the wood router in haste when I found the almirah doors were put together with channelled bits. The two bottom rails had rotted away and had to be replicated to take the panel boards or the doors would fall apart. In pre-machine days such channels must have been painstakingly dug out. With a router you can do the job in a minute. Slower is safer: with traditional tools, even with regular power tools, you cut downwards, iron or stone or wood, and you bring the cutting edge (facing away from you) to the material. Here you feed the stock *to* the tool, a naked bit spinning in your face at 12,000 revolutions a minute.

The wood router is a specialized tool. You can hammer with a wrench or gouge with a screwdriver, but with a router you can only rout. Or be routed.

—*Take the job in, Forest Dweller sir?*
—*Oh I would, boy, believe me. But jobbers do not exist in this town. And I want this wardrobe indoors before I leave.*

A day goes by in pure funk. You leave the machine in the box, study the brochure, parts and assembly. Surf the net (with the other router), delight in the cabinet making vernacular of America, so precise, so addictive. It seems absurd not to set the thing up. The parts come together with a kind of inevitability that could be logic or fate. You plug in the fluorescent orange lead.

—*The colour shouts danger, sir.*
—*Spare my nerves, boy.*

A power plane has a howl like an air-raid siren. Dhani will look up from his weeding. This is different. This is a harpy shrieking. The stomach actually churns. I switch off, pack bricks around the base of the machine to check a creep in it. Sweep the ground clear of leaves, a temple priest.

—*Today is a Saturday, Forest Dweller sir.*
— *Saturnsday?*
—*Not just that, sir. No Dhani to call an ambulance.*

Fear is a bad instructor. The router sits eyeing you. You cannot meet the gaze. You make a cup of coffee instead. Halfway through you turn sharply ('surprise your fear') and switch it back on.

Fear slips in ahead.

—*Consider also China, Forest Dweller sir.*
—*As if I could fail to, boy.*

I have a test piece to run through. But which way in? With the spin or against? Switch off again, reread the directions. They don't say.

Well, I think, *it is written*. I switch back on.

Go with the spin, sir.

The test piece is tugged from my fingers and shot through on the other side. I snatch my hand away in terror. There's a severed edge of aloe leaf at the verandah flowerpot, a drip forming there. Gravity. The universe going on its way. More coffee. So the feed was wrong. I see it in my head: the stock must push against the bite.

Switch on again. Feed, gingerly, from the other side.

Results. A satisfying grip on the wood, not the snatch of the first try. Under my eyes a perfect channel is forming in the rail!

Midway on a short piece is when your fingers are closest to the bit: here you are the most abject of believers. No atheists in foxholes. (With a long piece it wouldn't matter—you could just cut to length— but I haven't the will to do the timber market again.)

I push the test piece through. Without a break I insert the first good piece, then the second. Two rails, channelled. I switch off the router.

I will not use this machine again, not without a router table. An altar is a table between you and God.

—*Who sups with the devil should use a long spoon, sir?*
—*Boy will go far.*

11 May

All day long kissing my fingers.

12 May

The China visa arrives. The Great Wall snaking across it.

Send the reading passage for the translators. A droll excerpt from *The Trotter-Nama*, but will the jokes work I wonder as I watch the scanner beam glide under the page, will they cross over?

Poring over Chinese ideograms lately, finding small inset pictures I recognize from word to word. We are being housed beside the temple of the reclining Buddha in the Fragrant Hills outside Beijing. I google it and find it's in the botanical gardens. If I can find a ginkgo! That would wipe out the shame of returning from Italy without a cypress. I've learnt to spell the name after years of thinking it was *gingko*.

In the Khan Market Citibank ATM chamber, most luxurious in Delhi, with mirrored walls and mahogany-coloured carpeting, I'm intimidated.

The god in the machine I can handle (unlike the router), but I'm on edge because I've forgotten my pin code. Too many tries and I've heard the machine swallows up your card. To cheer myself up I imagine Dhani making a cash withdrawal. Frustrated, he wouldn't kick the machine the way a streetwise teenager might in the west; he has a respect for things with machined surfaces, like this satin-finish stainless steel module. He would look at the touchscreen in awe, but also in panic as he realizes he doesn't know how to get out of here. The button to release the heavy glass door is a little work of art in perspex and green light-emitting diodes, but Dhani belongs to another India. There is a security guard of Dhani's own class to keep people like him out for their own good.

With every button I press I'm conscious of my idiocy with the router.

MORAL: *Who gambles with his fingers could lose the Middle Kingdom.*

17 May

Emptying out the fridge before China: I want to switch it off while I'm away. Always this wish for a clean slate, Chairman.

GARDEN PLEASURES: SUMMER
To wander picking (with whole fingers) fresh leaves for the pot.

The stump of the old drumstick tree (the bitter drumstick, right beside the new one) is a gnarled remnant, its annual rings splitting up. A punk crest in the middle (where the trunk broke off before the saw went through) is less sprightly now, an ageing rocker's Mohican. 'To dig it out would be a *Mahabharat*,' Habilis said, meaning an epic feat. A Muslim citing Hindu scripture. Where else but here? Besides, it's a perennial source of salad greens.

RECIPE: **Lunch from nothing**
Poor Irv's Shahi Pilaf, for when the fridge is bare.

(Rice and oil you must have, girl, and for that matter continence and salt.)

A handful of drumstick leaf

A handful of curry leaf

These chiefly for colour, though the drumstick will fortify it and the aromatic curry leaf will lift the whole dish. Both leaves have served for centuries in times of famine.

Eight or ten chubby Malabar spinach leaves from washerwoman Sapna's creeper, not omitting the magenta stalks

Sprig of mint

Sprig of lemon grass

Two bay leaves

Chives from the shade porch pot

Half a withered onion from the basket on the gas cylinder

A few red chillies growing under the tea tree

An early drumstick or two, plucked tender. (If late, pluck them anyway, and steam: in the pulp you have the oyster of the vegetable kingdom.)

A wrinkled eggplant remnant at the bottom of the fridge drawer

From the spice jar:
    onion seed
    fenugreek
    cumin seed

A handful of cooked chickpeas, last of an elderly batch

Method: Fry seeds and bay leaf in a tablespoon of oil.
Add a cup of rice, turn once or twice till grains are translucent.

Meanwhile shred the eggplant and put to fry separately, no spices of any sort added. A pinch of salt, certainly, to sweat the flesh; if possible let it be rock salt for its martial thrust (a pinch of gunpowder did in olden times).

Add the chickpeas, all the greens, and two cups of water, and cook twenty minutes till absorbed.

Serve pilaf topped with faux mushroom eggplant. Garnish with young tamarind leaves.

—*Confess none of this to the Chinese, Forest Dweller sir.*
—*Never fear, boy. But you grow thin!*
—*A balanced diet, sir. The fruit of Home Science.*
—*Here. Crush this tiny onion seed between the front teeth. It floods the mouth with black urgings? Now, pass it to her on the tongue. She will forget theory.*

18 May

Tuesday, a good day to start a journey. Give Dhani an advance, hand over the gate key. Night train to Delhi.

God! I forgot to lop the mulberry.

China

Freeway from the airport: always this first shooting gallery glimpse of the natives—American, Russian, now Chinese—on the road, in the car, the truck cabin, on the bike, the electric rickshaw, the powercycle. Only the model changes across the decades.

Zipping along with small intent faces, little sealed Dead Sea scrolls you want to touch to life.

Beijing: all the women beautiful, all the young men puppies.

The Indian in China is a curiosity. Two thousand years ago on the streets of Chang-an, the ancient capital, London of its day, there would have been a sprinkling of us, men from the Buddha's land. (Can there have been a woman, a nun with small breasts and shaven head?) Every race and sort and kind from the lands along the Silk Route thronged those streets, pausing to admire a lantern, stopping to buy a steamed bun.

All the flotsam of the world.

Today a foreigner who goes to China, an American say, meets a gaze that is skewed. The eye behind it is either newly condescending, after the Olympic medal tally, the latest Forbes' ranking of presidents, or else frankly envious: we've come this far on your terms, *show us where to go from here.* Time and again I read this look, angled up or down at Westerners around me in Beijing.

The look I met was altogether different. For a start it was level. It grew narrower the smaller the town, the seedier the street, but it came straight at me. *You are—what?* it said. *One of the trans-Himalayans?* I would feel this middle-kingdom gaze brush my skin, linger on the brown in it, then rest on the clothing, take in the round eyes, the glasses, the evident gentility of a man who has not had to live by labour, who has lived off the fat of his head, Mao would say, and then the host of telltale but unclassifiable signs, processing the data, numbers spinning on the taskbar, crunching madly, until I felt drawn to return the look and catch the adventuring eye.

It would slide away, of course. But there in the hurriedly vacated gap between us, behind the apparition of a man coming to terms with a new thing, I would sense the ghost of something I felt approached brotherhood. After Beijing I saw no Westerners. In Xian, where I stayed in a hotel for Chinese beside the Great Mosque, the landlady in her crepe dressing gown nibbling at a crust of Hui bread as she played fan-tan with her teenage son would look up at me with a sad longing to speak. I might have been her country cousin, so long lost we'd forgotten each other's tongue. Only in Pingyao, where I came upon the international backpack brigade, did the skewed gaze return for all the time I was compelled to share those elegant lodgings.

I was happiest out of Beijing, away from Shanghai. I grew up in towns still half village, where streets were disorderly and a fancy shop stood out; the town limits were never clear, the start of the high road indicated simply by a row of upturned tar barrels at the verge and presently, enthralling as a tombstone, the first mile marker. Family outings were often tours of inspection with my father, the journey for me a gleeful delirium of milestones counted from the rear of the jeep as the white-gartered roadside tree trunks leapt back one by one and froze to wall a green tunnel. The holidays over, you saw the same countryside slowly revolving outside the window of a train, always the liberty of fields and more fields. A landscape repeated and still beckoning beyond the water boundaries of our boarding school, a prison house for nine months in the year. (The steppe was the hero of my first Russian novels: that vast plain that began at the edge of the page with solitudes where gigantic clouds paraded in a sky twice as big as ours. The discontents of the characters were beyond me: they had *all* that—and they wanted Petersburg!) Our big cities held no allure: Delhi a fearful place of politicians, Bombay an unreliable fantasy; only Calcutta, where my father had been on duty once, and ridden that chimerical thing, a tram, twinkled as a city should, just out of reach.

'Town-and-country's the ideal mix,' Padre Barkworth, retired British army chaplain declares, as we sit sipping our fresh-lime and considering the possibility of rain in a courtyard damped down from a watering can and gently steaming. Lame Ghasita baker has just delivered a roll of warm ginger biscuits, wrapped in an Urdu newspaper.

My almost-adult sister Janet lets the back of her new pointy shoes slip off the heel as she flexes her foot in an unaccustomed way. She frowns at my jiggling knee.

'That's *so* irritating!'

A glimpse of some quiet moment like this was what I dreamed of in China. Provincials are the same everywhere. We lurk at street corners, surprise one another in the Beijing metro; we might be freemasons exchanging secret handshakes, the middle finger bent back to point at that thirsty dust bowl, the palm. But the China conference was in the cities and could not be side stepped. China came with it.

At the hotel of the Wo Fo Si, the temple of the reclining Buddha in the Fragrant Hills of northwest Beijing, we sat across a table from the writers of modern China, pushing out notions; our interpreter restacked the freight midstream; then both sides watched the boats tremble on the brimming river. It was a scene out of Xuan Zang's journal. He had done countless debates with the learned all across India. I sat across from the poet Zhai Yong Ming, the beauty of

Szechuan, and sketched her silver spiral necklace. In the botanical gardens next door the gardeners, no Dhanis, wore gumboots and overalls and straw hats. During the week we read before the students of Tsinghua University. Lute master Li played Tang melodies of the eighth century. In Shanghai a green canal, impossibly clean, flowed under our arts-village-windows, crossed by a stone bridge in daily use since 1200. I sat in a billionaire's jacuzzi and sketched my vast pine bathroom with its fireplace and TOTO the automatic toilet ('Yes, Master' the rising lid seemed to say) and antique furniture.

Ten days of fellowship will end. The cook runs after our departing car: 'Stop!' she cries. 'Your *plants!*'

The billionaire overheard my garden plans and made a mental note.

In her arms not one but two flourishing ginkgos.

Dinner at Shanghai University

Frogs' legs, deep fried
Chickens' feet with red pepper
Spring rolls, scalding sauce inside
Fish-head soup
Prawns with a yellow bean sauce
Chicken with chestnuts
Broad beans
Runner beans
Bok choy
Sea lettuce
Marinated radish
Roast beef, cold
Squid with green pepper
Yangtze river fish, steamed whole
Hunan fish tails with red chillies (Mao's favourite)
Beef and tomato hot pot, simmering
Steamed rice
Congee with apple and pineapple
Dates in syrup
Watermelon

As a child Filo would insist on detailed accounts of grand meals she missed. (This one, Tochter, was one of the simplest; Beijing was where the banquets happened.) I chaffed our philosopher Ashis Nandy, the last free mind in India, for shaking chilli powder over everything. Afterwards we reconstructed this menu from the ruins as we sat around the table, picking idly, calling out favourites, wonders already half-forgotten.

28 May
An end to feasting. My countrymen go home, the journey begins.

I leave the ginkgos at Shuang's apartment and take the subway to the Beijing West railway station. 'Soft sleeper' this first night: wake to the yellow loess plateau. Hillsides dotted with cave dwellings. Here on the morning of 23 January occurred the greatest recorded earthquake of all time, the Shaanxi earthquake of 1556. A million perished. Akbar was 14, Elizabeth 23. Their thrones just months away.

Xian

29 May
At the Xian railway station I strike my first Indian-crappy public toilet, then catch my first city bus. It takes me to the Great Mosque precinct where I'm told the hotels are cheap. When I learn how cheap I'm plunged in gloom: I could have pushed back my return date, had a whole month in China.

Clean sheets, bright casement window. I open the window and the room is filled with the aroma from the bakery across the lane. I do a wild jig.

Hui miniature
The Hui people number some forty thousand. Muslims, they have lived clustered around the Great Mosque of Xian for a thousand years. They are descended from Silk Route travellers who stayed on in the Middle Kingdom. Their name means simply foreigner. They speak Chinese but their women headscarf and the men skullcap, and all revile pork. Their grilled mutton is not to be passed by, but

the trans-Himalayan must beware the third stall on the left where a certain hard-faced woman skewers the unwary. The boy waiter, who has surely stepped out of an Oxiana painting, is by no means to blame. His foot is on the ladder to heaven, hers is not. Let the foreigner mark the old Hui proverb: *fool me once, shame on you; fool me twice, shame on me.* Let him pass by on the other side next day. His landlady on the other hand takes a note off her son to complete the refund of his room deposit to the last Jiao. Six fabrics clothe her ethereal beauty, but here too the trans-Himalayan must pass by on the other side. Ah, the Hui are a handsome race! Hui soup is eaten with hard cakes of Hui flatbread broken into it. Notice the bakery below the window with the dervish. Eaten plain, the pasty cud approaches the universality of Esperanto. Herein is the brotherhood of man. Buy one, fresh from the griddle, and it will do service as a coaster; buy six and they will haunt you for the rest of your travels. True, in Mongolia, they will keep the wolf from the door. The border is of irises. The signature is woven into the gourd vine tendril.

Things I leave behind
At the Sunday market I cannot buy the sweet-tempered golden Labrador on a leash. Forgiveness flows from under its unicorn-pure eyelashes. But I buy, in their Chinese homeland, litchis, the fruit hanging this minute on our own tree on the 433. Other things I fail to buy:

    Loquats, pale orange, missed in Beijing, missed again in Xian
    Ripe jackfruit segments parted with exquisite polythene-gloved fingers
    Walnut butter, fresh ground in a jar
    Great fat wrinkled Bactrian dates
    Blue-glaze pottery jardinières
    A bushy paintbrush for washes
    An inkstone
    Green tea
    A silver necklace with a gyre down to heaven

A caged cricket
A hundred harassed songbirds
A child's lemon yellow suit, size 3, greatly reduced
A blown-glass ammonite
Imitation flat noodles in a china crock
A hollow wooden frog with serrated back and stylus croaker
Biscuits to munch on with hotel Nescafe
Imitation leather moccasins, soft as sin
Disco crispy chicken drumsticks
Mao poster (reproduction)
Red guard headband (perchance)
Tiger balm
City maps from old women

Bonsai junipers, canaries, pickled horse mushrooms, silk shawls, cow livers: where is a thirteen hundred-year-old pilgrim in Chang-an to pack these? Easier to overstay.

—*This Almanack, Young Householder, contains all things material to a good life.*
—*Indeed, Almirah Rentier, sir.*
—*Note, then. There is in men an impulse to record, and an impulse to enjoy heedlessly.*
—*Which do you advise, sir?*
—*The botched life is the life that succumbs to the one or the other.*

On the second day I visit the Small Wild Goose pagoda.

Then the museum with Tang figurines in clay, ladies on horseback with cats and mandolins, as if lifted yesterday from the kiln.

Then, sadly, the Great Wild Goose Pagoda.

—*A rule, boy. Take dictation.*
—*She has borrowed the pen, sir.*
—*Then commit to memory the following.*

MAXIM

The Almanack considers, *In countries as in men the ambition should be in the work, not in the plan.*

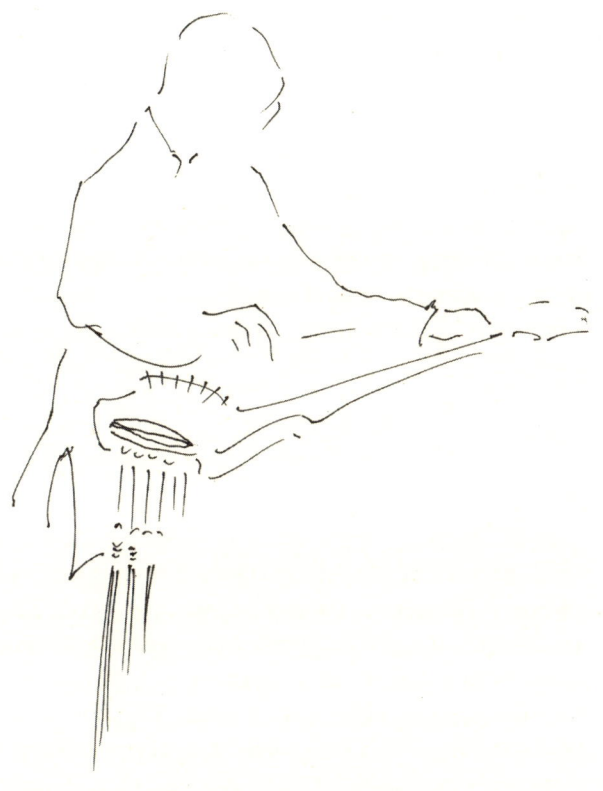

Mr Li, lutanist

June

1 June
On the third day I ride a bicycle on the Xian city wall, the whole circuit, thirteen kilometres. There is a lap when you are alone in China, as far as the eye can see. It is still possible. It's years since I rode a bicycle, and my calves ache on the home stretch. A boy plays the piha standing in an arch below. He is one of ten million migrants from the countryside.

On the last day I watch a thousand terracotta warriors face down a throng of ten thousand from foreign parts. On the last night the upstairs concourse at the Xian railway station has standing room only. No one shoves, no one pushes, and yet the hair is black like ours.

3 June

Pingyao
I ride the electric rickshaw through early morning streets, past the first trickle of workers, and shuttered shopfronts of what could be the set of a Western. The hotel is a courtyard hotel and I strike a bargain with the suave owner. Pingyao is tourist country, even for Chinese, a perfectly preserved brick city from Ming times, with hutong courtyards hidden from the street by elaborately decorated brick screens. There is little overt restoration yet a miraculous state of preservation that must have to do with low rainfall. I walk past yards and doorways, peeping as far in as I dare, catching tranquil moments of domesticity. By midmorning I'm sketching the intricate brick patterns over gateways and doorways on the alley just inside the city wall.

Four teenage girls stop their bicycles to see how the sketch is going. In a public square they might have hesitated; here there's nobody. One of them, Eileen, speaks good English and wants to know what I think of China. It's a marvel, I assure her with a sweep of the hand, a perfect marvel. Their smiles grow wider. I expect them to remount and go on their way. But they close in, simply and unaffectedly interested in the stranger. No, but really, what have I seen? Almost nothing, I say, except for Beijing and Shanghai. 'Shang...*hai!*' they chorus. But Shanghai is briskly set aside. Now I see how young they are, school-leavers from Wuhan on a tour: the rented bicycles, these funny brick lanes, the foreigner sketching, everything is oxygen, burning with an invisible flame and they are fire-eaters. Now I'm the one who's afraid they'll leave. I invent questions to detain them but I needn't have feared: they're in no hurry. Their enthusiasm is an undentable spacecraft, shining. I get them to write out their names. They leaf through my book. They ask me which of them is the prettiest. Both sides have found a private lane where they can be as nosy as they please. Only one of them, Shi Jiao, the shyest, appears to go by her Chinese name; the rest sign Western. I find this time and again among young people of their age, the ones most apt to seek me out when I'm sketching.

When they were gone, waving madly, a woman of seventy came by, and with the warmth of the girls still upon me I nodded brightly at her. She looked at me without the trace of a smile and turned her head away. But there was a still older man, of almost reproachable (and surely at one time dangerous) gentility who sneaked a look at my drawing and smiling approval bowed courteously as he edged away.

Hohhot

5 June

The train to Inner Mongolia runs through bare high plains with abandoned villages strewn on either side of the track. Little unwalled cemeteries crop up like market gardens growing stones. A weeping willow leans over a headstone higher than the rest: the two converse without noticing our passing train.

Hohhot, the capital of Inner Mongolia, is a Han city now, with streets so wide you shade your eyes when you peer at the far bank. It is crowded and empty at the same time, so you are forever running into snarls of traffic or pedestrians, then suddenly wondering where everybody went. I check into a hotel and then walk and walk looking for a park I can sit in. Highrises and unfinished malls line my randomly chosen road. Streetside escalators constantly block the way, and gantries with temporary boardwalks. Patient shoppers glide along travelators carrying bags whose brand names add to the silent cacophony, because it is quiet, unbelievably quiet for a big city. Finally I find a gap in the construction work and shear off down a dusty lane into the municipal gardens. All the benches that ring the blue concrete pond are taken; pleasure boats collide and quack. I find a little grassy plot beside the city conservatory and lie for hours under a laburnum, feeling the earth surge under my shoulder blades. In winter, I think every time I open my eyes and look up through the faded yellow lanterns, I would be under a metre of snow. All around me the lilac bushes have lost their blooms, the green seed still forming or I'd collect some to take home. Little girls in lavender leotards appear from time to time on a staircase, and a piano clunks Mendelssohn. A whiff of dogshit drives me to the next tree along for another hour. I want to be doing nothing, especially if all there is to Hohhot is what I've seen on the way here. I could spend the whole day here in the grass. A man and his young son come by picking dandelion leaves and dropping them in a bag: salad, not weed.

I spread a handkerchief over my eyes and see the girl in uniform at the Pingyao station last night: how torn between her need to stand at attention and her wish to talk! Duty won of course: her railway uniform was starched to a snap, and I had never seen such precise infantry evolutions performed in civilian life before, every platform with its presiding officer. She took my ticket and led me to where my carriage would stop.

'Here.'

A white-gloved finger pointing to one square inch of China. I did not doubt her for a moment. I came from a land where the margin of error was wider than the whole body of certitude. Having escorted me she felt obliged to wait till the train arrived. We stood there under the white lights on the empty platform, the emptiness a shock for the traveller from India, where a platform is a kind of gypsy camp. The train appeared to be late, in itself an incredible thing, and we filled in the interval with our need to talk, the will to connect trashing every obstacle of language. The usual question, the usual answer, with all the resonances of contingency added in: her unarmed beauty made piquant by that soldierish uniform, my susceptibility encased in my foreignness, the very circumstance of strangers, a man and a woman, thrown together in the half dark. I may have said I *loved* China. She may have said that was a *wonderful* thing. 'Welcome to Pingyao!' she said, her eyes shining, and immediately saw her mistake. I was leaving. More apologies, more answering self-deprecation; defences down to nothing. When the train left she was at her post at the foot of the stair, a statue.

I dusted off the little yellow petals, pea family, strewn across my shirtfront, shaking a couple into my book where I find them pressed now, a year later, and took another path out of the park. A student stationed under a tulip tree sold me a hammock, my only Mongolian souvenir. Would Genghis Khan have conquered the world with layabouts like me? By the Great Mosque were bakeries selling plaited bread: I pointed gravely at the stickiest loaf; gravely the man wrapped it, never once taking his sleepy eyes off me. I counted out the notes helped by all the housewives of the adjoining tenement halls. Then began an epic trudge, past salons where youths with orange hair sprawled before vast mirrors, and fishmongers whose eels lolled black and slick in buckets. A band of Mongol dwarves in wheelchairs paraded up and down, hogging the sidewalk, grinding out tabernacle hymns from a barrel-organ sized speaker in a pram. I passed and repassed them, lost. Finally a newspaper vendor set me right with a little map he drew me, painstakingly outlining all four sides of every streetcorner with a gel pen I bought off him. As darkness fell the streets came alive with prospecting girls and charcoal fires bristling with sticks of broiled mutton. I ate the sticky bread washed down with a peach bigger than my fist, the kind you can only eat naked and dripping in a bathtub.

6 June

Datong
In Xian I'd stood in a queue for a ticket to Yulin, once a border town on the Great Wall. It beckoned from the map, a place where nobody would want to go. No train, I was told at the end of a long wait, no train. So I went to Pingyao, then Hohhot. My quest was not for Ming courtyards or Mongol grasslands. I was looking for something in China that would compare with home. To see how someone neither rich nor poor lived, someone who might look a little like me. I was looking for a Dehradun-sized city, and at the last minute I found it, in Datong.

Datong is five hours northwest of Beijing by train. If you flew it would take forty-five minutes but the airport, like the airport in Dehradun, five hours north of Delhi by train, is not always functioning. Datong was once a coal-mining city (my hundred-year-old Bartholomew map of China shows a mineral smudge creeping under its black dot through the province of Shanxi, or Shan-si, as it was Englished then). As you approach the famous Cloud Ridge Caves with their Buddha carvings (the other reason for the prominence of Datong) you see the collieries. I might not have seen them had I taken a tour bus, but I was on a city bus, the long winding option, and it dropped me off on the highway where the colliery shuttle, a little yellow electric toy open to the sky, waited. To get to the caves I had to pass through the whole coal township to the far end.

We had mining too in Dehradun, for white coal, limestone. Quarried in the surrounding hills, hills not unlike those of Shanxi. Until the recent attempt to industrialize the new state of Uttarakhand, that was all the industry we had; you came to Dehradun to holiday or to retire. A hundred years ago or fifty you would have come to Datong to work the mines. You would be lucky to leave. Even today the colliery township, built in a hollow so you shuttle past at mezzanine level, has the air of a trap. The part that fronts the highway has a cosmetic look, like the garden of a factory, the gate painted white (the colour of heaven surely in a colliery) and the lawns kept up, but the back of town, which the shuttle serves, looks severe and harder worked, like the industrial end of an American town, only flimsier, clapboard and canvas, in danger of falling apart. No garbage in the streets, yet the buildings wore a light inexplicable coating of grime (coal was after all mined, not burnt, here) that clung to everything. The decrepitude was out of all proportion to the era of the architecture, from surely no more than fifty years ago. I last saw the like in certain tottering apartment houses along Picnic Garden Road in Calcutta, but it exists in every Indian city, and probably in one corner of every city on earth. A creeping civic despair rained from the frayed asbestos eaves and rubbed up against the broken windows; even the brave paulownia trees that lined the street we traversed looked dusty and resigned.

I had heard that the collieries had recently been privatized. I could not imagine the new owner; in Russia he would be a mafioso, and here probably a party boss's crony, but how would he dress? Where would he live? What would he drink? The workers I saw in the street belonged to another era too, wearing cheap mass market clothes but at odds all the same with the new China. It was not an insupportable condition: the women were shopping for fresh bok choy, the leaves not limp, and vegetables their grandparents could not have dreamed of, there were even racks of tee shirts and scarves for when you had money left over. An ordinary quotient of resilience would tide you over to the next week and the next. But there looked to be nowhere else to go. All those weeks would pile up here, and then you were done. I could not imagine the residents visiting the caves, if they ever did, more than once. That too was part of a larger inertia. I shuddered at the thought of the plumbing in those houses and realized I was never so glad to be passing through as on that shiny yellow shuttle. The little girl in the next row who kept turning around to stare at me and then giggle at her brother, and in the end to giggle at me too, had a local's curiosity but without the resignation that I felt would settle in in a few years like rheumatism. Still, if one had to be poor, better here than in the hovels at the edge of Dehradun or Delhi whose wretchedness looks more fixed and hopeless and medieval than this from a past within industrial memory. I didn't realize it at the time but I had found the answer to my naïve quest for a man like me: he did not exist in China. He was either streets ahead driving a Volkswagen Passat or in a place like this. If you pressed all the classes together under extreme heat, what you got was particle board, not wood but a new thing. Here was the underside of that board, whose veneer I saw in Beijing and Shanghai. The man who looked like myself did not exist because that social formation no longer obtained here (it was why the old gentleman who edged past my sketch in Pingyao looked like a ghost). India was something else again, our revolution stillborn, our classes poles apart.

Hohhot spoilt me. In Datong I grew choosy. I shouldn't have. I had just the afternoon to see the caves and I needed to find a place right away. I tramped the streets in front of the station, where you would think the cheap hotels would be, but they were all at three-star rates. I grew stubborn, the pack grew heavy, the sun hotter, the hotels further apart. My youth seemed a long way behind me. A woman, no longer young, was standing on the street corner under a red umbrella. I looked at her, she looked at me. The red in the umbrella troubled me. It sent out mixed signals, a bed but not for long. On the other hand I was back at the railway station, where once in old Belgrade I had found a bed for the night. I took the plunge and went up to her.

I fold my hands into a pillow and tilt my head in the universal sign for sleep. (Looking back, this could have been a mistake: with the male Painted Stork it's an overture.)

She nods.

'How much?' I ask, patting my wallet.

She holds up four fingers with an anxious smile. It's half what I paid at the cheap hotel in Xian. Incredulous, I produce a pen, a piece of paper.

She writes down 'Y 40.'

We turn together and walk down the street.

It was a room in a family flat. There was even a choice, another smaller room with a mended bedsheet, for less. I took the first and paid the lady. No sooner was she gone than I turned on the tap in the basin and found there was no water. The window looked out on other apartments just as grim. Well, I had wanted to see how the people lived. I had learnt to travel as the people travelled, now I would sleep as they slept. I rinsed off with mineral water and jumped on the first city bus heading east; at the edge of town I changed onto another that went past the caves. A man took the last empty seat just as I was about to sit (provincial behaviour, I thought with a justified smile, remembering the woman who offered me her seat in cosmopolitan Xian) and I stood the rest of the long swaying journey.

The caves are strung out along a bluff that meets a remnant of the Great Wall at one end. They are numbered from right to left as you face the hill and the literature warns you that no ranking is intended. But you start all the same with Cave Number 1, neglecting the broad staircase that leads up to the principal cave, Number 13. I sat in the first notable cave and drew the Buddha, alone for half an hour until a group of men I took to be Korean came in. Polite men who bowed appreciation of my likeness of their lord. A skylight, cut to let in a fall of light on the immense statue, varied the gloom of the cave from above and I was inclined to linger when they were gone, the solitude pleasing. Whistles began to blow in the distance. Closing time! I had still to see the principal caves. The guards signalled to me, a lost sheep, gesturing towards the gate. I scrambled back along the hillside track, ducking now into cave after cave as I went. When I got to the chief staircase I saw a small crowd gathered outside the principal cave, like the crowd in front of the Mona Lisa. Closed, the guard indicated, stepping in front of me. I held up one finger with a pleading air. He stepped aside good-naturedly and I ducked in.

It was a sight to knock you down. I knew at once I would never see the like again. Oranges, reds, viridian, oozed from the walls of the grotto, golds and ochres turned every sculpted surface to godly flesh. I hung in the womb again, time already seeded in there, its forceps threatening to reclaim me. I must have made some involuntary gesture because I felt the guard, who had followed me in, retreat. I felt utterly undefended, the way a pilgrim was meant to here. Then, as if a single glimpse is all you are allowed of godhead, I was ejected into the world.

Xuan Zang had such a moment on his journey through Tartary. Robbers had threatened to kill him and curiously relented when he reasoned with them. He must have had a honeyed tongue. Afterwards they went into the cave together and watched a candle recreate the world.

The water was turned back on when I returned to my room, so I didn't need to shower out of the two-litre bottle I'd picked up in the grocery store downstairs just in case. There was even a thermos of hot water. I had no alarm clock and didn't want to miss my train so when I woke before dawn I stayed up writing. Before I hung the key up I turned to the blank page opposite my drawing of the Shanghai billionaire's bathroom and sketched the cramped bathroom in this flat: a squat toilet you stood over to have a shower, the soap in constant jeopardy, with all the family's rubber slippers tucked behind the surrounding pipes, mute witnesses.

I never saw the family. But they live in my head.

7 June

Beijing
In the end the Chinese person most like me turns out to be Shuang, our interpreter. She has a middle-class apartment in the Drum and Gong hutong where my ginkgos have been cooling their heels. Time is short when I turn up from Datong, barely two hours before I must leave for the airport. We spread a couple of garbage bags on the kitchen floor and I go to work shaving the red-soil rootballs of the ginkgos so they fit into a zip-up bag. I want them to breathe but I don't want them too conspicuous on arrival. Half of me expects them to be confiscated by some officious man at the airport. When the job is done we go shopping. I want a common or garden Beijing wok.

'She would like to tell you,' Shuang translates for the wok seller, 'that you look typically Indian.'

I bow deeply.

'Not only do you look Indian, she says, you are the very essence of Indianness.'

I buy a cleaver as *well* as a wok.

Shuang drops me at the ABC terminal where I make a wrong turn and get on a metro line. Sensing something wrong in the crowd I ask the most likely young man. He sets me right and I get off at the next stop. Time is now very short. But when I get to the airport I take another wrong turn and find myself in the domestic terminal. Getting out of here is going to be a problem. Clearly a large part of me does not want to leave China. A tall Chinese official approaches me.

'Do you have 20 Yuan?'

When he is sure I do he leads me down a long passage to a forbidden door.

He pockets the note, I make the flight.

I arrive in Delhi past midnight: the botanical office at the airport is closed. I walk through with my ginkgos and climb into a taxi that heads straight out of town onto the Dehradun road.

10 June

Going away, I'd left Dhani with a key, but the thief was at the back of my mind. I raised both hands to the sky. Let fate dispose.

No one broke in. The whiskey stayed in the decanter; the jar of almonds was untouched. One by one I retrieved the bottles of scotch from their hiding places (among bottles of phenyl and bleach and toilet bowl cleaner). No one had dropped in for a peg of hydrochloric acid. I had cracked every seal for no good reason. Wardrobe doors shut, no heaps of towels on the floor, stained with betel juice. No rifled drawers, not one broken padlock! What was crime coming to?

But ravage there was, this time in the garden. The flowerpots had not been watered, the oakleaf hydrangea was in a bad way, the plumbago was a withered stalk.

I go from pot to pot snapping off dead twigs, thinking: 'You've not been by *once*, Dhani!' Here is breaking by *not* entering, an inside job.

I rehearse cutting things to say.

'Was the garden tap *so-o* hard to turn on? The gate key so stiff in the lock?'

But no, Dhani was immune to irony, innocent of it. I would have to distance myself. Instead of the usual pleasantries and chitchat about the weather I would say to him: '*I said to myself, "let's see what this chap's been up to while I've been away",*' something like that. The reported speech, the *chap*, would impose its distance, while *this* chap would make it a touch more offhand than *that* chap, a little closer in and yet higher up; in Hindi, as in English, the shade of meaning matched precisely. A single tic could put him in his place, a place from which I would normally be at pains, by a different kind of patronage no doubt, to rescue him. A Mughal or Tudor prince might twit a presumptuous companion in just this way: *You grow familiar.*

Familiar! In truer democracies that shade of meaning is three centuries dead. Here rank and distance still come built into your choice of pronoun. Besides, when he refers to this house, Dhani will say: 'Oh, this is family'. We *are* familiar.

And then the bottom fell out. I called on my good friend DP down the road, and learnt Dhani was ill.

Now followed remorse of conscience. All the harsh words I rehearsed I took back and turned on myself. Each was an edged weapon, and I did not spare me. What was an oak leaf hydrangea, even one from Scotland, compared with Dhani? Plumbago, was a *weed*, for godsake! My penitence was medieval, self-serving. *I'll be good to him, Lord, just let him come back. Spare him and see!* Not that Dhani's life was in danger, but in recent years he's wilted. A simple bug could carry him off. The fact is I would be lost without him, and knowing this, how far was my concern concern for Dhani? Could I be sure of the purity of my motives after that disgraceful inner scene?

I took his wages and went to call on him.

11 June
A mongoose! Proof no one has been by since May.

How easily these 433 sq yards could turn jungle is demonstrated every time I go away. Word runs through the ranks of the buffalo grass. Oxalis pushes up in a hundred places. The whole iris battalion takes one step forward. Lantana rolls out its barbed wire, and a fine rain of litchi mast begins to clog the guttering.

The terrible thing is you long for this to happen. I *want* the mongoose to feel free to roam (it has a family), oxalis to sprout, the barbet, our coppersmith to come down for a drink. Half of me wants to bury the birdbath and make a proper waterhole of the lawn where mice and seven sisters and stray cats can pause on their way through the urban jungle. Perhaps this future is already out there, once Dhani is dead and my strength fails. Forest Dwelling in earnest. From childhood I remember an ancient lady whose cottage garden ran to seed around her and her forty cats. There's a Jean Rhys story written in her old age from what looks like a garden shed: the whole job of a day is to tackle a rat.

12 June
A fine yellow dust has followed me from China, chasing along high overhead, then raining down on the valley. DP tells of the sky turning a dark gold last week and I think of the 'yellow storms' of my childhood in the plains. The garden is parched, the brick walks caked with ochre. A handful of litchis on the tree. I pruned too vigorously last year and the tree is sulking.

13 June
Today Nergis is ninety. I make her a card from a Pingyao sketch, a detail from a granite stele border showing a songbird on a pomegranate twig. Jump into the Fiat and drive up to Nayantara's where her friends are getting together. Nergis trim and ageless. Her supple yoga paperback has failed me, but her cookbook is an archive. Her son has travelled back from Illinois to be here today. He decides the Fiat is *racing-car* green and I defect at once from emerald. Nayantara presents a downy cheek to guests. She is editing her uncle Jawaharlal's letters; the photographs on the mantelpiece are of a Nehruvian vintage. I'm kneeling at the fireplace under Ho Chi Minh's gaze with one arm exploring the S bend in the flue when an architect comes up and draws me a cross-section of the correct chimney. Friends throng the verandah.
    I'm home!

17 June
Wake the hibernating laptop. A week of house and yardwork in hottest June. Clearing a way back to this book.

18 June
Daily power cuts. I want to clout our linemen, our engineers. When you've watched a foreign people go about their lives you come home with a changed heart. Shuang said she could remember just two outages—from her childhood. *Two* power failures in ten years! Two a *day* is our average.

—*Perhaps we're easier on the planet, sir?*
—*Now there's a thought. On ourselves too.*

Dhani comes by. He's been a month convalescing, wants to be up and about. He squats by the almirah.
'How's it going?'
I tick off a little defensively the jobs I finished before leaving: 'The back's done, the baseboards, the legs. Just the mirror left. It would be done by now, if I didn't have my inside work to do.'
Inside work is what I call writing with Dhani.
With Habilis I say *computer* work. He likes the sound of the modern word, and if I leave it out will find a reason for supplying it himself. 'When you get back to your computer,' he'll say as we cut stone. Kam-*pu*-tar. Computers mean figures to him, not words. In his head I sit here crunching numbers. (Mathematicians must share this prejudice against words: if the universe is a series of equations, of what use is this book?) But of course it's not *real* work. Hard slog is work.

I'm trying to write about work, the work they do, two men who can't read or write, and the work I do, a man who lives by the word, and how these regimes overlap. And I'm getting nowhere. Because my head is full of China. The two things needn't clash: after all China's spectacular development is only partly to do with inflows of capital; the other part has to do with the upheaval in social relations when her classes faced off in a way ours never have in all our history. The return of a class society in China doesn't alter that fundamental shift in the old conception of work and value. Although neither Dhani nor Habilis understands the work that gets done in this study (office is their word, *daftar*), they are in awe of it. It (along with money) is what makes me respectable. Whereas the work I do with *them* (perhaps because it blurred what until that had been in clear focus) was for the longest time a matter of faint deprecation. I was not a true sahib *because* I worked alongside them, doing that lesser thing: real work. It was work because it was *not* respectable. In the old days when gentle people fell on hard times the ruler let them join public works after dusk. So no one would know them as they dug.

19 June
Another night-long power cut. Sleep out on the Stoneman lawn under a mosquito net. Grateful for a cool spell at dawn. Grateful to gravity, that feeds a shower without electricity.
Water trickling into the ground tank all night long.

20 June

The small rains

Storm before dawn. At the nameless hour when you've mourned every misspoken word, listened for the first bird (magpie robin, of course; the milk truck, that low-flying harpy, a close second), and slipped back into sleep, this grim churning that jerks you upright. *Dust!* Blind scramble, glasses misplaced, just this morning naturally, to shut every door and window. Seven doors, thirteen windows. Stumbling in the dark because the local substation switches off the power before a storm. The first gust sent all the fallen mango leaves skating together down the Bengal-side alley; now they go skating back. The cloister gate slams. Black air seething with sand and grit and China loess. The first drops of rain sound on the fibreglass sheet above the bathtub (fourteenth window). A different sound on tin and another on aluminium and another on stone till the rain gathers force and beats down on all the surfaces equally.

Still you wait, for the downpour to steady, for a plashing from the gutters.

Then you go around reopening every door and window just shut—the doors first so a cool draught blasts a passage clear through the night's fug—and lastly the vents with their more intricate veins of air, moving easily now between furniture lit by continuous lightning. At last the house is aired.

Two external doors are considered quite enough in these parts, for reasons of security; three at most. There have been kidnappings and robberies all round in this largely business people's suburb, most notoriously the gang that timed their raid to coincide with a return from a wedding and took all the women's jewellery. *Seven* exits would be considered inviting trouble if word got out. Even Habilis looked sideways at me as we punched out yet another wall.

And we were, after all, burgled. But then the burglar came in by the front door anyway and left with an old camera. Imagine the privations of life with three doors: you want to get into the garden from your bedroom but you must traverse the living room and one verandah first. You want the steam out of your monsoon bathroom but you must wait till a tiny window exhales it draught by draught. So one by one our windows have turned French.

21 June
Summer solstice. At midday I upend a brick on the Stoneman lawn. Brick, Stoneman, and I, stand facing north as the sun passes overhead. There is a slight shadow off me, it could be stomach, off the north face of me, but it's there under the brick as well, and a black moustache not accounted for by Stoneman's chin. The fact is we're just north of the tropic, so there's bound to be a fringe of shadow on all three, but here we are: the sixty year old, the sixty million year old, and the six year old, lined up on our given latitude, saluting the sun as it tags meridian and tropic.

When the honour guard disperses I realize I forgot to salute my mother. Today was her birthday and she celebrated four such in this house, arthritis slowly crippling her till she succumbed not to the disease but to the treatment.

This was to have been a school, this house, her school, a dame school. But it got no further than four little tables, one red, one yellow, one green, and one blue, and four matching chairs.

Dame school
Some hours past the city of Allahabad, where I was born, the train from Calcutta to Dehradun, passes through the town of Fatehpur. Just

past the first level-crossing after Fatehpur station, on the left side of the track behind a row of ancient mango trees stands a whitewashed bungalow. It has a tiled roof, four corner bedrooms and a central axis on which drawing room, dining room, back verandah, and passageway to kitchen are disposed. In an armchair on the front verandah, within a wooden paling, sits a woman in a cotton frock, still young, raising her voice. She is my mother, and the verandah is her dame school.

I learnt to spell in this school, along with my sister, Janet, two years older, and I can't remember who else, perhaps the Civil Surgeon's daughter. In our earliest years my father was posted in small towns of the cow belt. No English was spoken there, except what we spoke. In such towns, overgrown villages really, my mother taught the children of the two or three government officers—the District Magistrate, perhaps a Treasury Officer, or a Sessions Judge—stranded there like my father, back of beyond.

Quite how old the dame school was in India I didn't realize until I was researching my first novel. For near on four centuries countless Anglo-Indian women made ends meet by teaching at home. The verandah was where such classes were conducted, with all the distractions—a monkey in the mango tree?—that entailed. From small town to small town my mother follows her officer husband; where there are proper schools she teaches there. She wouldn't mind a big city, which for her is Allahabad, old capital of the United Provinces, with its broad roads and fine university campus where she read English literature, but my father is never posted there again. In the past Anglo-Indians got preferential advancement; in independent India the boot is on the other foot. She is a good teacher, the small town officials recognize this: when my father is transferred to the next small town, their wards come with gifts, a thermos flask, a set of tumblers. In Dehradun at last, our first venture into this city of sparkling canals, she is appointed headmistress, and four years later principal of a proper school, but again my father is shunted away. Enough is enough: they decide to emigrate. But when she arrives in Australia her Indian degree is not recognized, and Dorothy Sealy, BA. LT, sits in the cramped basement office of a Sydney stationery supplier. She will not forgive this slight, and twelve months after emigrating she returns to India for good.

In a famous minute of 1858 Lord Macaulay proposed to make English gentlemen of young Indians, and legend has it that the spread of English began there. Not so. The British Raj did not introduce English to Indians. Anglo-Indians invented English education in this country. A hundred years before Macaulay Anglo-Indian women, teaching from home, from their verandahs, spread their native tongue through the land, first in the three port cities and later upcountry. Men too, but mostly women, women who wore gowns on skin as dark as my mother's. Dames who spoke English at home, with an accent already sneered at by the British. It shaped the accent of Indian English to this day, but Indians do not know this. It is to dame schools as much as to the church schools of the competing Catholic and Protestant clergy (where again the teachers were routinely Anglo-Indian, not British) that today's Anglophone middle class owes its ancestry and its ascendency.

23 June

First rain bath of the year, on the Stoneman lawn. Water spouts from the gargoyle on the roof, a pleasure as old as the naked body.

26 June

The garden is full of unfledged birds. Two baby sunbirds on the olive: their nest is concealed by the swords of a flax bush at the harp seat. The mother spends all day feeding them. One is well-groomed and the same size as the mother; she gets all the attention. The smaller and scruffier sib perched lower down gets every third worm. Suddenly I realize this bedraggled brown creature is the male, the future sun king: by the end of the year he'll be in regal purple.

28 June

Misery. The small rains have made it insufferably humid.

This morning I pull up a chair beside the almirah and stare balefully at it. One small job remains but I can't bring myself to act. Idly I scribe a line and begin to pull and push the saw (the push, the cutting stroke, especially light: this is rotten wood) at the bottom of the mirror door. Moronic action eases you in. When the cut is made I slip in the rib, like God with Eve. Waiting for the glue to set I pick up a rag and dip it in a flat-bottom oval mackerel tin. Two hours later the cupboard is transformed, the paleness of scrubbed teak mellowed to a dark brown gloss from twice-boiled linseed oil. I sweep the sunporch and tarp the finished almirah.

A sense of release. But the book is still bogged down.

30 June
Thunder to madden a deaf dog. A cloudburst. The big rains at last? Scribbled in cursive Mandarin, lightning over the hills: *Hunan Fireworks Factory # 8.*

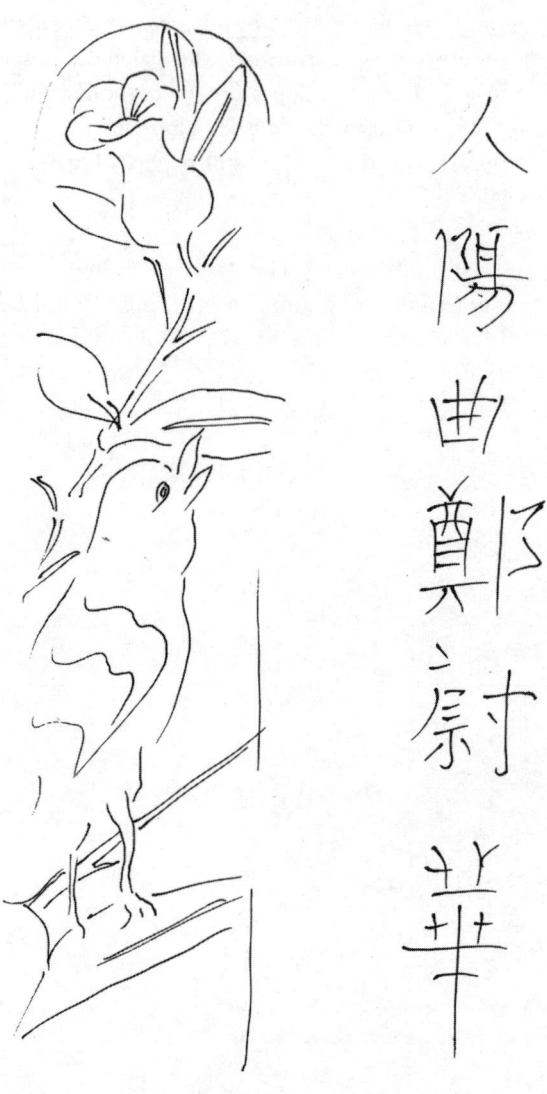

Pomegranate songbird

July

The rains
The long hard summer is done, the dust settled by the first showers. Sun hidden, air cool, earth scented with rain. From classical times the sky has been black over lovers. *Her brow clouded over* means something else here. Grass springs up underfoot, the hills are green; bushes beckon with soft bedding, and there's that brimful pond to dip in after love's exertions. A landscape made for love.

Two characters, mountain and water, unite to form the Chinese word for landscape. Resolutely material, Chinese art always had a secular ear to the ground; in painting, the depiction of landscape was considered the true test of an artist. With us, south of the Himalayas, the focus in painting is on faith, the god in the centre, let nature go hang. Landscape is a distraction, even a stumbling block; perfunctory and decorative, it's a kind of frame tacked on within the picture, a border with flowers and leaves.

Except in these hills. These very foothills of ours—go up on the roof and look south: that jagged ridge where the lighting forks—were the home of Pahari painting, the Hill School, the most rarefied and least acclimatized of Indian schools. Just along the way from here occurred something of a miracle in Indian painting. A painting that celebrated love, and in the same breath nature, as if the two were one. Provincials active two centuries ago, a long way from the centres of political power that nurtured the sophisticated Mughal School, the painters celebrated a radiant union of nature and man in the classic pairing of Krishna and Radha. It was a turning aside without precedent, as though lightning earthed in these hills and made them glow.

The lovers sit on a wooded bank spread with banana leaves. It's late evening, to judge from the smoke blue sky, but every shrub and vine is in vivid flower. Lotuses avert their pink heads from the lovers;

their great leaves tremble from something other than the tossing of the wavelets. Cream and meadow blue are the grass flowers. In the darkening grove he sits with one arm about her shoulders, drawing her to him: one hand strokes the tresses that ripple down her back, the other presses the tender flesh just above the elbow. She sits in a trance of love. She whose visible eye is shut (his are wide open) as her dreaming forehead burrows deeper into his chest. The forest canopy is dark with approaching night, the tree trunks, this snaking creeper, already black. Snow-white egrets patrol the far bank, a dove on a branch pecks under a lifted wing, all nature goes its way as nowhere else in all our painting. She who calls with little inward notes is yours this monsoon night. She in the late-night sales tax office, where a gecko is moulting. She on the still-warm concrete of the railway siding, where a rat gnaws at the parcels. She who laughs you.

—*Young Householder, that is some sort of wooden toy for the child?*
—*Forest Dweller sir, Her-at-the-helm is still in the family way.*
—*Then why this haste?* (Examining it.) *It looks like a harrow.*
—*For flesh, sir.* (Bashfully) *She requires a nightly application.*
—*Aha. China-made from the look of it.*
—*Oh no, sir, from the Shakumbari fair, just beyond those hills. It works wonders.*

1 July
The Silk Route keeps creeping into my life. As if China were still calling, the long way round:
On a paper bag, handmade, this page from a school history of India: *the Turkis from the land of the Oxus (Amu Darya) and the oases at Bukhara and Samarkhand settled in this country a thousand years ago, and founded a sultanate and made Delhi their capital.*

7 July
I file down the sharp edges of the Chinese wok with a German angle grinder: the races meet and spark. It's a crude enough pan but I was after a street wok, light and handy, not factory finish. I stir-fry quick easy things from the packets I brought back, I nibble at the

pale watercolour candies Zhai gave me, but I need serious food and lack the will to cook. Takeaway food tempts but betrays: *E. coli*, old sparring partner. I hanker for bread and cheese, but the yeast is flat.

Where is Habilis?
Victor turns up instead, his dog Sairu with him. His waitering jobs at the EC Road wedding point have dried up during the monsoon; black skies are all very well for lovers, but grooms on horseback see things differently. I have him putty windows, but his touch is not as sure as Habilis's.

11 July
The breath thins, I think, waking in the middle of the night, laying one hand on my chest, a fingertip on the breastbone where the spirit-stuff seems to come and go through a blowhole, no longer the tingling rush of childhood, not the fat silken cord of youth; now a skein.

15 July
Sitting out the monsoon, leafing through the China sketchbook. Hearing Mr Li in my head. Nudging the book that way, herding China this way. Into the lion-mouth.

18 July
Gardeners go home to their des for the rains. It's too wet to work, and often they have simply to sit and stare. This is a time of luscious unkempt lawns. Who will push the mower? Not the owner. Who will scythe the grass?

Dhani often takes the day off, stays put in his garage. He has no ancestral home to go to any more. Half the family migrated here anyway, and those left behind don't want an old man turning up on their doorstep. I ask him when he was last home. A pause in his whetting of the sickle blade.

'Years,' he decides.

Nowadays the carrier on his bicycle clamps trowel and sickle together in an emblem that looks vaguely like the old Soviet flag.

Next I look the bank is shorn. A steady stroke beats speed every time. The tortoise, if we had one, would be Dhani's true emblem. (Habilis is the hare.) Dhani's neck has stretched and curved with the humping of a back bent right over: his head comes prospecting out from under the shell at a stiff collar.

The lawn is ripe with worms: some days it quakes like Gorgonzola.

Earthworms
Wormcasts minaret the green. Dhani steers around them. He's not squeamish about worms. Will slice one in half when turning the soil without even noticing. He is more than half soil himself, this lifelong vegetarian, so it's always with a start that I realize he won't return to it. He'll be cremated. Worms will never traffic with him, never get their turn.

I took him to the cemetery once, and only once, to plant some lilies around my mother's grave. Was he uneasy? I kept wondering, too late, as we walked down the long cypress avenue with tombstones stretching in every direction. He would no more have seen a graveyard than the inside of a butcher's shop, and for the rest of our visit I kept seeing the ground with x-ray vision on his behalf, and cringing. After that I went alone, with whatever clumps of violets or lilies I had to. Nothing took, just weeds.

Everybody knows Darwin's study of earthworms. He educated the Victorians on the vital role these creatures play aerating the soil. Less well known today is this paragraph written before he was born:

> *Earth-worms, though in appearance a small and despicable link in the chain of Nature, yet, if lost, would make a lamentable chasm. For to say nothing of half the birds, and some quadrupeds which are almost entirely supported by them, worms seem to be the great promoters of vegetation, which would proceed but lamely without them, by boring, perforating, and loosening the soil, and rendering it pervious to rains and the fibres of plants, by drawing straws and stalks and leaves and twigs into it; and most of all by throwing up such infinite numbers of lumps of earth called worm-casts, which, being their excrement, is a fine manure for grain and grass.*

Without worms, says the author of the above, writing in the 1770s from a little country parsonage in England, the earth would become 'cold, hard-bound, and void of fermentation, and consequently steril', but thanks to these hermaphrodites, 'much addicted to venery, and consequently very prolific', there is no danger of that.

Gilbert White's *The Natural History of Selborne* would have been one of the earliest books Darwin read; at one time its popularity was exceeded only by the Bible and Shakespeare. It has a special place on the 433—our copy an 1840s illustrated edition, a gift from my mentor Dan in Scotland—should really be on a shelf by itself. I owe it a new set of eyes. The boy Darwin would have memorized whole pages; why does the old man who wrote the treatise on worms mention White only once in passing? Can it be that he thought the passage too well known to warrant acknowledgement? Or was it that he saw White as an amateur—in just the way White himself will acknowledge the help of friends, 'an inquisitive gentleman' or 'a curious personage' and pass over the countryman's contribution as that of 'a great looby.' Is all this simply a matter of class, or is class itself simply a matter of sedimentation? Are we at bottom geology? Is geology itself just an episode in gravity? Or gravity God? Hafiz, who knew this all along, laughs and fills the cup. Then frowns, finding verdigris on the lip.

19 July

Housing
Entry for this day in my parents' accounts diary for 1982, a penciled note in my father's handwriting:
GREAT DAY!
WE BECAME LANDOWNERS!!

Registration tip	50.00
Stamp paper	5.00
Typing & notary	11.00
Pani wala's tip	2.00

68.00 <u>Cough!!!</u>

When I was a child my father came home every payday and put his pay packet in my mother's hands. If he needed to buy something he stood behind her chair and said: *Cough*! I loved this ritual.

My mother has written in ink alongside this entry:

Paid on 20/7

and underneath:

    Eggs and Bread   4.85

    Veg   4.50

It must have been a long hot day at the courts, so the water-carrier would have earned his tip. Today six eggs and a loaf of bread cost ten times what my mother coughed up; the land value has gone up a hundred times.

All the same those excited capital letters would have mystified my father's father. My father himself speaks of the pleasure he once took in writing across his tax form every March: 'NO PROPERTY'. Owning land was not something Anglo-Indians went in for: home was somewhere else. Home, if at all you could see it, and most never had, was on the wall, a thatched cottage beside a Kentish millpond with the motto: *He leadeth me beside the still waters.* (In a land of flat roofs, the pointed roof of Europe still symbolizes a house, and not just for Anglos.) During the Raj you rented, the British rented, Anglo-Indians rented. Buying property was for adventurers, an eighteenth century breed who prospered beyond any sober reckoning, and for that suspect class in British India, businessmen. Even the box wala, the salaried executive of a foreign company, rented his mansion. So our action was bold for where we came from: not altogether without precedent, but as unusual as the leather sandals my father had taken to wearing, or the salwar kameez my mother wore nowadays.

Community leaders who understood how Anglos despised property tried all along to encourage little Anglo enclaves across the country. In Bihar a whole township was laid out by colonists who felt India, not England, was home. McCluskieganj, still served by a railway station on the Calcutta line, is a ghost town today. Such a colony flourished in Dehradun too, a little settlement called Clement Town grouped around a couple of churches at the edge of the forest. But we lacked a Land God; no Jade Girl, no Gold Boy among us. The colony fizzled out around independence when most houseowners sold their properties to Sikh refugees from Pakistan and went away. It took half a century for those who remained to begin to put down roots: the more enterprising families took to running schools on land they owned, while one or two even went into business and the professions. I wish more had. I like the sound of *Harry Maclure Design Studio, Chennai,* run by a friend. I toy with a verge-garden company called *Frontage* for Filo, studying landscape architecture. Or *Palmyra Gallery,* for myself.

—*How go the applications, Good Householder?*
—*She is squeamish, sir.*
—*The job applications, boy.*
—*I could run your art gallery sir.*
—*Art gallery? A pipe dream, son. An excuse to build around the palm tree at our Andamans corner. Say nothing of it or Maeve will laugh.*

20 July
Maeve arrives from New Zealand.

21 July
M asleep behind the bedroom door I just pushed to, so I dry my face with her blouse on the chairback. That sweet old musk!

'First Things'
A video series at the Palmyra Gallery. What the eye sees on opening, shot close-up. Just that first click.

Today, 24th *July*: selvedge of white Genoa pillowcase, thread count of pale blue Bombay Dyeing double sheet in focus up front, discoloured length of off-white lamp wire looped from bedside lamp, green mica headboard, swell of forearm sprouting new grey hairs. That one frame.

365 shots in a loop, projected for the duration of Chennai Dutchman Maarten Visser's breathy experiments on sax, Track 4.
Voiceover to music:

A new title forming for the book after waking at half past three and going over in my head Chekhov's 'Gooseberries,' read out softly and surely by Maeve before dinner. She lies beside me breathing hard, the woman whose breath I've often watched come and go at this hour, leaning on an elbow and wondering what storms are sweeping through that skull. Email from the student in Beijing asking whether prosperity is not more important than democracy (polite censure of India's way?) recalled Giono's acrobat discoursing on socialism in the shepherd's hut. 'Enough for all is more important,' I think. 'But prosperity?' Lying here in the dark wishing for but not finding my blank sheet and pencil. Thinking: Victor could have helped me carry in the almirah. Crick in the neck the whole day (fan or wasp sting?). Went up onto the roof to waggle the power line: sure enough the power was on when I came back down. For five hours we thought it a power failure. Computer man says a burnt out transformer in the old UPS caused a short circuit. M's breath coming in bursts. Muezzin's call slips into the night air. Getting out of bed I tangle in the sheet. Dawn now, a conch blown in prayer somewhere. Pickup speeding by hits the judder bar so all the iron rods on the flatbed jump together. Now what was that title?

My new title has gone! Clean out of my head.

Idling, irritable, I look in a book I've just picked up at the rag and bone market, Freud's *Psychopathology of Everyday Life,* which includes an 1898 essay on the forgetting of proper names. It's one of those blue Pelicans published the year the war broke out (the year things went bad for the Jews of Vienna, providentially the year of Freud's death) and I take it to bed. It has the stamp of the Universal Book Depot in Hazratganj, Lucknow, a bookshop I visited regularly as a schoolboy, and is signed *R.K. Wanchoo, 1945* on the title page.

Freud puts my loss down to the 'incessant stream of self-reference' in my head and means to uncover the 'lawful and rational paths' of this forgetting, refusing to accept 'psychic arbitrariness' as a cause. It's only as you emerge from the essay that you realize you've been swept along by a logic inside rather than outside it: the force of the argument is in its rhetoric. Beauty has led you on, and at the end of the garden path you find a murky pool, Pathology. The itch to name and classify fishes this pond, the way drug companies dream up maladies we didn't know we had. It's while I'm on this roundabout attempt at retrieval, after the pleasures of Freud's essay, that the title pops up again.

The Small Wild Goose Pagoda.

Life flows from thought to thought, feeling to feeling, now connecting, now not. 1. I have a notion. 2. I draw a blank. 3. I recover the notion. More plainly: I forgot the small wild goose because I forgot it, and I remembered it when I remembered it.

It looks fine by broad daylight (the acid test).

24 July

Dhani's going blind. Today he knocked over the rubbish bin while looking for the broom. Yesterday he almost fell into a hole I dug at the gate.

A bit of polished iron lying in the shingle path. When I go to pick it up I find it immoveable. It's the root of a greenbelt fencepost someone broke off. (Looking back now I remember a grinning face on a teenage ragpicker.) Angle iron will keep its virtue only till it takes a nick in either leaf: then a girl can simply lean on it and bend it back and forth till it snaps.

I gave up digging after half an hour. Corner posts are buried eighteen inches deep but the foot is cloven and the ends turned up and shod in a concrete gumboot. In rocky soil the lump finds further anchorage. You think the post has begun to yield but your job is just beginning; a dentist would grasp this at once. Finish it tomorrow, I thought, and meant to flag the hole with a white cement sack, but forgot.

Dhani walked straight into it. Pushed his bike straight into the hole.

I hang my head. He could have fallen *on* that sword.

Years ago there was a young eucalyptus tree he cut down by the portico, right at the boundary. In those days neighbour walls were low, run up to elbow height for comfortable gossip. Dhani, younger by twenty years but already past middle age, shinned up the tree with his machete. I spelled him in the sun and we watched the beautiful heartwood leap out of the cut like chunks of Spam. At some point he tired of his cross stroke and thought to change to a backhand cut. Changing, he lost his balance and fell. I watched him go, as the machete spun from his hand in slow motion. He was lucky. A second before his head hit the top of the wall his free hand found a branch. We cut down the tree the next day.

Today, after work, he parks his bike and sits there rubbing tobacco in his palm while I tamp back in the fresh earth at the hole. Mosquitoes hover around his new haircut.

'How's the widow?'

'She keeps saying she wants the garage vacated. I say to her, Let me find a place and I'll clear out.'

Not that it's easy to dislodge a long-time tenant.

'In the old days your mother used to say she'd build a room for me.'

'How's the leak?'

'Oh, it comes with a heavy shower. She keeps saying she'll have it fixed but when there were workmen she didn't get around to it. In the old days your mother—'

'We can do it.' I mean Habilis. 'There's cement, there's gravel.'

'I was looking at the cement the other day. One shouldn't keep cement over the monsoon.'

I went to see. The sack was rock solid.

GARDEN WORK FOR THE RAINS
1. Shift yellow bottlebrush to swing seat
2. Red oleander to the red stone patio
3. Ivy to clad the new wall. (While I was away Pak raised the roof on their servants' quarter. We've lost two feet of western sky in the cloister.)

25 July
Habilis comes in the gate without rattling the latch. He stops to greet Dhani, stands over him where he squats weeding.

'Maliji,' he says (he doesn't need to use my voice), 'Take this willow tree and put it in that corner over there.'

Dhani grunts amusement just as I come up from behind. The rains are when you plant out things, but he's not one for shifting.

'You do it,' I suggest to Habilis, who jumps, but quells the jump.

'Or have you become some kind of big-shot contractor?'

He grins. The grin tells me he knows he's moving up in the world. Unlike Victor, Habilis is in control of his life, mostly.

'Job too small for you?'

I remind him that he used to lop for me, with me.

'Give me a contract,' he laughs.

'Let me work out the design.'

He's been working out west, in Gujarat. 'Out there,' he says, 'it's the Hindus that are good-looking. The Mohammedans have habshi hair. The soil is black, sugarcanes fat as trees. The sea is right next door.'

House style

In-flight entertainment: a maze of a Chinese movie on death and ghost-writing. *Written By* rehearses the obsessions of the American ghostie but from the perspective of a new master race anxious to get it right. A noodle ghostie, mumming Hollywood in all essentials, the way a tandoori ghostie from Bollywood might match its American original frame by frame. The old curry Western was a humbler form of tribute, a costume drama whose cosmetics wiped off. The dusky ranchera discarded her crinoline, the Madras cowboy hung up his hat. *Written By*, like many of the new Bombay offerings, comes across as a surgical makeover. The makers, you feel, will not be returning to normal life because there is no normal life to return to: they have successfully erased wherever it was they came from. They must live the story now.

Something of this sort happened in our painting, a generation of painters lost to Paris, figuring their modernity by mirrors. And something like it afflicts our literary life now. No home-grown tradition of experimentation exists. You could sit down and try to hammer out some new shape, but it's simpler to fit an old one out with native content. And since the thing must sell where it counts, you relocate to New York, acquire house style. True, the price is raised on arrival: you find yourself assigned a brown beat. You could live there forever and not get beyond covering the country you left. Strangely, the country you shook off is proud of you. Nor does it resent the travesty: even as your caricature passes for the real, the real adapts itself to the representation. Notice abroad is still the bottom line, and the only ticket is race.

Household gods

Chinese factories turn out flawless Hindu gods for the household shrine. In this house, two Chinese gods: a folding aluminium stepladder, and my Trek bicycle. Each an engineering marvel of its kind. The ladder was bought from the local hardware king, a last piece he parted with reluctantly. The bike was a gift, for an essay I wrote.

A local ladder is a desperate thing, the aluminium ones rickety and downright dangerous. The Chinese one is no heavier for being braced and channelled; as it slides open the steps fold down and lock with bionic security. A local bike, well, they last, but just look at Dhani's dowdy Atlas. The Trek is the work of a divine watchmaker. When will we make such things?

The prototype of every device and science known to man is, we are taught, Indian. Vedic science engineered flying saucers. Yet the hardware section of a Beijing department store had this remarkable sign in English: FOLLOW THE JAPANESE WAY OF PRECISION.

A break in the clouds. I ride the Trek down the centre of the new highway to Rishikesh, so new the white lines are not yet painted on. The road runs blank and undiscovered through scrub forest washed clean by rain. Partridges call in the early morning light.

Land God,
Jade girl and Gold boy
Shuanglin Temple

August

Cabin-fever month, tree-topple-over month, rain-lily-spill-scent month, frogs-skitter-like-green-hail month. Month of sweats and breezes, floods and malaria and moss and monstrous leaves. A pomegranate tree, heavy with fruit, leans right down to the ground, must be stood back up, lashed to the wall; red brick goes moss green, then sooty. Foreign windows open in the air, Vancouver Island peat, Greenwich sedge, Kalamazoo roof shingle, Maori fern-green. Salmon-ladder sunset. To the east, against black thunderheads, a lone silver kite.

1 August
It takes Dhani so long to turn his bike around on the way out I think I'll do it for him. When I've pointed it at the gate I think I might as well take it as far as the garage for him, past the thorny privet bush he grumbles about. But now it's starting to rain so I carry it as far as the gate where it's just under the garage awning. Only, once there I realize it'll be in the way when he comes by with his wide wicker basket of weeds under one arm, and he hates that. So I bring it back and stand it under the eaves only I turn it to face the gate so it's ready to wheel out. But when I do I find its front end, where he hangs his Holland America luxury cruise carry bag, is sticking out into the rain. So I shift the whole bike a little closer to the verandah where neither nose nor tail will get wet. But then I realize I've cut off his approach since he needs to get at it from the left and if he squeezes in there there's the risk of its toppling over and his overbalancing with it. All in all it would have been better to let him slowly turn it around himself.

I put it back exactly as he left it.

2 August

Rain, rain

Every morning I watch a little old lady in leucoderma socks lean into the neighbours' garden and strip it of flowers to place before her idol. That's what gardens are for. The Chinese garden is nature taken in hand, made over to man. Here, nature belongs to God. There's a story from the *Ramayana* that every child knows. I came to it late. The monkey king Hanuman is sent from Lanka all the way to the Himalayas to pick a vital herb: it alone can cure the divine Rama's wife, Sita, at the point of death. He reaches the sacred hill he was directed to and searches frantically but can't recognize the herb. In despair he tears up the whole hill and flies back through the air with it. It's a scene from a thousand miniature paintings, the god in the middle—at the very centre—and all nature balanced lightly on the palm of his hand.

Where are our gardens? Where does the secular start? In nature tamed, agriculture. At the end of that line is the garden. The Vedic peoples worshipped nature in the abstract, dealt with it as pastoralists; they took it as they found it, culled herbs in the wild. By classical times the garden, nature invited in, seems to have evolved no further, a distraction at the back of a mind focused on grammar, aesthetics, the decimal point, God. In Kalidasa it is nature that is beautiful, in itself, without improvement. Lily ponds, the white siris, the pure clouds above.

So where *are* our gardens? The ones that come to mind are imports from Persia, from Araby, Transoxiana. Was there an indigenous tradition of gardening? What did Xuan Zang find outside his carrel on the campus of Nalanda university? Flower beds? Espaliered fruit trees? Had the cultivation of the mango already been raised to a fine art? By the end of his long sabbatical, did he feel let down in those mango seasons when he hadn't had his fill? Babur, the first Mughal, sets about remedying the lack in his 'charmless and disorderly' Hindustan. In my favourite miniature of him he stands in a walled garden with pomegranate trees in flower and fruit.

'There,' he is pointing. 'No, nearer.'

The bare brick wall, the pomegranate trees, the tranquil foreshortened enclosure, could be our cloister here.

And where are our garden *tools*? Do we have a single digger earlier than the medieval period? Toys, yes, all the way back to Mohenjo-daro, kitchen tools by the thousand, weapons, ornaments, pelt-scrapers, ploughshares: but not a single spade. If I want a good spade, I must go abroad. In foreign stores I've asked for just the steel head of a spade, but spade-heads come already mounted. A full-length spade is just longer than a suitcase, and you'd feel silly importing a naked spade, tagged and clanking along, snagging on the carousel. The nearest equivalent here is Dhani's *phaura*, half hoe, half mattock, with a curved blade that is mounted at right angles to the shaft, so you hold it like a weapon. And since the shaft is always short, you *grub* rather than dig. The simple dig-down spade does not exist: there isn't a squared off blade with shoulders you can put your foot on and push easily and accurately into the earth. The very word for tool, any tool, in common use up north is foreign, from the Persian, *aujar*. Until the Muslims arrived with their chahar baghs and spades—there it is in the foreground of the Babur painting—the plough ruled.

Tools down, I sit on my redstone seat and miss the sign Maeve painted for our herb garden in Christchurch, a rough plank with two lines from Basho:

> *Sitting quietly doing nothing*
> *Spring comes and the grass grows by itself*

Again just too long for a suitcase.

THREENECKS
Corn-on-the-cob seller: the flap-flap of his wicker fan under a charcoal brazier penetrates all the way into the cloister.
Water-chestnut seller: purples and greens and magentas such as only jockeys wore at this bend in the course.

8 August
3:30 AM At the gate watching a stray dog standing motionless in the centre of the road. He's watching an old man workout under the streetlamp on the traffic island, our Sri Lanka. Just the three of us linked in the cool breeze of this soft dark morning.
Three days since I opened this laptop. Victor here all week. Absolute gardening, the whole day every day given over to replanting, shifting, digging, cutting, lopping, so I fall into bed at ten and sleep till two or three. Wake rested, watch the white head bob rhythmically on the traffic island, a cop bike past in uniform. *Slosh* in the milk cans as the milk truck hits the Threenecks judder bar. Police gong strikes four.
'*Allahu Akbar!*' calls the muezzin. '*God is Great!*'
'*Motherless* rain coming,' the corn wala says at noon.
Gave him the tenner the kabari gave me; four cobs of corn swapped for newspaper and tin.
4 PM Race (race *who*?) up onto the roof to watch the rain sweep in. Heart singing.
Yesterday, shifted the frilly orange hibiscus. Sweat running down my lenses, hint of impatience in Victor, a man normally unflappable. Take the axle shaft, get him to bend back the plant, strike blind at the last hidden root: three, four, five times, till a muted *click* sounds through the soil.
Released, we sigh simultaneously: free! A cool breeze sweeps over us right then, running ahead of rain.
Habilis comes by just as the hole is being filled in. A bit peeved at finding Victor here, Victor whom he introduced to me. He aims a kick at Sairu who jumps up and scoots away; for a thickset moth-eaten brawler he has the most craven way of flattening his ears and looking put upon when threatened. This morning he slept in the garage, then found himself a shady spot in the greenbelt.
'He gets a packet of sweet biscuits every day, and twenty rupees worth of meat,' Habilis notes proudly.
The pride on Victor's behalf. It's a tenth of Victor's wage. Victor says nothing. He has never spoken of Sairu, and it was Maeve who realized this dog with great mooning eyes who appeared from time to time at the gate was his.

'He was rescued from a street fight,' Habilis continues. 'If Victor hadn't stepped in'—his hand flies to his throat—'he was a goner.'

Victor reruns the moment a long way back in his head.

'We've found him a wife,' Habilis says to me, nodding at Victor now.

'*What!*'

I stare at them.

Victor smiles feebly. I'm amazed by the simper; it says there really is something afoot.

'So when you die,' Habilis turns to him, 'there'll be somebody to bury your bones.' He nods at the hole. Their faiths share this one end.

Victor's eyes screw up into glints.

'Save up a couple of thousand and borrow a bit from Sahib here and do it. She's not going to wait forever.'

Victor tamps the soil with an unsure foot, the missing middle two toes pushing hardest. Has the girl heard about the toes?

'Where is she?' I ask. She gets a handsome head up top; Victor's a looker.

'In her village. It's all been set up by a woman here.'

Housing (2)

The lapwing builds its nest on the ground so the young must run for cover as soon as they are hatched. A cat finds a window down in the Fiat and has her kittens in the back seat. Dhani sets tin cans to catch drips from his roof, a private gamelan. Victor must leave a crack at the bottom of the rolling shutter or get no air in his garage. A Young Householder and his Good Wife, rent my almirah (to judge from the creaking). Habilis has one room and a muddy yard for six. There was an old woman who lived in a shoe. The girls of Hunan Fireworks Factory #8 sleep under dormitory mosquito nets. My mother sleeps in a narrow grave. My mother's mother had an acre in town with a four-bedroom bungalow, four attached dressing rooms, four corner bathrooms, four verandahs and a grand portico. My father's architect placed a shoebox in a lion's mouth. Pak has put a servants' quarter on our west boundary. There are one million new flats lying vacant in China. An opera box hangs on our roof. The snail carries his house on his back. Wormcasts Gaudi the shingle.

10 August
Walking on the roof this morning it comes to me like revelation.
There is a way to block off that balcony!
There *is* a way of building the screen I want, right on the line, without starting at the ground, without touching the existing boundary wall, that will return our space to us completely and forever. How could I have not seen it!
A simple cantilevered slab that goes right out to the boundary, to the very edge of that opera box.
And one fine morning, when the concrete has cured, I run up a wall. On that line, in the air.
These guys are history! Ancient history. (Well, modern history.)
I spend the rest of the day cantilevering.
Cantilever, *v.* to walk on air, to gallivant.

—*Revenge is sweet, Forest Dwelling sir?*
—*Fermented even better, boy.* Make haste slowly, *the Almanack says.*

11 August
Let the new thing be a pagoda.
A Small Wild Goose Pagoda! My new title is contagious: who said books make nothing happen? It's only later that the design begins to flow the other way, so the tower and its making shape the book.
With a third storey, now that the roof slab will be concrete, a pavilion on top of the rain room that overlooks even the main roof terrace. Three stories will make a fine tower.
With a skywell let into the rain room study, through which the monk seated in the chamber can see the stars.
Pagoda *n.* **1** a Hindu or Buddhist temple or sacred building, esp. a many-tiered tower, usually with an odd number of tiers, in India and the Far East. **2** an ornamental imitation of this. [Port. *pagode*, prob. ult. f. Pers. *butkada* idol temple] *Concise OED*

12 August

Madly happy. Woke out of a dream of Datong. Buried my face in the pillow, exulting, shouting softly: *A SMALL WILD GOOSE PAGODA!* Maeve asleep six inches away.

On Sunday gave Victor his trousseau (some bride stuff in there, silks and cottons for the village belle). Raining, so dropped him home. Home! His street is one house-row from a river-turned-drain. But a street all the same, so there are those still worse off. He sleeps on the garage floor, on a mattress spread with a foul sheet. There's a mysterious chalked-out rectangle on the floor beside him (where her mattress will go?) leaving just enough room for the kerosene stove she will cook on, dipping into the iron bucket for water. The common bathroom is down a short passage that serves dwellings to the rear. When Victor said he had a bathroom he meant he had access to a bathroom not shared with the world. The wife will take herself there mornings, early to avoid the queue, will have to teach herself not to want to go during the night, which would mean stepping over her husband and lifting the rolling shutter with a great iron crash.

Our one thousand square feet looks immense on return. By pushing out here and there Habilis has given us an extra three hundred square feet. Pushing westward we could get another hundred now.

We have a long plot, rectangular, roughly 90 feet by 45. Roughly, because the irregular shape (the lion-yawn) makes measurement hard. When you stand on the street facing the plot, the boundary to your right is at right angles to the front boundary. (The house is aligned with that boundary.) On the other side, the portico side of the house, the left boundary angles in. Any projection from the portico, such as a cantilevered roof from the room on it, will be slightly irregular, with only two sides, front and back, parallel.

Rich, *adj*. To have a meadow on the Shanghai Bund and do nothing with it. To have a bare roof in Racecourse and do everything with it. To put a pagoda on your portico. To have garden rooms open to the sky. To be known for what you do not build. To have stocks and shares in air. To have no opera box.

13 August
Now the monsoon is looking finite I begin to think seriously of building. Simple questions arise: how many sides to a pagoda? Sadly, the broadband line is down.

14 August
Still circling the pagoda looking for a way in.
Reading in bed I'm conscious of little browsing sounds on the front lawn. Has a buffalo has sneaked in? There was a bull in here once. But then I hear a pebbly clink underwrite the grassy cropping: Dhani. He glances indoors; I show myself. When he sees my silhouette against the back door he turns away satisfied. He doesn't like an empty house. That, not just his sickness, explains his dereliction of duty when I was away. He won't work for ghosts. Vanishing into a book is bad enough; vanishing to another country is craven. Let the house be full, and he will turn to his routine.

The scorn of those who stay for those who go.

Delhi? He was there once, and that was enough. If I say Chennai I might as well be speaking of China. If say I'm going abroad I get the look I once got from a man in a log cabin in the Yukon.

'To the Yucatan,' I said, looking down at the new boots that took me all the way. He fetched from his depths a pitying look that is with me still. (The boots are too. I saluted him when I reached Sisal, standing on the shores of the Gulf of Mexico.) Today it's *his* shoes I stand in, in that doorway, looking out.

I try to picture Dhani on a bus or a train. I just did. There was a small nervous smile on his face as he craned his head to look out the window. The fact is he'd hesitate to take even a tempo, the two-stroke three-wheelers that ply along the main road at Dharampur-Antarctica. His bicycle is now a walking stick. Only my aged aunt in Calcutta, stuck in a second-storey flat, gets around less. Dhani sticks to this square mile.

Till the new century his attendance on the 433 square yards was more regular than mine. Only in the last ten years has my acquaintance with their surface been as close as his. Inch for inch I still lag behind on certain lawns. His archive has no gaps. Plus he actually *is* closer to the ground. He squats there, day in and out (he would squat in his garage too) at a level I seldom reach, and his progressive hunch has touched his squatting too.

I want to measure it exactly and am tempted to take the inchitape out to where he is and casually extend it to the ground as we talk. I can't bring myself to, and must lecture myself sternly. If you're going to be thorough documenting this plot, these 433 square yards, you have to measure depth of field as well. I compromise. Measuring my knee against this door, I then go stand beside him.

Twenty inches. Dhani's altitude.

Where he lives and works. His country almost, so in a sense he emigrates every time he rises. When he uncrouches, as now, it is to wheel his bike to DP's house, where he sets it on its stand—only to crouch down again. His eyes are knee-high for most of the day. Dogs and pigs are the only other creatures I see dwelling at that level. (I hesitate before writing those words, insulting names for ten thousand years.) Cows and buffaloes roll their great liquid eyes at *chest* height as they go past the gate, higher than Dhani.

To test a condition older than animal husbandry, as old as hunting, I take a folding bed, twenty inches high, out to the back lawn and lie there for a bit on my stomach, looking down. So this is how he sees. This is what *Homo erectus* was trying to escape. It's what our own *Homo habilis* left behind in his village when he quit stoop labour and turned painter.

I turn over on my back. The sky seems further away down here.

15 August
Brushdown of the kitchen: a hundred spiders perish on Independence Day.
　　Broadband back!!!!!!!
　　Then lost again.

16 August
China dreams, but they fade as I wake. Instead I travel with Robert Hillenbrand in Transoxiana, returning again and again to a black and white photo of the courtyard of the Turbat-i Jam Shrine. To be buried

there I would die today, or just as soon as the pagoda is ready.

AUGUST PENANCE
A barefoot tour of the Silk Route for the designer of the parking lot at the Great Wild Goose Pagoda in Xian.

17 August
Seven power failures today, maybe eight, I lost count. No power, no phone, no internet. Ashamed, Shuang!

Last night the old Fiat took Maeve to the train station in the heaviest downpour of the monsoon. Groping our way, headlights flickering, cars veering away, wipers coming on only on the way *back*. Ploughing through axle-deep water, cheering her on desperately:
'You beauty, you *beauty*!'
She came home and died right outside the gate.

Racecourse Crier
Dhani crouches under the mango, no songbird, but a single bar of four notes escapes his red-scarfed head.

Who would have thought this hornbill was (under his breath) the Racecourse tabloid.

RC: *Didn't you know, then? That man you'd see walking the course with his minder? He wasn't born blind. Oh no. He was in Kashmir, with the State Bank. One of those terrorists walked in one day and demanded the safe key and he said no. The gun went off in his face. He gets a pension from the bank. He's sold and gone off to Chandigarh.*

Me: *A planned city, Chandigarh. They have sidewalks there.*

RC: [Rubbing tobacco in his palm] *Gardens outside every gate.*

Me: *This is the armpit of India, Dhani Ram.*

RC: *This is a* louse *on an armpit* hair.

19 August
I go up on the roof to rehang the telephone cable and find a simple break in the wire. Two weeks without phone or broadband and the fault was right under my nose!

20 August
Nights out in the rain for the Fiat. Looking glamorous in the morning, her emerald green skin glowing. Twenty-five years I've hung on to this car of Terry's, her forward-opening front doors, the anti-clockwise bolts on the left-side wheels, all appealing to a contrariness in me.
  —*Time to give in, Forest Dweller sir?*
  —*As in make for the forest?*
  —*No, sir. The car. You have a State Bank term deposit maturing.*
  —*Speak lower, boy. She has ears, forward-opening.*
  —*That* [lowers voice] *Volkswagen salesman was here again, sir.*

21 August
To the families Sampsell, Clark, and Wellenkamp, of Kalamazoo County, Michigan.

Forgotten anniversary, fortieth. A young man from Muzaffarnagar, a boy really, hardly twenty, arrives in Kalamazoo, Michigan with seven dollars in his pocket, an exchange student. The Honors College at Western fete their hostage: his parents needn't have worried. He's rich. He will always have more than he can spend, and less than he imagines. The curriculum is familiar, literature already a madness in him. September the pleasures of the New World pounce, November he's in love. April his fellow foreign students are gravely crafting resumes; he laughs and lets his hair grow long. Hitchhikes around the mitt of Michigan, to California and back, subs at the local coop, weighing out granola and pinto beans. Buys a bicycle, a tent, rides to Indiana. There is no tree as lovely as the maple in fall, no street as enchanting as Eggleston, no woman like the woman at number 73. He gets a summer job at Flugelman's on Lake Michigan, where the kitchen staff are black, the busboys brown, the waitresses blonde. The Jewish owners could be Anglos, but breakfast is lox and bagels. For weeks he thinks: '*larks* and bagels?' Big Larry sets him right. He has never known snow, car radios, an inland sea. *Muzaffarnagar*, do you hear? From there, Kuwait Air to red maples in fall. Hot showers, live music, *and* ready waitresses?

How could a boy not go wrong?

22 August
Scratch my thumb pruning bougainvillea, watch it puff up.
The south face of the willow trunk is worn smooth where generations of passing pigs have paused for a scratch.
I remove the iron tree guard from the flame tree because it hides a handsome trunk now five years old. When I turn around there is a two-ton milch buffalo gashing the bark with its horns. I put the guard back on.

23 August
The ginkgo is dying! One by one the leaves turn black and fall. I feel sick, physically sick, betrayed, by what I'm not sure. Bougainvillea thumb pustular, wants lancing. To the quack or wait it out?

24 August
Merciless monsoon, the roof holding out. My father's roof. Tackle the cracks in October.
Go away rain, I've a pagoda to build!
Thumb infection subsides after three anxious days. Luck?
Lilies eaten to the ground, the leaves blasted: a race of velvety black-and-white-and-orange caterpillars swarming. The mason's trowel finds a new use, slicing them in half, but after a while you tire of kindness.
Rehang the grapevine. The last brown leaf hanging there in heavy rain, dry as a chip, is a butterfly.

25 August
As if a day skipped. Two days and nights of the heaviest rain so neither Dhani nor Victor shows up. Reading Broch in bed, then gutter work with three-inch pipes: too late but who knows, another month of rain to come. Thumb almost healed.

—*Are we too quick to the quack, Good Householder?*
—*Sir?*
—*The body is a good enough doctor, as a rule.*
—*True, sir. But do your guttering before the monsoon, as a Rule of Thumb?*

The Small Wild Goose Pagoda   119

AUGUST CHORE

—*Bail out vile flood waters, boy. (Rule of Benedict, see* insubordination*)*

Mesh room flooded, our only room at ground level. (The kitchen is up one step, the house sits on a two-foot plinth.) A lone firefly takes soundings. Heaviest monsoon in half a century. Surely all aquifers are recharged by now. Every room has a drip except the living room under the roof's trusty watershed; up on the cambered roof the spine dries first. I begin to share Dad's hatred of this season.

26 August
Wake at four to the Ramzan sirens—half conscious of the earlier announcement at half past three: *Brethren, awake. Be quick! Wake your neighbour, prepare your meal, prepare yourselves for the fast*—from a dream of burning cold. Freezing shins—in August!

Drift off to Zhujijiao, to that canal lined with camphor trees where I trudged with Ouyang Jianghe, poet militant and calligrapher, in search of a chemist for our Bengali poet's medicines, past stall after stall of pig's knuckles. On the way home our boat collided with a boatload of Chinese tourists. Nailed together by the impact, rubrail to rubrail—it took a crowbar to prise us apart—India and China were last this close during the fruitless border skirmishing of 1962. Our young boatman told off by his seasoned other as we disengaged, but without the squabble we would have had at home. The passengers in the China boat, reserved at close quarters, began to send gruff helloes over their shoulders when we were almost free of each other, practising the only English they knew with shy smiles that turned to hoots and catcalls across the wobbly water.

Almanack vs calendar
I buy Chaturvedi's calendar (the one from Deep-Fryers Lane in Varanasi) not for the table that lets you keep track of your daily milk account and your newspaper account and your weekly dhobi account, but for its list of national holidays. Today is not a holiday as Maeve feared: she can go to the Foreigners' Registration Office with her sealed letter from the Delhi office where she waited all day with

Afghan and Pakistani wives.

Calendars are for nitpickers. They serve the keepers of the sabbath. Minders of observance, observing not the world but its shadow. Ritual-mongers, cabalists, keepers-off. The purist, as well as the drain-cleaners' union: either is likely to black-ball you.

—*Take your pick, Good Householder: the Royal Bombay Yacht Club or my Lady Sweeperess's clique.*

The wait-maker in every public office, lording it over the queue (let us say the queue in the Foreigners' Registration Office, Dehradun) is a calendar man, will have one nailed to the wall behind his desk. Yet his neighbour at the very next desk, dreaming of his wife and counting the minutes to lunch, is an anarchist who lives by the almanack. Trapped in that dismal office, with that riteist, he looks out the window, considers the lilies, and is no less efficient, or no more inefficient, than his calendrical friend torturing the woman who has failed to fill in Form 19-H Part III.

The calendar is party to every tyranny. In the book I'm reading, in the old days in these very hills a Brahmin woman, young or old, had to run *naked* to the bathroom, on winter nights too, because caste law obliged her to. Calendrical law abets such hallowed poppycock: see *Gormenghast*. It may regularize the year—so January doesn't slide into summer—but along the way it pettifogs and torments with pernickety rules. The modern calendar simply puts all faiths on an equal footing (it loves faiths, not faith) and sidelines those it can't fit in. This is called secularism. Secularism in India has acquired a meaning you will find nowhere else in the world: it means a parity of rituals; not a liberation from dogma but a dogmatic liberalism.

—*Fraud, Good Householder, beware!*
—*But ancient and colourful, sir.*
—*Most picturesque, but fraud.*

The Almanack is for Everyman. On whom the sun shines with equal vigour everywhere and on whom the rain rains without partisan wetness. In recent times it has been demoted to a yearbook, a treasury of facts, but *fancy* was an important part of old almanacks: poems, stories, riddles, advice, all found a home in that rattlebag. Do you wish to kneel at the tideline tomorrow night and tickle crabs? *I* will tell you when; Chaturvedi Sahib will merely roll his eyes. Sow your black-eyed peas at the equinox? *Here* is how. Scale your lover's wall on the night of the dark moon? Go nimbly.

—*Packing for a journey, Good Householder?*
—*Her-under-the-Quilt must see a holy man, sir. We would like to make us a child.*
—*And what stands in the way?*
—*Saturday is not a day for setting out.*
—*Leave the planets to Chaturvedi, boy. Your Almanackist advises a Saturday above all days.*
[Returning from train station]—*Saturday's waitlisted, sir.*
—*Then try dread Tuesday. The Gap, remember?*

On the fifth day of the moonlit fortnight in the rainy month of Shravan, when snakeholes fill with water and snakes are obliged to seek shelter in your house, falls Cobra Day. His day who makes your flesh creep.

Today the vagrant rules, the aborigine, the outcast, the sadhu, the ragpicker. God stands up for bastards. It's the nearest we come to the World Upside Down, that roisterous medieval trope of Europe. Today life trumps order. The young bride returns to her village. Look! A swing rigged up on the gular tree for her to be a girl again.

—*She dreams of a lily bank, sir.*
—*Try ours. We'll be out tonight, boy. Make you a wee girl.*

She'll be a new thing. You get a small cash award in this country if you marry outside your faith. It's a brave and appealing and daft notion, one to set alongside those wonderful exceptions in the railway rulebook governing who shall be entitled to a reduced fare on trains.

27 *August*
Any day now we start to cantilever. Sick of waiting! The rainy rain room on the portico will get a hard dry hat.

Xuan Zang would approve. Here he is from a late etching I saw at the Great Wild Goose pagoda, the Himalayas behind him, that prissy look in his eye.

Koel (Eudynamys scolopaceus) 1: off season

In the rains he goes quiet, our cuckoo. Sitting it out. Today he emerges in plain view on the Mexican silk cotton, contemplating the first sunshine in weeks. He can sit for minutes together on a chosen branch, simply looking around him. Alone as always, distrustful, vigilant, insecure. Without any lapse in his looking, he will ruffle his gorget and peck in there for fleas. One eye on the crows that fly aimlessly past in twos and threes: any of them could be an enraged cuckold. Neither the hawks that nest at the top of the cell phone tower nor this peaceable white egret wending its path straight home overhead is especially interested in him. He's marked them both though, missing no one who goes by, especially egrets with nothing to hide.

After ten minutes facing west he turns south with a little hop and spends the next ten minutes studying that quadrant. Suddenly I realize: he's a sailor! (In the crow's nest, naturally). This is his inland sea with islands of vegetation where he can rest and take stock. His flight is a swift passage made when the coast is clear. No pleasure in being airborne for him, the tumblings of swift and bee-eater leave him cold: it's all to do with getting there, and getting away. Longer hauls are half glide, half flapping from one tree island to the next. The gliding is done with his tail held straight and spread a little—its length at last an asset—to fletch him like an arrow; none of the hawk's carefree tiller variations for him. The flapping is in earnest, in short bursts, each making for a little rise, and then another, and another, in crests that repeat themselves into the distance.

In his fallows he studies the inside of his glossy black head, nursing longings confessed to nobody, polishing old grudges, stoking desires that would scandalise a crow. He's happiest sitting still, making his camouflage work for him as he ponders the next move. A wife in every port, his harsh call a drunken shanty. On shore leave he'll twitch the glossy black coat with the green speckling he secretly thinks is the best thing in the world, after maybe the blue silk caftan on the Emir of Bokhara.

29 August
Dhani groping in the shadows the other day as I went ahead of him poking holes for the brinjal seedlings.
  Victor turns up looking sick. Wants 500 rupees. Says he's been laid low since the last day he was here. Habilis owes him 500 he'll never see again. Go eat a plate of liver, I say. Build yourself up for the roof work. More likely he'll drink a jug of country liquor. Habilis claims he's often to be found in a heap on a certain widow's floor.

30 August
Long power failure. *Cucking-stools, boy!*
  Maeve on the back verandah, fanning herself with a straw fan.
  Three clearings make up the backyard, outdoor rooms set off from each other by shrubs or masonry: the redstone patio at the kitchen, the lawn at the centre of the garden, and the mulberry rise, a grassed over septic tank. The sky lends each infinity.
  There's also a hillock. Years ago the rubble of the old concrete drive was brought around to the back and heaped in the Afghan corner. Next we covered it with earth and put in lilies.
  'You'll get rats!' the Bihari labourer warned.
  We got a family of mongooses.
  And today, suddenly—Maeve comes in and whispers, 'Guess what I saw'—a rogue monkey.
  He came down off the roof of the new three-storey apartment block to lunch on the green seed-straps of the new mimosa. Sat on the lily-bank wall, undid each pod, neatly unzipping the two bands as he ate down the middle, seed by seed. Then went back up to drink at the big plastic roof tanks whose lids he's worked out how to open.

31 August
Tuesday. (Dog day, Chaturvedi Sahib.) Brakes jam when I go out

to pick up the rewound adapter for the Chinese speakers. Drive home steering around women walking on the road to avoid lake-size puddles.

A pack of pi-dogs, every head and body imaginable brought together, trotting along near the clock tower. They have the scarred look of a foreign legion patrol, armed to the teeth, wary but not worried. Maeve reckons they're being disappeared on the orders of a new-broom health officer. She misses the frolicsome black-and-white bitch of the Rita Ice Cream lane that she cured of mange last year by stealing up and squirting doses of disinfectant. Also the gay black male of the Police Lines eateries, pushy, psychotically friendly.

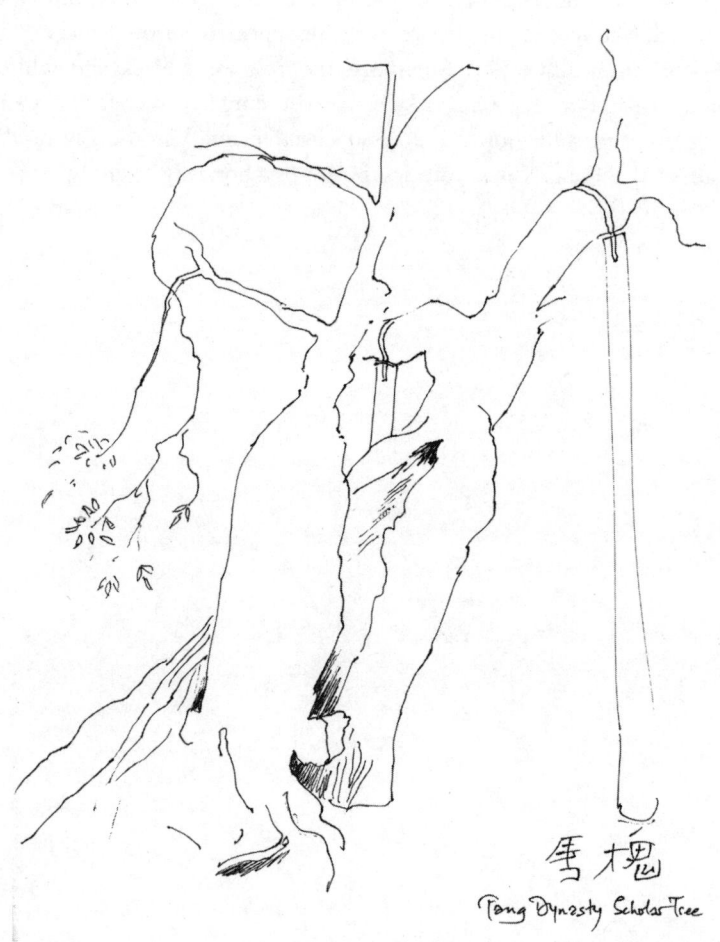

September

1 September

PAGODA MONTH!
Breakfast at the kitchen window, gold flecks in the granite sill: fried bread with Maeve's monsoon-liquified grape jelly (from the derelict Christchurch vine) poured on.

    A little frog, the first of the monsoon. At the monsoon's end! It hops onto the shingle and sits very still. So still it's there at the end of breakfast. I go out and see whether it's not a dead leaf after all, must lean right over it till the morning glitters in its eye. Once frogs *were* the monsoon. *Video, video*, they taunted me through nights I sat up writing a celluloid novel, *Hero*. That great shrill chorus silenced. Saved as a ringtone. This one from its unfroglike markings could be a young toad. But where is the jewel Pliny put in his forehead?

2 September
Drips off the roof tink on tin, bet on pebbles. The same pearly half light that has haunted us for months.

    I recall a great stone basin brimming with clear water in the courtyard of the Great Mosque at Xian. Leaves sank to the bottom, clouds stayed up top. Rainspots on the page as I sketched. Nothing except the orientation was remotely Meccan.

    Chalked out the skywell on the floor of the rain room, directly below where the concrete slab will come. Hung the inchitape as a plumbline, found centre, drew a square, then rotated it so it points forward, aligned with the cardinals. Crept up the iron stair just now to peer at the stars through a hole not yet there. The stars not there either, but faced north and shut my eyes to see.

    Tower month!

Babel

Among Bible stories, for a small boy in a small town, the story of Babel beats Noah's ark hollow. A tower that scrapes the sky is bound to tease a child more than a wooden zoo. It's also the first muddle in the Bible, the first account of confusion, and it makes Eden look impossibly remote. The expulsion of Adam and Eve resorted to props: an apple, a serpent, an angel, a flaming sword. With the ark the deus ex machina was even more brazen. With Babel for the first time it's all man's doing; you listen to the story biting your lip, because after all you *want* them to reach the sky. You haven't learnt about limits, and can't credit adult failure. In the whole of the Old Testament there's no more vivid image of human folly, and it brings you up short. Babel is the simplest overreaching: you run out of stuff, simple. Unity, mortar, will, in the end even bricks. And the sky stays where it is.

Enter any Chinese provincial capital and you wince under the gaze of the latest Babel, yet another giant Drum and Gong pagoda. In Datong the city bus carries you past white hard hats bent over endless blueprints. It's like some terrible mistake in a surgical ward: '*Wrong bed!*' you want to shout, rapping the glass. '*Wrong man!*' But there's no stopping a nation bent on refashioning itself. It could be just availability: of engineers and funds and concrete, hence those ponderous turned-up eaves repeated upside down in ponderous lily ponds. At every epic bulge you long for the simple pinprick of irony. In India, where plaster is our forte (tellingly sand, not shingle) the result may be no more imposing than the three-storey blue Shivas that preside over any cow belt town. But the motive is the same: another fitness gym for building national deltoids, a Great Wild Goose Pagoda.

Why not build small? Before small can rejoin precious in a people's mind there must be an intervening stage of irony, of deflating laughter whose object is the self. Hell bent on epic, Asia isn't ready for that.

In every epic there is a tower on fire. Then the age passes. The comic epic has no time for skyscrapers, for great wild goose pagodas. In every comic epic you watch a vaunting tower put up only to be taken down. I built such a tower with my first novel, *The Trotter-Nama*, a chronicle of the Anglo-Indian race. The *nama* was a medieval historical form that encouraged invention. In that novel the bloated hero, conjurer of the whole tale, pops up again at the end, taken down a peg or two and talking demotic Anglo, for all his puffery up front. The book charts a long decline from imagined greatness to a plain but oddly satisfying present. But mock epic will not satisfy cultures of ostentation, nations with something to prove; only their own gout will bring them down.

So the pagoda is my *second* tower. In the same way as you change tack from book to book, your form setting a limit, and life hemming you in besides, as a builder too you cut your coat according to your cloth. With the present tower, our portico and the offending balcony (the opera box) are the givens: they delimit and enable. I don't need to start from the ground, for example. And I don't need to scrape the sky.

Enough things can go wrong as it is. A falling tile impressed me early, the one that brought down the wrath of the Roman empire on the rich Jew Ben-Hur and made a galley slave of Charlton Heston. The governor is passing in procession in the street below. An excited girl, of *course* (I was eight and had almost set fire to my father's police issue Norton motorcycle because I felt any liquid, the petrol in the tank for example, should behave like water and douse a lit match: if I dunked it *really* fast it should go out, right?) leans over to get a better view and dislodges the tile that falls on the governor's head. Years later a residual fear would spoil my first visit to New York: what was to stop those limestone slabs that faced the Empire State Building working loose and falling to the street?

Actually there *is* no guarantee the bond will hold. It's a healthy fear; breaking is more natural than joining. I find more cutting tools than joining ones in my cupboard, though perhaps the score in nature is roughly equal. Every accumulation, the geologist Charles Lyell observed, is the result of erosion somewhere else. He might have spoken as an economist, or a historian; possibly the law is universal. So what are these skeletons in the closet under the outside staircase? Have I really emptied a hundred cement sacks rebuilding this house?

I have built with lime mortar, a low wall, but I'm afraid to go up high without cement. Our local supplier, a Sikh, like half of Racecourse, has a stranglehold on the business; his bricks and gravels occupy the verge outside his monsoon-proof warehouse. I'm a small-time customer, but long-time too; most of his clients build once and for all. He knows my ad hoc habits, knows this gate, and so do his deliverymen. The best bricks come from Shamli, halfway to Delhi. Gravel is running out locally. And the same is true of shingle and river sand: all have to be trucked in from further and further out every year. This city has doubled in the last ten years. Twenty years ago Racecourse stood at the edge of town, now we're inner city.

The fact is we are in the middle of a building boom. Habilis is harder to get nowadays.

5 September
4:30 AM Old man Gout singing tunelessly in bed next door. Also: mosquitoes, cricket, dog, autorickshaw, milk van, faint login chord from removed headphones. Suddenly the keening of the Ramzan sirens. Hawks skirl the sun up.

Phone in monsoon form, dead, but broadband fine: no bad arrangement. The phone's an enemy, the computer a friend. Rain at least gone.

6 AM Lie in, barren, thinking: *the heat of China has gone off me.*

Victor to marry this month. Doesn't look enthused. Habilis says he'll accompany him to the girl's village. They plan to go after Eid, take the overnight train to Lucknow, then the Sultanpur bus to the girl's village. I keep thinking of her in Victor's airless garage. In that fancy silk nightie a village girl might abominate (but Victor would fancy her in). Will she sing the old filmi hit from *Sangam*: *What do I do, oh what do I do? Sold off to an oldie, pray what do I do!* And Victor? Will he be bowled over and besotted, or drunk every night? The slight hunch has given him a hesitant manner in life, both gentle and shrewd. He has the small man's watchfulness and patience and dandified way with clothes. His refusal to ever answer back, to life or a mason—heroic and probably infuriating when it's Habilis taunting—could be a natural philosophic bent, an inwardness that the girl if she's dense will resent or try to take advantage of till she gets a beating and habit takes root in that little garage.

7 September
Weeds poking up everywhere. Dhani not seen for a week now. Last Monday he turned up to explain why he can't come. He has cataracts, an operation coming up.

Why didn't I see that? In the evening we drive to the dyers to pick up a shirt—olive-greened and grease-spotted moleskin trousers gone a rich black. In a vat seething right on the kerb, spilling poison into the gutter—

—*frogspawn black, Forest Dweller sir?*

Next door I spot a weeding fork. I'll need to run the cutter up the blade to fork the V properly. The tooling action not thought through because the designer will never use the tool himself—a slave will.

It may start at the top, but it's everywhere. The minister planting a tree will find the hole already dug for him, and expects to. The mortar pan on the head of the activist will have not a trace of mortar in it, and is not expected to. It's theatre, or rather magic, a mirror trick that leaves the drudge exactly where he was. The hostess at dinner will say: 'I put in a pinch of this and then I put in that.' She means the *cook* does, but sincerely believes the dish is hers. Servants have done this class no good: 'Can you get me a glass of water?' is a normal request. So the busy editor of the online magazine vetting a report on the treatment of domestics as I sit across the desk from him, a man who has only ever entered his kitchen to set down a plate someone else will wash, can turn to me and say: *So, what do you do all day?*

—*What do you do, Forest Dweller sir?*
—*Less cheek from you, boy. It's a rest cure I need.*
—*Better a retreat, sir.*
—*A retreat from a retreat, boy? That's the world.*
—*Then play dead. Yoga prescribes the shav asana. The corpse position. Lie flat upon your back, feet apart, arms extended, palms open. The posture of perfect rest.*
—*That too will come. For now there are yawns trapped deep in this living chest.*

A strange claustrophobia, not of space. For a long time I worried that this place might begin to pall, that I would tire of these 433 square yards. That I would wake up one morning and step out onto the back lawn and feel penned in, and mock the walls I'd built, and find myself longing for another place. To test myself I sometimes step out suddenly from the study into the garden. The result is always shock at the beauty of the place.

But that doesn't help the crushing monsoonitis, the fag-end torpor, after a summer of power cuts. And perhaps after all a nagging doubt that this is far enough away. Or near enough—to *what*, it's still impossible to say.

—*Is your peace made with the world, Forest Dweller sir?*
—*With some not yet, boy.*
—*Should a pagoda come up in enmity, Forest Dweller sir?*
—*This one will bring equilibrium.*
—*Peace with justice, Chanakya sir?*
—*Go play to the opera box. Its days are numbered.*

Chanakya, third century philosopher of statecraft. Author of the *Arthashastra*, today he would tweet and be followed. Master strategist, he'll snuff out your grannie and manage your grief.

Which reminds me: where is Habilis?

Monsoon woes
Salt clogs the salt-cellar, mustard mildews, seameal curdles, bread won't rise, curtains sag, doors stick, windows jam, ovens slow, kettles fur, rubber perishes, leaves rot, cobwebs lurk, garbage stinks, the carburettor sweats.

The infallibly stuck-in Beijing wok-handle comes unstuck.

—*Do not, Good Householder, demoss the roof mid-season or damp patches will appear on walls and ceiling.*
—*A map-maker's delight, Forest Dweller sir.*
—*And only his. Give Victor his hire and let him go. Gently release the wire-brush from his hand.*
—*Sir, Her-at-the-fridge-door has cravings. Today's is fish.*
—*Best wait another week, son.*

September marks the return of fish months, months with the letter r in them, the hot weather over. In the days before refrigeration my father's mother knew this. She gambled with housie, her lucky pencil stub tucked behind her ear, but not with fish. She came from a poor family, Chloe Beulah Murray. Dad has a faint memory of her telling him *her* mother would gather twigs for their Allahabad kitchen stove. (Kindling started the coal fires I grew up with too.) It could explain the gambling. I remember only her moles, on golden skin, and the hairs on her chin. And sensing that she was genially past caring which of the ten grandchildren I was.

Clements

A photo arrives from my last surviving maternal aunt. I sent it to her for a gloss and it's come back with pencilled annotations. It shows the Clement family gathered around a little pond at the Bank Road house in Allahabad, 1931: she is paddling in there with my mother and two other sisters, while my grandmother stands with her sisters-in-law and her children from her first marriage. I think of the futures awaiting these placid souls gathered about that concrete pool and my heart wants to break, but it's just the normal run of luck.

Millicent Rose Clement, nee Cleophas, is already twice widowed. Her first-born, a schoolteacher son, stands beside her with another year to live. How is he to know? But he looks nervous. The next son, who played piano in a band and drank himself to death, has probably taken the picture; his wife is there, cigarette in hand. The achiever sons are not there, off somewhere, achieving. One will become a sea captain: look at him leaning on the taffrail of their Bombay balcony reading off the Morse code messages flashed from one ship to another in the harbour—the cleverest thing I ever saw anybody do—but unable to see what his wife is up to. The other, the bachelor whose car I drive, will become an aeronautical engineer, the Fiat his modest last car after Chevies and Fords with running boards. The daughters disposed about the little pond are expected to marry, and do. But here too are the maiden aunts. Four spinsters, Paul Clement's sisters, among the earliest female graduates in the country: a doctor, an inspectress of schools, a botanist, a wallflower. Happy (or not) to be left on the

The Small Wild Goose Pagoda   133

shelf by men all unworthy, they sail to England (the inspectress), to Ireland (the doctor, trained at the Rotunda), to the continent, and one befriends Gandhi's lonely wife on the ship coming home. IC's, Indian Christians, unlike my Anglo grandmother, they wear saris, like a point made. They no longer despise 'the Wid' who brought their beloved brother six ready-made children before producing four more. Today they rub shoulders with a woman who has just buried her second husband and is raising a family of ten children alone. They would like their four nieces to follow their studious example, but my mother is the only one will go to college. For now she's in a frock, kicking water as she bites into an apple, my father, growing up in the same city, so far from her thoughts he could be a Lapp. My favourite aunt, Maureen, 'Big Clem', marries an English soldier who disappears Home after the war. The piano-player's wife, reflected upside down in the pool, sits slightly apart. 'A bad egg,' notes Aunty Maureen, without further explanation. She's dead now, the rotter; living she seems no worse, perhaps a little more tense, than the rest. Aunty Maureen is the last of all these alive.

9 *September*

Labour Day
Today I must go to the clock tower to find a labourer.
    I never go willingly. Always I must work myself up. Always I park short of the clock tower and run an eye over the crowd. I'm looking for a reliable face in an able body. Not easy in a milling crowd: faces cross and pass in front of each other, a head can wander off on another set of shoulders. There are some three or four hundred men, rough and not, mostly rough. In their best clothes most would be rough and here they are lined up for work on Monday morning. Many will not find it, so there's an air of despair that grows with the advancing hour. No one shows his desperation, not this early. For now they amble, those who can't stand still. The painters sit with their cans and brushes, the masons with a little bag of tools. The rest are on their feet, the shifters shifting from one group to another, catching sight of a friend in the crowd, or looking for their gang, the stayers content to stand

alongside strangers without a word. Tense, the way a kerchief will be flicked back over a shoulder. Most are loners, older brothers who've left three sisters at home. Or younger brothers who'd rather be in Bombay (these last you avoid like the plague). The young tend to club together, the middle-aged look lost. The family men are sternest, young husbands the most edgy. The old hands have a watchful look, their eyes ranging further out because they can see a job coming at fifty metres. I wouldn't be surprised if they've spotted me already sitting in my car and are trying to size *me* up before approaching.

Sometimes if I can't make up my mind I get out and go among them, but then you can't dawdle. Mostly you drive up alongside the crowd, madly scanning the inner circle and picking the one whose eyes look trustworthy, though your glance widens straightaway to take in his build. If that's OK you point straight at him.

YOU!

He just happens to be on the wrong side, the driver's side, but you hold him with your eye, moving him on the point of a finger towards the passenger door which you keep shut until he comes round. Then, grateful for the forward-opening Fiat doors, you open just wide enough to let one man in. The car is now completely surrounded, mostly young men who are drumming on the roof in case you need a second pair of hands. You turn to the man (this has to be done before you start) you've picked because he's not old, not even middle aged, though there you would have made an exception for someone with the right eyes. (It's not good to be an old man and a labourer.) '*The work is such and such,*' you say, your voice unnaturally compressed, '*and it's for two, maybe three days, and I'll pay you 300 rupees a day.*' He'll ask for more, but he knows you know the rate and in any case he's not getting out of the car, so already you're easing the foot off the clutch and the Fiat is rolling. A thumb squeaks on the windshield, men peel off the sides and fall away.

You have kidnapped a man. The stranger beside you is a technician in plain clothes. He carries in his head formulae, and will put them at your service. The Chinese understand this; we do not. They respect labour; we do not. This man can measure out one part of cement to two of gravel to three of shingle, or one of cement and seven of gravel, or two of cement and twelve of sand, his lips moving as he repeats the total to himself so he doesn't lose count while Habilis heckles him. He has already twice shifted the mound of sand and cement, sifting once so it's beside itself, then returning it to where it started. Two strokes of the shovel carve out a dip in the crest. He fills it with water, stops up the gaps that keep appearing in the crater walls, shoring up the sides against runnels, heaping dry gravel over the top till a bucketful of water is buried in the heart of the hill. Now he will hash and flip and hash again, before filling the pan. Every labourer at the clock tower knows the routine—or gets a cuff on the ear from Habilis. He thinks on his feet, can also sleep there. Count on him to appear with a refill when the other pan is empty, in between fetching bricks and tools and tea and staring into space. Sand runs in his veins and dulls his dreams. Count on him to swallow it if necessary, to get it in the eye, and ear, and down his shirt and inside his collar and stand perfectly still, the pan on his shoulder, or on his head, because the mason is on a stool. What does he do when the mason belts him for tiring? Nothing. At pay-up time, if Habilis is the paymaster, or Contractor X, he will get three quarters of what he is owed, to make sure he turns up tomorrow, and tomorrow he will again get three-quarters plus the offer of regular work and the promise of the rest by the end of the month, or failing that by the start of the next job, or most certainly on the 12th of Never.

Today's man expects a shovel but finds himself holding a machete. Garden work.

10 September
4 a.m. rising, along with the milk van. Frostbite in the feet because the fan was left on. Weather all wonky.

Maeve wakes, sees I'm wearing socks and stares.
'If you're cold why are you naked?'
'If I weren't I'd overheat.'
'Can we turn the fan back on?'
'OK. Did you hear the owls?'

Going all night. I realize last night was the first dry night in ten weeks. They're celebrating.

'I thought they were bats.'
'You're as bad as Terry. Forgetting how to brush his teeth.'
The Fiat uncle who lost his mind to Alzheimer's.
'Did he? I don't remember that.' She looked after him too.
'You're next then.'
People who've returned from abroad misremember simple things.
I should do a rerun, but don't.
'Those are screech owls. You remember them, surely?'
That's how she would have put it.

11 September
Dull thump as a motorcycle helmet falls from the balcony flat. Again.
'Hell-met,' the man, the pisser, calls to his wife. In Hindi both syllables toll equally.
I think, for no good reason, *Hail-fellow-well-met*. It jingles jollily in my head all day. Soon, *very* soon, an end to this rain of helmets!
Habilis appears at the gate as if he pushed it off the edge himself.
Says he'll take a contract on this job, cover all labour, everything but materials. He's seen through my elaborate unconcern about a starting date. 'I'll do it for fifteen thousand.'
Why don't I automatically halve the figure, so he climbs down and I climb up and we close at ten?
I shrug meekly, and the quote solidifies. I realize two things: how I hate going looking for labour, and how much I want this pagoda.
'When do you want to start?' he says, his eye sizing up something not there yet over my shoulder.
'Yesterday.'
Sadly yesterday, *kal*, also means tomorrow, so the irony too is lost. He focuses. 'Two more days at the Khandoli site.'
'So that's where Victor disappeared to.'
'Oh, you needed him?' Knowing well I did.
'Not really.' I did, but I'd sooner die than let him know. He borrows the shovel and goes off. If I weren't sure he needed work I'd say a longer goodbye to the shovel.
Two days later I don't look out for him. He won't come midweek. And then there's my faith in his Friday and his faith in my Sunday,

so those two days are out, and why would anybody start work on a Saturday? Best start fresh with a new week, he'll be saying. Except that on Monday I trust my gut instinct and again don't bother. He'll take *one* more day off, start on Tuesday.

12 September
Dhani's eyes will be in bandages. How did the operation go? Take him his pay today.

13 September
Every year on this day, Founder's Day, our school body would congregate in the chapel, a baroque powder-blue-and-white fantasy out of Versailles, to honour the name of General Claude Martin, Frenchman. Founder of La Martiniere, a school for boys that took forty years to get off the ground after his death on 13 September 1800, in the city of Lucknow. Adventurer, turncoat, soldier of fortune, though crazed Swiss confectioner will do too. Martin built the vast wedding cake of a mansion that later became our school and was thus an accessory to my incarceration on the banks of the Gomti River sixteen decades later. I wrote him up as the Great Trotter in my first novel, *The Trotter-Nama*. He was so troubled by kidney stones he invented a crusher, a glass rod he inserted up his urethra and into his gall bladder to do the job manually himself. I did not know this for the seven years I was held there or I would have looked differently at the man whose bones lay in a bat-dung-scented crypt forty feet below the chapel. On the thirteenth of September each year we were allowed down there. In 1857 his grave was dug up by mutineers looking for treasure and his bones scattered about. He never showed himself again, except to me.

14 September
Tuesday. Four sharp raps of the gate-latch.
  Homo habilis.
  His Eroica entry, harsh, metallic, assertive. Meant to unnerve. Today especially bold. I've just heard the hubba-hubba of a two-stroke diesel tempo pulling up outside. The crash of poles and planks and

ledgers begins right off as labourers chuck them anyhow from the truck. The scaffolding has arrived. Always these first minutes shatter the neighbourhood calm with uproar and chaos, like a beach landing. I imagine the frighted spirits of the place taking cover in the trees, and secretly love it. Blood lust. Afterwards the crew, a man of eighty among them, shelter in the garage while it rains, haggling over who got paid or not yesterday.

The first advance has just changed hands, two thousand rupees. Thirteen thousand to go.

Sunshine through rain: *fox's wedding and the monkeys dance!* we'd chant as children. Dancing, now I don't have to worry about accounts: labour and scaffolding Habilis's headache. I reckon ten thousand for materials, say three each for cement, gravel, and iron rodding. For the concrete roof he has agreed to two raised beams (9"x 9") that will take the main load and three others, 'digested' beams (6"x 4") that will merge with the roof slab.

15 September
8:55 AM The second lot of scaffolding arrives. Habilis, the old hand, always punctual up front. His team of labourers:

1. a younger old man, 75 (not yesterday's old man), Afghan-bearded, in skullcap
2. the female labourer, 30, today with her handsome head covered
3. a lad, 21, with a scowling old man's face on a pinhead, skull-capped
4. Victor, 50, unshaven, in my old pyjama top

Habilis has fielded family, not a crew. The faithful, anyway: all Muslim except Christian Victor. One by one they carry the poles and planks up to the roof.

9:30 AM Habilis and I go to the brick surdy for shingle. Now all we lack is a Jain. Returning I go up onto the roof and encounter the female at the door; she frowns from head to foot. Painted nails. The lad has a folded towel for padding on his shoulder as he carries the heavy poles. Old man and young woman carry three or four decking planks at a time.

The crew need to be watered. Stainless steel tumblers are set out for them on the front verandah; the sound of their being set down empty, a gritty echoey ring, will soon become familiar.

10:30 AM We take the old roof off, unbolting the two arches joined at the breastbone. My ineffective screen. Beauty takes one corner, Beast-Victor another, Habilis and lad the other two, carry them across one by one to the mango tree corner. Meanwhile the old Afghan is carrying headload after headload of gravel up from the gate where the pickup dropped it. Habilis goes back to working out where the joists will fit, knocking out bricks to stick poles through walls, sending Victor to fetch the sack of hemp cords left over from past builds.

I'm still a little jumpy. What sounds like a hammer-blow on the gate turns out to be a brick falling on Habilis' new iron horse scaffold.

I look the beast over. 'Give it a coat of primer.'

'I did,' he protests, but there's not a lick, and rust are scabs forming.

'Well, give it another.'

'Where's the time?'

I know what he means: maintenance is leisure work, the other stuff brings in the money.

12 noon. The fat gravel arrives: pebbles in it so (Habilis says) there's no need for the edged shingle that's usually mixed into concrete. Shovelled from a small flatbed truck onto the already delivered heap of sand. I hand over the money: the driver counts note by note, twice.

'All OK?' Habilis asks.

'If Sahib has counted it, it must be OK,' the driver grins abashed.

After lunch Beauty demolishes the brick curtain at the far wall, then sits knocking the cement off the old bricks. The rest resume the gravel haul. The lad I now remember having seen here before; his scowl natural, not put on. Habilis everywhere, heckling in his customary way. His team pay no attention, a regular Dad's Army; not one able-bodied man, so he'll be paying them what he pleases. He's often alone with Beauty, and I begin to wonder if she's family after all. She has a dozen silver bangles on each wrist, a gold nose ring.

'Bet you've never had a labourer in more jewellery,' Maeve says, watching the show through windows front and back.

We've never *had* woman labour. This one wears black plastic hoop-earrings as well as studs higher up the ear, a yellow mirrorwork headscarf, black and yellow plastic sandals and frosted crimson nails.

3:00 PM Habilis on the roof setting up the scaffolding with Beauty; the rest shifting matter.

'OK, let go the rope now. There. Now did it slip? *Did* it?'

His secretary, if not his mistress.

Abruptly he will leave her and remember a prop Victor was supposed to fetch.

'VICTOR!'

It's meant to cleave the house in two. Victor doesn't jump. He's with me on the other side of the house holding steady an old eucalyptus trunk while we cut it to size. We're a few poles short—Habilis saving on rental—so the trunks of garden trees past, silver oak, ashoka, mango, bottlebrush, get drafted for use as putlogs, sawn off or mounted on bricks. When we bring the log around Habilis stands unmoving, his head thrown back, his eyes scanning the bearer he'd like double-propped because his instinct tells him it will buckle. This Habilis I trust. The rain room has turned into a greenshade tree-house with a flat roof of planking whose cracks let in the sky. The concrete pour will come on this platform.

16 September

Neck aching horribly. Long sleep coming. But such a thrill to see the platform up! Stood on that wooden deck for the first time this morning and surveyed the country from a new vantage. Is that Xian on the horizon?

The scaffolding in place, we use the garden hose to establish the level for the slab. The water column leaps and dips as Habilis and the hired mistri call out readings, marking the surrounding walls. Victor pedals off to the hardware shop for twine, held taut from the high point at our roof to a low two inches below the pencilled line on the enemy wall. The slope is to the corner directly above the kitchen drain and the downpipe water will run off to the stormwater drain by the underground pipe Habilis himself laid ten years ago when we first built the kitchen in the former portico.

Pagoda upon kitchen: the domesticity of it appeals. *Small* wild goose.

3:00 PM I have Habilis remove the piffling pillars he built on the roof-jut yesterday to support the two main concrete beams, his lean-to instinct. I require a triple-wythe wall at the main roof. It's been worrying me all night. The hired mason sees it at once and nods. Cowboy H was about to hang a concrete slab on nothing. Habilis tries to wriggle out but has the decency to laugh it off when I take him below and show him just how skimpy the jut is. I realize just how much he plays by ear. The new support will now come directly on the load-bearing wall.

They set to right away. Rain slows work but doesn't stop it; the hired mistri works under his red-and-white gamchha. Habilis Contractor turns bricklayer under no hat at all. Beauty cutting up cement sacks in the garage, slitting them with the knife blade I use for puttying. Old man labourer fetches and carries; as I type up proceedings in the green study he trowels cement from the sack in the back verandah.

Up since 3 a.m., looking up concrete on the net, worried about the mix. *Cement : gravel : shingle 1 : 2 : 4. Water proportion critical.* Watched the white-haired walker exercise in the middle of the road before dawn, arms stretched out, wrists wriggling. When a goods truck roared up in the dark he kept wriggling, luring it onto the traffic island like some demented naval policeman.

Bricks arrive at midday, seconds mixed in from the stack the wily surdy swore he wouldn't touch.

Beauty has just cut her finger: Habilis comes to the back verandah with her and wants Dettol. I give her a bandage as well, and she exclaims at the fuss.

'What do you know?' Habilis says, shushing her.

He holds the finger clinically because I'm there. Sends her to sit in the garage for a bit.

The bed for the pour will not be the iron trenchers Habilis grandly promised: he's cost-cutting now the contract is his. It's the usual boarding, that deck of hired planks laid on hired cross-poles with Beauty's cut-open cement sacks spread out on them (to stop the cracks) and a bed of fine gravel laid over and tamped level. The concrete poured directly on that.

Typed that whole paragraph before remembering I had cement on my fingers. The precious white laptop baptized, now just another machine.

Victor carrying load after load of bricks up, five at a time in a sack; this morning headload after headload of gravel.

12 noon. A grizzled ironworker, his beard steel wool, appears on the roof. Here, subcontracted, to measure the platform. His sons will lay the grid. He steps up onto the deck, looks this way and that, plucks a figure out of the air. I ask him to write out his estimate, then wonder if he can write. He can. I will need:

1 ½ *quintals (150 kg) of 4-sooth* (16 mm) *rods*
1 *quintal of 3-sooth* (13 mm) *rods*
15 *kg of 2-sooth* (8 mm) *rods*
1 ½ *kg wire (*for tying)

Sooth, *n.* string, folk measure. [Hindi]

2:00 PM To Shiv Shakti Iron on threadneedle Raja Road, parking the Fiat right up against asbestos sheet store while rod is weighed. The 8mm rod is for the stirrups that bind up the beams. Delivery by rickshaw.

6:00 PM All gone home. On and on it rains, shower after shower, just a slackening from time to time so you're lulled into thinking: now the cement sacks are safe.

18 September

No entry yesterday, frazzle day, day of the surprise pour. *17 September,* LINTAR DAY.

Lintar, *n.* lintel. A lintel is *not* a beam over a doorway. Nitpick, and people will laugh. A lintar is a *roof slab,* so go teach your grandfather to suck eggs.

Lintar Day

Rodset day, I thought. Slab day, too, as it turned out.

The two rod-wrangling sons worked all morning measuring and cutting and setting the iron grid for the slab, using a little truss fork to tie the crossovers. Watched with pleasure this deft elastic action repeated over and over at their feet, like tying shoelaces. The rod-bending done with a hand-held hickey. The cutting done on the main road with hammer and cold chisel on a rock. (Maeve, watching from the window, said they looked around the garden and considered Stoneman's head for a moment, then decided against.)

For nights I've been trawling the net, to figure out how to centre the hole in the concrete slab where the skywell will come. In the end I abandon theory and plumbline and work by simple arithmetic: find the centre on the floor of the rain room, mark off a square, then repeat the measure on the platform above, drawing the matching square in the freshly tamped gravel (the yellow pencil-stub stylus preserved for posterity). The rodsetters observe the proceedings as they go about their business, but a hole in the roof wants explaining. I explain *skywell*. Satisfied, they mark off the centred square with a formwork of bricks and lay the rods around it. Occupied with the skywell I fail to inspect the general grid: there'll be time for that before tomorrow's pour. Or so I think.

Tomorrow's pour! Habilis had other plans.

As the rodsetters worked he had his crew carry the last of the gravel onto the roof. Somewhere in the mid-afternoon he had the cement carried up too. Next he cut short the rodwork, enough was enough, against the protests of the setters. He was not going to pay his crew just to look on. If he could fit the *pour* in today he would save a day's wage bill for four: two old men, Victor, and Beauty.

Looking back, I thought the rodsetters—rodbusters of American skyscraper lore—looked a little underbusted: they seemed to be standing around as the pour crew stepped up. Habilis sent them home saying he'd pay their father.

'Why not pay us?' they seemed to say.

'I'll drop in later,' Habilis insisted. Wearing his *something-I-can't-say-right-now* look. To negotiate a discount for abbreviated work?

19 September
Daylong net search. Trying to discover whether the structure put in place yesterday is safe. A good plain book by James R. Mihelcic, *Field Guide to Environmental Engineering for Development Workers,* doesn't say but points out another simple omission: the rod ends of the slab should tie into vertical rod ends at the walls. I slap my forehead. *Such an elementary precaution neglected*—and after I built a triple-wythe wall precisely to rest the slab on!

I learn a new word off the net for the shuttering that is removed once concrete sets: *falsework*! I learnt the word *shut-ring* from Habilis, but should teach him this.

Well, it's fifty-fifty. Scaffolding and shuttering faultless—and that's not a little, Habilis's forte—but the pour a fraud.

THE ALMANACK ANSWERS

Q. *How did the cement get up onto the roof, Forest Dweller sir?*
A. *It was invisibled up, Habilis-ed up.*

Fifteen years ago he pulled his first swiftie: he flattened one of the S bends in the swung wall in the fifteen minutes it took me to pick Filo up from school. So the wall has one perfect Euclidean curve and one flattened Habilis-ed curve.

So. At a certain point Habilis looks at his watch.

'*Enough rodset.*' And swings into action.

Who spirited twelve sacks of cement up onto the roof? Not the old men surely? Beauty? Victor? Half a ton of cement? Not Habilis himself, that's for sure. Then who? All of them? And when? I was there, but I was figuring the skywell.

Homo habilis, Houdini.

I heard about the mix only when he called for the pump to be turned on. I switched it on and *still* didn't realize what was happening.

And once the water goes in there's no going back.

Homo habilis, Napoleon.

When I got up onto the roof, sent for, they were sitting around, the concrete mixed, ready to begin. Nothing to do but go ahead now.

Victor was despatched to the tea shop for the ceremonial sweets;

we ate together and began.

Beauty surprised me by taking the shovel: the two old men delivered, and Victor, up on the platform, received and poured for the new mistri, who squatted on the grid with his trowel.

When there are no metal plates concrete is poured directly onto the sandbed. The rodwork grid levitates on the sandbed like a box-spring mattress, 3-D geometry. When the concrete sets it must figure midway through the slab, like a floating rib. To stop it sinking to the bottom under its own weight it is propped up on bits of brick at intervals: where it sags, the mistri lifts it manually, poking around with his trowel, shovelling, filling air pockets. (In big projects they use a vibrator.) I worry that the sand will draw off the water in the mix, but Habilis has sprayed the bed lightly before starting. Wetted newspaper is sometimes used, but here the grid was already in place.

They start at the far corner, the lowest point, where the drainpipe will come, and work their way across along the precise line of the opera box railing. The moment I've waited years for.

Very soon, *very soon*! I mutter evilly to myself like Merlin as the parapet is matched, level for level.

I want to do a crazed dance.

It's evening already. We should never have started this late. This was work for another day, with the team fresh, not tired from having already hauled all the gravel and cement up onto the roof. All morning they have carried headloads from the garage, around the front of the house, down the rough side, through the back gate and up the staircase, ducking each time at the bedroom sunshade, which will knock your head even when you don't have a pan on it, through the gate at the top and out onto the roof where they dump it in a heap. Then twelve sacks of cement: quartered, each headload would be some ten kilograms: say fifty trips.

Two old men, a young woman, Victor.

Now they are delivering the same material as concrete, the weight of water added. Same day.

The pour is happening at some four feet above the level of the main roof, at roughly chest height, so the deliverer must at the last moment hoist the pan, some ten kilograms every time, twenty pounds, to Victor leaning down from above. Over a long haul such a load would normally be carried on the head (not the shoulder, the great divide between Asia and Europe) but here the mix is happening some five or six paces away from the pour.

After a bit the young old man takes the shovel and Beauty takes his pan. Habilis keeps up a steady flow of directives all through the pour. He has a reliable mistri but his word is law. His heckling is crucial, support of a kind. And his eye is busy too. The mix can't be too thick:

'*Keep turning it over! Why is that edge of so dry? Mix it in, moron! Is that a shovel or a walking stick?*'

The old men are flagging. It's clear the older one is done in. Each time he reaches the deck that final hoist hurts. But somehow he gets it up.

'*Higher!*' Habilis snarls. 'What are you, a woman?'

'Woman!' the gaffer grunts, snatching the empty pan from Victor. '*You* try lifting for a change. Woman.'

I'm tempted to step in, but I don't. I've never heard him answer Habilis back. Not even when Habilis taunted him yesterday as he began to boast about his son.

'If he's such a good son how come you're still working?'

He half glared at Habilis, but faltered. The dropped look said: 'Pay me right and see.' His wide irresolute eyes childish beside the old Afghan's narrow stare.

Victor comes down off the platform to spell Beauty. The light is failing. I too am biting back anger. The whole thing is out of my hands. It's not how I would have done it. But a contract is a contract. You surrender the right to intervene. Not with the team, not with the tactics, not with the timing. In any case, there's no stopping. There's no such thing as half a pour. A slab is a slab.

'Get on with it!' Habilis calls.

'Come *on!*' the mistri echoes from the almost-slab.

Victor surrenders the shovel to the Afghan and goes back up to his post by the mistri.

They've reached the fore edge. It's the one edge without falsework and concrete is oozing out and spilling onto the roof. Habilis grabs a six-inch ledger, slaps it in place and wires it to the rebar grid.

It raises the bar for the gaffer. He must now deliver the pan those six inches higher than before—just when his strength is gone. He's eighty if a day. He manages once, twice, three times, then the pan slips from his hands and falls to the roof. Habilis says nothing. I shovel the mortar back into the heap while he picks up the fallen pan. The Afghan steps around me with his pan: the chain can't be broken. The next pan I take and pass it up to Victor. But Beauty, who's been squatting to one side, resting, comes and stands in the way: she will not let me work.

'Here,' she says and takes the emptied pan away from me.

'You shovel,' I say, 'I'll lift.'

She will not be moved. *Not your job,* her look says, closing the matter. Gaffer hands her the next load. She has a female way of lifting: an abrupt twist and thrust using a different set of muscles, the whole trunk, and maybe the legs too, to hoist the pan over her head, arms straight up, then tilting over towards Victor.

The pour is almost done, the mistri and Victor crowded together at the final corner. Pure cement puddles and laps over their feet like mercury as they pour the last square foot. The two old men wiped out, the old-old one already squatting in the twilight smoking thoughtfully.

Habilis's hands are clean. I've never seen him so masterly.

Right then the rain starts to come down. Beauty runs for the black tarp at the arch. I run downstairs for plastic sheets.

I'm past exhaustion. Bills, rates, measures, contingency plans, chasing though my head, but the mess at the mix has to be cleaned up or our roof is spoilt. Habilis says he'll clean it up tomorrow, knowing very well it won't wait. I start to scrape at it myself and he sees I won't be budged. It's too dark for a thorough job and I'm reluctant to push an exhausted team. Beauty is the only one scraping seriously. The two old men simply can't and Victor pretends to be checking something up on the slab. He's borne the brunt of the pour.

I let it go. The team disperses with less ceremony than I've ever seen.

Cement harrows skin: my fingertips are destroyed. Maeve offers apricot kernel oil.

'The old-old man kept dipping his hands in a bucket,' I tell her.

'Beauty was teasing him.'

At night I read Mihelcic. 'Remove forms after three days of wet-curing. Wet-cure for a total of seven days.' Fine. Then: 'Most masons and local workers prefer to add too much water to ease the transportation and placing of the concrete. However, added water weakens the concrete.' The stuff at the tail end of the pour was just slop. Next I read: '*cold joints should not occur within a beam, column, or structural member.*' The main beams, designed to stick up rather than down (my fault) were poured only to the slab level. On another day we could have built up a formwork of bricks and continued the pour. Thanks to Habilis's haste I have a pair of do-nothing beams.

19 September
Two days, of incessant rain.

—*Stay home, Householder, or stick in the mud. How's your connectivity?*
—*Lovers have off days, Forest Dweller sir.*
—*Also days off, boy. I mean the Net.*
—*She has made holes in it, sir. Mosquitoes fly in and out.*

Idle days. Surfing, I come across an etymology of *brouhaha*, that's an exact echo of our *hobson-jobson*. From 'barukh-habba', a Jewish nonsense stage-murmur, their 'rhubarb-and-custard'. Souvenir of that vanished age of Europe's Asia, the age of Pierre Loti and Marie Corelli, when excitable natives chattered, gabbled, hobson-jobsoned, hubba-hubbaed, ran amok.

The rise of China redresses all that.

20 September
The almirah ready! I mount and tack the mirror, putty the edges and polish it. One year boring like a woodworm towards this luminous moment. A miniature pagoda.

Tochter not here to fill the looking glass. I transfer her things and take over her little cupboard for my tools. Its four shelves impose a loose taxonomy: *Cutting, Joining, Gripping, Grinding.*

Sorting through Dad's wooden tool chest. His US Army surplus carpenter's tools, wooden-handled WW II jobs, can go in the cupboard with my hand tools; my power tools now occupy the chest. Its tray still for keepsakes: Terry's automobile souvenirs—labelled in his no-nonsense engineer hand: '*FLOAT JETS*', '*SCHRADER VALVES*', mysterious fuses like cyanide capsules—in their tobacco tins and cigar boxes.

Cigar fancier, Uncle Terry, and a pauper's funeral in the end. The Little Flower nuns of Kathgodam buried him, and by the time I visited their town there was a second grave alongside with its identical heap of stones and no one was sure which heap was his. The Fiat his mobile tombstone.

12 noon. Half-day cleanup in progress overhead where the concrete was mixed. Too late, but Beauty chipping away with adze, Habilis prising with trowel. Victor spreads the tailings on the grass outside where the rear wheel churned up mud. Weak sun drying out clothes, mats, cordage, and garage floor where the last four sacks of cement perch on bricks.

Looks like Habilis is preparing a skedaddle, the cleanup is so thorough. He saw at once there can't be a cold joint along the whole length of the beam. Agrees the four high-and-dry 12-foot rods are better cut off and used elsewhere.

21 September
Last day of cleanup. Hose down the new room, wash away the silt that's turned the kitchen ceiling below into a dripping sponge.

Damp patches everywhere in the house: black mould, white mould, green mould, yellow mould. Never such a monsoon. Fans on in every room drying out mattresses, underlay, musty pillows, damp curtains, sweating ceilings. Let the rains end and the scurvy vanishes.

I pick black leaves off the diseased ginkgos.

Yesterday Habilis built little dikes, ponding the slab so the concrete wet-cures over the next ten days, rain or no. Obliging now, a little penitent, sensing his tenure as preferred builder is at risk. Pointing out little details he attended to, picking up litter he normally leaves for me: plastic bags the takeaway tea comes in, newspaper bags the samosas come in. Beauty gathering up the tools, helping me spread the black tarp out to dry. She's Habilis's other woman. When I appeared suddenly with the broom and pan they were sitting close together and Habilis made a sudden guilty movement. Victor sitting there sipping tea as if accustomed to the pair.

22 September
2:15 a.m., wake to two thoughts.

1) The far wall must be anchored at the base: the pressure of the new slab is not just down but *out*. Add another wythe to bring the wall to load-bearing girth.
2) Today's online report: Mao's Great Leap cost 45 million lives, a finding from newly unclassified state documents. The look that nagged at me on older faces in China. Stunned. As after some great trauma only the gods can contemplate without madness.

Weeklong Habilis drama in my head. From: '*You've had a big lump sum, mate. You can fill up your tank and ride a long way from this place!*' To (to myself): '*It's catch as catch can, boyo, wake up!*'

The slab has things going for it structurally, despite the cut-off beams: a wide overhang all round the small rain room (so there's as much roof outside as in); the resistance the whole (Pak) nation offers to its out-thrust; and support where the slab hangs (a bit cheekily) by its fingernails *on* the opera box.

9 AM Dhani back at work—in dark glasses!

'Salman Khan!' Habilis teases him. Bollyboy.

His vision's fine, he says, no pain, still on medication. But he shouldn't be bending over and looking down, Maeve thinks.

A groundsman not look down?

'Go home,' I say, 'rest.'

But he *wants* to be on the job.

24 September
Train whistle mourns: the track is open again after last week's mudslide, the week of incessant rain. That makes us the rainfall capital of India.

Habilis arrives on the dot of nine, to make amends. Today he adds the second wythe to the outer wall. The iron merchant set my mind at rest yesterday, giving me a little tutorial, drawing a grid on the back of a bill.

Drying out
The first dry day you go from verandah to verandah marvelling at the strange amber light. What's this! The world dipped in tea and hung out to dry. Step out onto grass, unyielding lawn. Who took the sponge, left this pumice in its place? The haze overhead not yet sky but no longer cloud. Release! No more drought porn from the Thar Desert, from Mali. Topaz glint from dry shingle. The frog's jewel? It tinctures gravel and grass, air, earth, and Mars. Ghost of sunlight flaps at the black-mossed wall. Butterflies throng the willow.

ROOFTOP PLEASURES
 5:15 a.m., the hour when colour returns, the bat panics, ducks under its own cape like an old-time photographer hell bent on black and white.
 A breeze caresses the drumstick leaf fans. Fresh, sweet, otherworldly, luring you over the balustrade.

GARDEN SOLACE
 —*Putting away the gardening tools, sir?*
 — *The Jerusalem artichoke is best bought from Lamboo's pushcart.*
 —*You mean gentlemen's toes, sir? And okra?*
 —*Ladies' fingers are still best home-grown. And, for that sly toe dig, you will pull up the rotted radishes of June.*

THREENECKS
Every year about this time I regret the loss of my mother's kitchen garden, sacrificed to the cloister. Then, at lunchtime—always in the middle of that meal—comes Lamboo's call: *'Here be potatoes, be onions, be eggplants, be tomatoes!'* and I come to my senses: why grub and carry on when in another month or two, the summer finally behind us, there will be no glory like that of this approaching cart? Of the

finest vegetables in the world, old mellow seed strains, among the last on earth.

The monsoon is in retreat. Nightly now this manic laughter from the power lines: the screech-owls are back. The wires shake with their bitter jests.

The compleat almanackist
Dhani squats on the front lawn in his Bollywood dark glasses, consults the sun, like a cautious welder. Has always looked to the sky for tokens. (I've never known his umbrella to appear without cause.) In settled rain he'll absent himself, but let it start while he's here and he'll go on weeding in the drizzle. I sometimes call him in just to hear him scoff.

The compleat almanackist is not pious, like Thrifty Ben, but he has his days off. If I need him on Ram Navami, his namesake's birthday, he's not available. Three such days in the year, the other two Shiva's night and Krishna's birthday. But here he is on Independence Day, on Republic Day, on Gandhi's birthday.

He fasts, he has his feasts, because that is what all creatures do. A tuning fork or chip in the cortex tells him how to act and when. He knows what he wants, knows what he likes. The black mulberry, for example, he finds insipid, even when I tell him it's from his des, out east. He'll pick a lime, just the one, from the laden tree, when prompted; Habilis would fill the bag. Dhani will accept a bunch of litchis, but fresh figs, even mulberries, not sweet enough, he'll turn down. He's learnt to appreciate the drumstick, though, and has taken to the sweet and sour Natal plum, a new hybrid that lights up the yard with its spotty red wattage. He pops one straight in his mouth and finds it good.

'Down Kanpur side they have lots of *karaunda*,' he says, munching, 'a black kind and the small sour pinkish pickling kind.' When he was a boy he ran away to Kanpur. 'I must have been ten or twelve. Two years I stayed. It was a different city then, with jungly patches and groves, all cut down now and built over. They had karaunda hedges they kept clipped.'

'And food?'

'Oh I'd run errands, go marketing, they'd feed me. I didn't go back home. After that I came here.'
But in another version he went to Delhi as a young man.
'When were you in Delhi?' Of course he can't give dates. 'Was your hair still black?'
'Oh, getting on for grey,' he says.
'How long were you there?'
'Two years or so.' Two years is a handy number with him. 'I spent two years in Meerut too, after, then I came here.'

Habilis covets this thorny plum and wants one in his yard some day, but Dhani just chews and nods approval.

I've never heard him exclaim over the beauty of anything. This one is colourful he'll say, planting out seedlings, or this has a pink flower, or this is perfumed; but a beautiful pink, a sweet scent, no. Solitude has bred an austerity in him. That and his natural reserve have made him a sage. People seek him out for counsel, often on this ground, at the lion-mouth, and he gives them a hearing, frowning into the dip at the Adam's apple as if something in the voicebox held the answer. He delivers his prescription in two lines, kicking a little soil as he does, to give them the option of doing as they please. Soil is at the root of his calm, the way Habilis' flint comes from brick.

So why do I see him hunched over a brazier in the widow's garage, reading catastrophe in the embers? On such days I see him wheel his Atlas into a mountainside and vanish. And watch this garden clap shut and rush howling after him.

I wonder what he makes of the pagoda. Building matters he habitually sidesteps, working away from the chaos on days when Habilis and Victor preside. Usually he retreats to the opposite end of the 433: if work is in progress at the pagoda entrance you'll find Dhani on the front lawn, weeding minutely. By such punctilious separateness was caste maintained for centuries. But that doesn't mean he's not interested. When he's done his two hours he'll come around to the redstone patio and cast an eye over the building works, and if they're of sufficient interest he'll squat down and start to rub tobacco in the palm of his hand. Habilis will greet him without turning around, addressing him always with the honorific, Mali*ji*, and they will exchange notes. A chirpy young labourer might explain a fine point in the folding grill that is being hung on either side of the picture window, and Dhani will humour him. Habilis will give the boy a withering look. He and Dhani go back a way on the 433 and they're not going to truck with pipsqueaks.

They also have in common, I suspect, a slight skepticism of my projects, because they're out of the ordinary, and possibly unnecessary (though of course professionally desirable). The pagoda especially has the makings of a fine tower, but what's it for? For that matter what is it? The very word *pagoda* is unknown to either of them: as for the plan it exists in my head alone. It's only lately that I've begun to speak of China, and the new study versus the old. I've sometimes thought of Dhani as a sorcerer, but now it occurs to me that in his view there's a better candidate for that title: myself. Who puts a hole in his roof? Now I look through his eyes and see me, divining and carrying on under the skywell.

1:00 PM Still doubtful of the slab. Nicky, my architect friend, holds one hand out and presses down on the knuckles. Her fingertips rise up.

'The tension in overhangs comes along the *top*. As opposed to the tension at a span. Compression below, tension above.'

So the overhang at Pak can take a brick wall along the boundary edge. Physics is with us.

26 September
Holiday feeling. Sunday for one, but also no rain, and no workers, no work, the concrete curing peacefully.

27 September
The first pumpkin flower jolts with its ten thousand volts. It's the tennis ball at Wimbledon.

Behind it, the first shy violet.

Lay awake till four this morning, then up on the roof at five, under a waning three-quarter moon so bright it shows up the plume of smoke from the baker's ovens. Orion overhead, the Plough stood up on its handle, Pole star faint. Heart singing.

Three nights since I watched the full moon rise over the slab ponds.

Now we need steps up from the roof onto the new terrace: four steps and a landing. Drove a 12mm rod in under the new slab yesterday, a landing feasible there. Projecting steps—treads without risers—hanging free, so we respect the rule that nothing shall ever be built on this roof. Habilis looked skeptical when I described what I wanted.

Make them before he comes back!

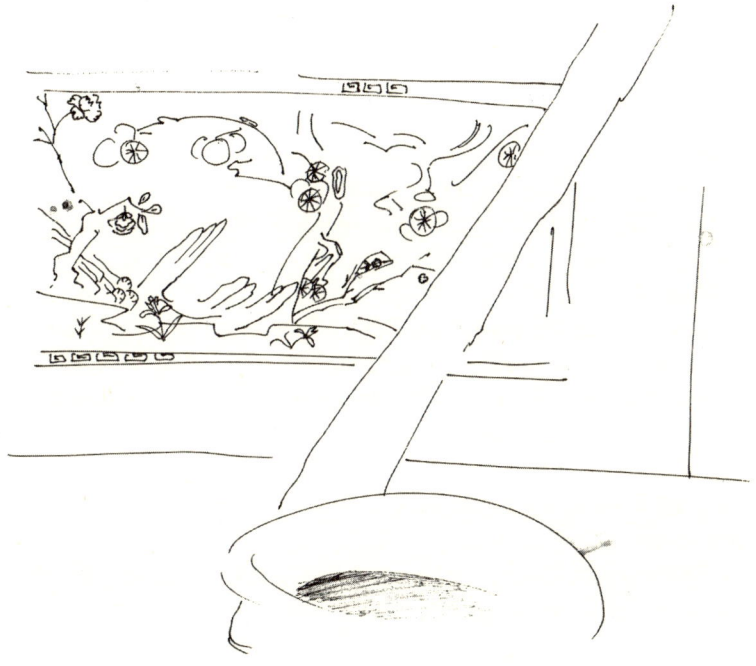

Rainspots
in the courtyard
of the Great Mosque

October

1 October
    —*Mattress Turning Day, boy!*
    —*Her-under-the-Quilt is sleeping in, sir.*
    —*Rouse her up. Burnoff Day too, the Almanack says. Tell Chaturvedi Sahib, Uncle Ben Franklin, Poor Richard, Poor Robin, Poor Irv. Bring out your old wicker chairs, your cribs, your rickety stools. Your crusted woks and frying pans. They come out of the blaze new-minted.*
    —*The crib will shortly be in use, Forest Dweller sir.*
    —*Why, you sly begetter! Almirah not crowded enough for you?*

THREENECKS
'*Pay-por!*' comes the kabari's call. Which Filo always took for 'Tea-pot!' The newspaper recycler's are back on their bikes after the monsoon. You wait forever when you want one, then when you've locked the gate they come by in threes.
    'Kainchi tez, chhuri tez.' Knives ground. Scissors ground. Cried with great authority by an ancient surd who uses his bicycle wheel as a motor.
    'Kursi-palang bana le-o.' Chair-and-bed-rewebbers, always juveniles, often in pairs, always rogues.

Gandhi's birthday

2 October
He's the bald guy with the stick in a thousand city parks. But he's also the worker, spinning cotton. He was not so dull as to imagine machines couldn't do a better job. He had a simple point to make: full employment.
    He's had a hard time lately, but Gandhism is not the worn-out doctrine industrialists pretend. They forget, like our weathercock

middle-class that now dismiss the man as a repressed crank, he had reason for his bias. A class that have never made a bed or washed a shirt are not going to distinguish between anti-industrial and pro-labour. Village labour, for obvious reasons, in a country predominantly rural: that was where labour was most disorganized. And believing a doctrine empty unless practiced, this practical man began to spin cotton himself. Spinning was the simplest, and most telling, form of praxis: something he could do, and do daily, in the midst of a hectic political schedule. It was his way of saying: *put up or shut up.* For all his austerities he did not recommend a suppression of self, or a life of unrelenting toil. That mystifying schoolroom sign that dogged my childhood, WORK IS WORSHIP, could more helpfully have been replaced by his challenge, one so radical it beggars the political mind:

BE THE CHANGE YOU WOULD LIKE TO SEE IN THE WORLD.

Teachers' Day comes on Radhakrishnan's birthday, children's day on Nehru's birthday. (Now what *he* taught—pinkish noblesse—doesn't amount to much.) A home-grown Labour Day, as opposed to the international May Day of parades, could come on Gandhi's birthday, an occasion for small wild goose awards. In a country with an atom smasher, an award for the inventor of a hand-held rock splitter. (Millions of women squat by our roads wearing their joints out with ten thousand little hammer shocks a day.) Or a simple rope lift for loads up to the second storey, since that's still the level most commonly reached, and cranes at every site are still a distant dream. (The gaffer would applaud.) A hardware-store block and tackle. A dig-down spade. The ultimate garden axle shaft. Victor would happily expand this list.

Dhani and Gandhi
He looks a lot like him in fact, with the glasses.

Dhani and pasta
The other day he found a furrowed piece of penne pasta in the gravel and examined it as one might a tiny spaceship fallen out of the sky.

5 *October*
4:00 AM Still shaking my head over Inam's visit yesterday.

He arrives in the afternoon with young Sanjay to test the brakes. Asks for a nail and some thread and the smallest spanner. Winds the thread around the nailhead while Sanjay takes off the front wheel. Gets under the car, accustomed to a garage jack.

Sanjay gets in the driver's seat. I freeze. He's right above the pillar jack!

This very jack once toppled over because the back wheel hadn't been secured. The back wheel is unsecured right now. But the forward-opening door won't let me past to slip a chock in. One slight shift from Sanjay and Inam will be simply crushed.

His cell phone rings. Coolly he takes the call under there while tightening a nut.

10:00 AM Sit on the sunporch this morning simply to enjoy a space hogged for a year by the almirah.

Noon. Sun ray passes through a chink in the boards at the skywell, through the picture window, onto the red flagstones two storeys down, to spotlight a snail horn. Detail after months of fuzz.

But Victor and company vanished as if they were never here.

GARDEN WORK FOR OCTOBER
- Fork ground around the dying oakleaf hydrangea. Pray, girl. Down on your knees.
- Transplant the Persian rose.
- Dig up and spread oxalis corms. To think that for years I treated oxalis as a weed.

—*Tart but toxic, my lovely, best not endanger the child.*
—*Rackrenter sir, will we upgrade from almirah to rain room any time soon?*
—*No rain room, boy. That's my study you're coveting.*

6 *October*
6:00 AM Sitting in the rain room, the heart of the pagoda, after sweeping it clean of sand and grit, I get the first feel of the finished space.

Tons of concrete floats above my head, the iron grid gone to work. Three weeks since the pour. With every day of cure the rods loft a slab that otherwise would flatten me. All around me in the little room are trunks of dead garden trees turned posts. They bore the whole weight for the first day, standing put under the five eucalyptus beams that underlie the planking.

I'm in a magic forest. Dying to see naked concrete, yet eager to preserve this sylvan half-light. I take out the inchitape and measure the swept floor: one inch short of seven feet from door to picture window; eight-and-a-half feet across: a shade smaller than the kitchen below. This will be my study.

A white ginger flower on the lily bank leaps into view: the picture window at work. In the doorway opposite, this maculate giraffe neck is the rosewood trunk. When we built the rain room the first work was an arch to accommodate the rosewood tree leaning over the portico. I wanted a tree in a room but settled for a tree in an upstairs patio.

Monkishly happy. Already I see the room plastered and whitewashed, tiled underfoot and furnished. Half the glory of the Alhambra, we forget, was in the vanished rugs. This room will have: a desk lit by falls of light from the skywell. A chair. A daybed.

'But what is it?' DP wanted to know, inspecting the works, and I couldn't say. I should be able to tell him: he is the friend you trust before you trust yourself.

It's a bolt-hole. It's a tree house. A monk's cell with the sky allowed in. It's a screen, of course. (Aching for that last wall when I walked up on the roof terrace this morning.)

Pagoda, another of those Eurasian words from the Portuguese, like *kamra*, from *camera*, room. *Pagode* from the Persian *butkada* or ghost house.

It's a spirit room.

[Exit kissing inchitape rosary.]

7 October

Inam arrives with the car so I go with him for a test drive. When I drop him off he leans in the window.

'Chalti ka naam gadi.'

If it runs it's a car.

BROADBAND
Online I find a photograph in Christopher Hawes' *Poor Relations* of a sampler embroidered by one Anne Jennings, c 1790, in a Calcutta military orphanage. Tears, two centuries on. Her mother would have been 'a slave named Fanny', or 'a Portuguese named Dominga'; some mothers remained nameless, 'a Coffre belonging to Captain Gordon, Master of a country ship'. By the late 1760s, just a decade after Plassey, the records for Bengal show half of the children brought in for baptism only by the father's name. The mother some anonymous Indian or Portuguese or 'East India' woman. I know Anne Jennings in my bones.

8 October
Sandstorm in the rain room. Habilis, an Arab with his head in a towel, Gaffer loose-turbaned, Beauty headscarved with her yellow gauze chunni (stuck with mirror sequins).

The scaffolding removed, the whole ceiling is a beach of yellow sand, upside down, with the imprint of the dislodged planks. My magic forest of standing putlogs vanished too, replaced by this Saharan mirage. Gaffer is jabbing away at it with a crowbar. Habilis, red-eyed from a fever, perched on a single-wythe wall, looks on in disgust. 'Long strokes, *long* strokes, father,' he calls, then leaps down like a young man and shows him. He loves this life. Beauty, slashing with a trowel, gets the angle right instinctively, her yellow kameez lighting up the room. An iron rod falls on her, fault Habilis, and she brushes it off without a pause in her scraping. Noonday sunlight drops down the naked skywell onto her head and ricochets off every tiny mirror to dance on the four walls.

It's a particle collider.

9 October
PLASTER DAY. Cowboy H astride the boundary wall balancing a great eucalyptus pole while Beauty binds the far end to make a plasterers' scaffold at the boundary.

'*Won't* fit?' he growls, as Beauty looks doubtful. 'It'll fit and its *father* will fit.' I leave them to it.

While I'm in the shower, the plastering sand arrives, a trolley load. Beauty rings the cowbell. Grit in my ear and the tractor men impatient, I dry off and find some plastic sheeting so they can dump it on the shingle path. They drop the tailgate and shovel it out. I pay them, wondering if Habilis gets his cut here too (he placed the order). At one time I thought him on my side. Now I know he has just one side, his own.

10 October
Sudden shower, brings a power-line crew scrambling into the garage for lunch. They squat down and open up their tiffin boxes while Beauty, also looking for shelter, sits nearby, looking away, accustomed to being the only woman.

After work, Victor stands in his undershorts in the garage and unwraps his good clothes from the polythene bag he stores them in. Doesn't mind showing Beauty his legs I notice. Sairu looks up and sniffs.

'And the marriage?' I ask Habilis.

Beauty, leaving with a headload, appears to smile. She was the broker, the girl from her village.

'He can't save a rupee, how's he to marry?' Habilis says.

Have you paid him? I should ask, but don't.

'Just three hundred rupees so far,' Victor reports when I ask him. One day's wage. A little amused at my surprise.

No more contracts, I decide.

11 October
'Oh he's sharp, very sharp.'

The new mistri from Rae Bareilly, a young man, Hindu, married, earnest, chatting with Gaffer. Gaffer is Habilis's neighbour, knows the family, may even be family. I took him for a Hindu at first, beside the bearded hawk-eyed Afghan.

Habilis is back in the afternoon, smoking and half listening to Gaffer when I appear.

'Chup!' comes the instant command.

Gaffer stops mid-sentence, his mouth open.

Later I watch the mistri egging the old man on, partly for entertainment. Gaffer's a kind of tradesman's radio maundering on in the background. In plastering, more than in brickwork, especially on wide stretches of wall, the labourer has long spells of doing nothing while the mason jobs away doing something that's both heavy and skilled, earning the extra money the labourer can only hope to merit some day. Gaffer's past it and knows he'll end his days a labourer, so he squats by the mound of plaster he's mixed and gossips. I get the impression Habilis's wife is upset (over Beauty?) and catch the word *wrestling* used in a figurative way. Has he thrown away the money I've advanced?

'That sand did me in yesterday,' Gaffer tells the mistri. 'No joke carrying it upstairs,' he says to the air between us. He headloaded half a ton up onto the roof, marching steadily back and forth from the garage. Habilis will be underpaying him too. He crouches under the silver arch to eat the lunch he brings; the mistri wanders off and has a snack at the shops.

Habilis just has a cup of tea.

13 October
SCREEN DAY!

Today they build the crucial wall: at the far end of the cantilever slab. I work all morning on my projecting steps just so I can watch it go up.

It looks like a theatre now, this stage five steps up from the roof terrace. We're building its backdrop now, but really we're wiping out Pak. I want to write an opera, sell tickets to the show. My set would have a balcony that overhangs a garden, and justice would be served at the end as the wicked General is bricked into his own box at the opera.

In the afternoon I'm up on stage as Gaffer's assistant, passing the mortar he mixes on the roof, dipping bricks. We work in the sun. Wobbly at day's end, but the payoff is palpable: *no more opera box.*

A whole pagoda consecrated for this moment. And now it's past.

Everything beyond this consummation is a bonus, a gift.
In the evening I walk up and down the roof.
It's gone!
One task remains. An arm of their washline-T (that once rained pegs and socks) still projects into our space. Ducking down, this afternoon I cut my scalp on it. When the wall reached that point we considered a moment and decided: nothing for it but to keep going. Now it sticks through the brickwork like a dagger from the other side. To be cut off at leisure some day.

Yes! On Small Wild Goose Day, a ceremonial cutting off of this last thorn.

14 October
3:30 AM
Very like a stage, now the plaster's going on. For small one-act plays, the audience seated on the roof.

Yesterday I had the mistri build a post to hold the rail across the front of the new terrace where it overhangs the rosewood court. Halfway through the day, I saw it was too near my steps: you would graze your shoulder on it going up or down. Several times in the afternoon I looked for the right moment to tell him. With bricklaying you have six hours to change your mind.

Finally I said, 'Mistriji, I may have made a mistake.' I demonstrated the clearance needed.

'No problem,' he said considering his handiwork a little ruefully. 'But it'll be a little weaker than before.'

'The plaster will bind it,' I offered.

'The plaster will bind it,' he agreed.

Beauty looked on gravely. Gaffer bemused, turned gentle, fatherly. 'Here,' he said, 'let me help you.'

Brick by brick we dismantled one end. Peace in the air.
Habilis off. *No alarums, no excursions.*

'I wanted to see how a contract would go, and now you've shown me,' I said to Habilis in my head.

But this morning, I see his side. We had an understanding, not an agreement, not even a handshake, but each of us had a slightly different picture in his head. Contracts are great wild goose documents. For a Five-Year-Plan, a Great Leap Forward. With an understanding you *can* be shown another side. I see now why he's eager to wind things up: because I could go on simply extending the work in a small wild goose fashion and he would be obliged, out of politeness and deference and friendship, to do it. It can't be done. A crossing of the two species isn't possible. An efficient India, a relaxed China: you wake from the dream rubbing your eyes.

Habilis unnaturally agreeable yesterday, making trite remarks all round that must have been wormwood and gall in the mouth, all because the contract is drawing to an end.

Knocking off, Gaffer whines: 'I'm just an old illiterate. Who cares for an old man?' And, glancing at Beauty, 'No one's going to give *me* a ride on his scooter!'

Habilis obliges and rides off with her.

5:30 AM Shut the bedroom door for the first time: winter in the air!

8:30 AM New mistri here early: *pal-as-tar*, he says, and *joun* for *which*, an Easterner.

4:30 AM Tea break. Gaffer looks older without his headwrap. Giggling as sand whacks him in the back; as if it hasn't happened a hundred times before. 'Well, if you *will* sit in the way, uncle,' the younger man calls, not letting up for a minute. Whiplash must plague his arm from flicking all day.

15 October

Precise half moon last night over the theatre.

At the bank this morning the cashier did the usual double take with 'Sealy'. A small inconvenience but should I have to deal with it? Anglo names came from every corner of Europe. What made them Anglo was they all stayed on in India, those adventurers, to speak our English. But you wonder. Could Rencontre, now safely in Melbourne, have ever felt at home here? Vanspall, now in Toronto? Marazzi? *Tremenhere!* Imagine spelling that out for the cashier in a crowded bank. How to explain that small ordeal to a Singh or a

Verma? Or even a Khan? No wonder they fled. Imagine a dark-skinned Gudmunsdottir, first name Ingrid, born and bred here, trying to cash a cheque. Spell that out, lady.
Scalp wound from the dagger almost healed.

16 October
Today Habilis arrived at closing time in a new hat: *Developer*. With aides in attendance, almost visible. He bustled around, chivvying old Gaffer, pointing out defects in the plasterer's technique, noting details of the day's work, drawing a long chisel from his tool sack to knock out the dummy pipe at the new drainage hole. Attended with inclined head to my list of matters outstanding, said he would have two mistris on the job tomorrow, a squad of labourers to clean up. The job would be finished by the end of the day. The plasterer looked doubtful, I simply laughed, but Habilis the conjurer carried the day. The day after tomorrow, he said, speaking with quiet urgency, he had to start on a new project up in Rajpur; tomorrow at seven he needed twelve labourers. I thought he was trying to impress the mistri but it turned out he'd impressed me: when he was gone I felt a whole team had left. That *seven* and *twelve* had done the trick.

The plasterer a sloppy worker after all. Now the iron stair must be repainted. A simple cloth thrown over was all it needed (and Habilis at hand). In future withhold the last instalment. Lessons in leverage.

17 October
Yesterday was Ayudh Puja down south, the day you bless your tools, including machines that serve your trade. This laptop.

Last night the finale of the popular outdoor *Ramayana* drama down the road. *HAHAHAHAHAHHA!* went the wicked Ravana into the mike, quite often and quite late. Our plasterer says he went. *Huhuhuhuhuhuhuuuuu!* wept kidnapped Sita, the harmonium whingeing pathos. Windy night too. Through it all the clink of bricks being unloaded off a truck backed up to the jewellers at Threenecks. Tonight the torching of the demons.

4 PM Enter Habilis the Hun.
Mistri and labourer, free and merry all day, turn meek schoolboys.

Habilis pays the labourer in front of me, the whole amount owing for the day's work, but not the mistri, saving his payment for when I'm out of earshot. When the man leaves, he wears a deep frown. Next evening Habilis appears at sundown, looks briefly over the day's plastering and issues his instructions to the labourer. He addresses all his remarks to the labouring man, utterly ignoring his superior. Then, still without looking at the plasterer, he curls a finger at him and, with his face turned away, delivers his lines in a kind of future imperative.

'Tomorrow you will sweep this slab clean and you will mix a strong mortar and you will apply it with care in one go and you will make very sure, every, little, dip, is filled, and the floor comes up *perfect*.'

When the men are gone I make small talk.

'Cement is up five rupees a sack every time you turn around. The surdy has us by the short and curlies.'

'Ah, but his *manager* will fleece you where you stand,' Habilis retorts.

He plucks a mask off the new stage. Rubbing his hands together and hiking his shoulders right up:

'*Oooh Sheikh Sahib! What can I possibly say! Just yesterday we were paying the truck wala sixty over and above to come straight here, and today he says,* Two hundred, *or I go first to the other guy. Our hands are tied!*'

Next he's off telling on his clients. This one gives him the keys to his house (where, it occurs to me, he takes Beauty), that one has an aquarium with scarlet goldfish opposite the posh girls' finishing school. He has built him a tiered fountain descending from a range of Snowcem Himalayas. I should have known one day I'd meet Habilis the Clown.

18 October
Yesterday, Habilis Highwire.

Balanced on a plastic stool set on top of a rickety table, he grades a runoff slope where the slab overhangs the iron stair. The front edge done, he shifts to the side, but there's a tree trunk in the way. One by one he passes every tool he needs around the giraffe neck and lines them up within reach on the far side. He has an arm on either side of the rosewood trunk, like a tree-hugger. Then he finds a toehold on the trunk, leans out—the stool strains—and mates the screed with the side edge, tilts it for gradient, and trowels mortar. Mortar he understands, will play on its nature, tease it with water, withhold a drop. Without looking he exchanges trowel for float. Starting at the low point he draws the mass back up the slope, negotiating the blind spot, caressing the surface as if it were alive with strokes that get progressively lighter and more notional. It's late, I need a shower, but Habilis, master of the feather touch, the extra minute, won't give up: and for the past ten minutes, at the end of a long day, his left hand, the wrong hand, has been doing another man's job, holding the screed deadlocked.

19 October

Cleanup day yesterday: wire-brushed the plaster crust off the trunk of the rosewood, hosed down rain room, iron stair, garage, verandahs, every surface that has hosted grit since work began. Then sprawled in the back bedroom reading. *Reading!* In the afternoon put the leftover iron rebar 'Away': the Venturi canyon now bonus covered space.

The pagoda looking new-clothed. Plastered.

24 October

4 AM Full moon floodlight, that cold bewitching lamp, a light to end by: daylight executions must be harder, on everybody. Far away, a woman's tuneless quavering solo, then tabla and rhythmic clapping buoy up a choppy chant.

Chanda mama chanda mama chanda mama, uncle moon uncle moon uncle moon.

At the same horizon, a steam engine chuffing along! Poor knackered horse let loose by night. Then the town's twenty muezzins are off, jockeying.

25 October

Sent the mistri home. I don't want my cement used up. He's not the best of plasterers (who is, after Habilis?) and his technique of sloshing a pure cement slurry undercoat leaves icing-like dribbles that he never

bothers to smooth off: trapped under paint they're there forever.
The second day plastering he needed the toilet. No look more complex than from a man caught short. There's a latrine by the Police Lines, I said at first. Later when I asked him if he'd been he said he had shut the need off. I went downstairs impressed and put the situation to Maeve. She frowned, but prepared the guest toilet. Easier, though, to let him in at our bathroom, off the master bedroom, nicely named: one step through the laundry and he's in.
Afterwards found his shoeprints on the seat. But glad to have him breach a vile taboo.

26 October
Today dug out the dead tea tree, failed transplant, and put in the new one brought home from the nursery on the roof of Wayne's Maruti 800, flapping in the wind.
Third step ready for concreting. Each step has a skeleton of two heavy iron rods with a lighter one set in between; short bits laid crosswise on top and trussed with wire. Mixing mortar in the bucket now, instead of on the roof. Shingle, gravel, cement, brought up at intervals, in between broadband, coffee. The peace of solitary work.

BROADBAND
Browsing the net I come across a familiar line: 'We live without feeling the country beneath our feet,' a Mexican writer retranslates Mandelstam, and again I think of the stunned look on many Chinese faces of a certain age. The soles of your feet must never recover.

28 October
Stage steps done. Onto the landing now.
Fresh down from the bash, arm trembling. The landing takes five rods spaced at five inches, hammered in like giant nails under the roof slab. Bought a 1-kilo club head for the job. Blunt-tipped, the first rod took some pounding; pencil-sharpened with the Bosch grinder, the rest slipped in. More misses than hits at first, then the average improves. With each hit the head mushrooms, widening the target. Sweet the centred hit.

30 October
Today added a buttress wall using up all the brickbats, even small bits and pieces, just to remind Habilis, who grandly scorns anything like a fragment. The landing slab built directly on the old tabletop, that knackered workhorse. Give it a month to cure. Concrete takes its time: Roman concrete roofs are *still* curing.

31 October
The skywell needs a grill, something simple that won't hide the stars. I find a fine motif in an old photo of the wrought iron gate at the Bibi Khanum Mosque in Samarkhand. The design could use up Dad's old archery arrowheads waiting fifty years in the tool chest.

GARDEN PLEASURES
In October, everywhere and anywhere.

ROOFTOP PLEASURES
More than any other bird we watch the swifts, their ways learnt from Gilbert White. First up and last to bed, our swifts, joined now and then by swallows, canton in a ruin I once coveted just down the road to Antarctica. At any time thirty zigzag in the upper air, an ideogram in motion, always in danger of dispersing, hiving off like poetry.
    Contrast the steady prose of this paragraph of egrets.

Now let a year pass.

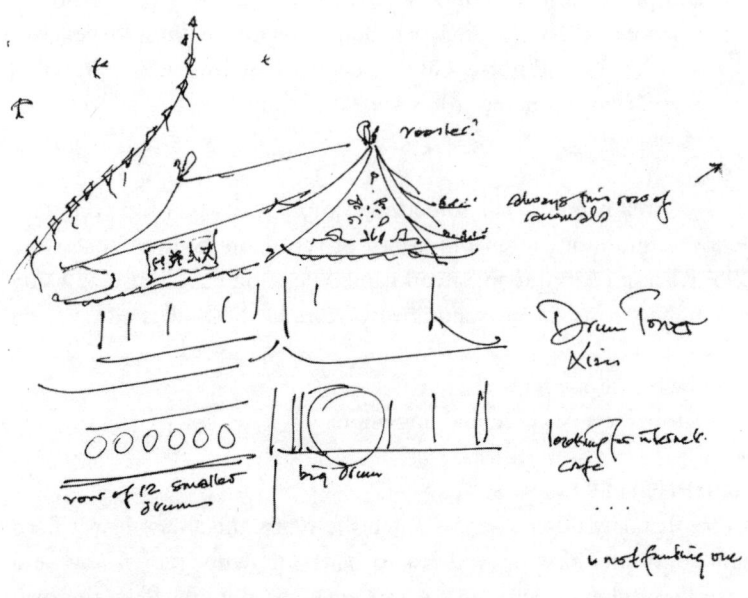

rooster?

always this rose of animals

Drum Tower Xian

looking for internet cafe

a not funking one

rows of 12 smaller drums

big drum

Suddenly swamped or @ any rate swept by this sense of the bl*dness of this new nation — on this swept and garnished terrace overlooking the bell tower — which strikes as I write! —

then a lightfall swallows and a string of kites. The swallows hawking insects attracted by the floodlit drum tower

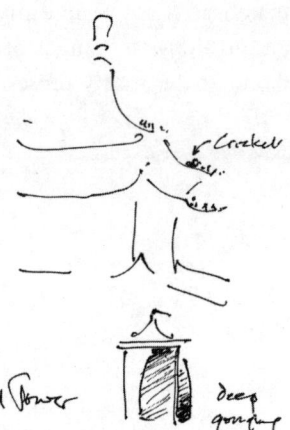

Cricket

Bell Tower

deep gonging

Kites and swallows

November

—*Can the godchild be walking already, No-longer-young Householder?*
—*And glad to escape the almirah's four walls every time, Ageing Forest Dweller.*

1 November
Quack Day, one month late. Every quarter should spark a small fire of renewal.

Still dark at six. Winter a serious possibility now. Lay in bed an extra hour, reluctant to leave that warmth. Thinking of refuge, of the Aharon Appelfeld hero who returns home to find it occupied by strangers who shunt him off with a curse.

Maeve seen from the redstone seat last night. Switching lights on and off in the house. First the kitchen light, then the laundry light on the other side of the house, on and immediately off, lighting up momentarily that whole dark Bengal gulf, then Filo's room where she lights up a cigarette and takes a deep satisfying drag, unsmiling and calm and simply there.

This is her book.

3 November
Watching the Rem Koolhaas maison video Filo sent last night. His twisted pier-glass the only exciting building I saw in Beijing.

Is the small wild goose pagoda a folly? Now the silver arch has gone on, the pagoda roof looks suspiciously like a pleasure dome. In the shimmer I see Habilis, the day we mounted the aluminium sandwich board, holding down the bowed sheet while I drill. I'm sitting in the igloo drilling blind, up and out (through holes welder Mohan put in the iron band) calling '*Mind your hands!*' And he calls back every time, '*Minding.*' All through the hot afternoon that antiphon. I could be his confessor.

All is forgiven between us. But it takes a new job to clear the air.

'Let it stay,' he urged when it was time to peel off the protective layer. Meaning, keep it new a little longer, the way people leave the plastic wrap on car seats. So I did, till his back was turned.

It's only part pleasure dome; I'm building a workplace. A beautiful one, true. More time than money spent on it, its beauty spare but cumulative. The silver arch is a kind of crown for the domestic levels below, but its plain function is to keep rain out of the skywell. Now one monsoon has taught me the skywell needs a glass chimney for a shield as well. And if so, why should it not have a tin frieze of animals on each face? Those cut-out silhouettes you see on the eaves of Chinese drum houses.

You build for beauty: Habilis living on a rooftop understands, Victor living in a garage understands. (Victor scorns blacksmiths and snakecharmers not for their lowly trades but because they'll live anywhere. Just stretch a tarpaulin, he says, and that's enough for the likes of them.)

THE ALMANACK ASKS

—*Who do snakecharmers look down on?*
—*On the crematorium doms, Not-yet-Ascetic sir.*

Living is a sober business that the almanack with its bunting of eclipses and harvest moons can only hope to lighten. Trivia, oddments, puzzles, prophecies, make life bearable. (Or why does it matter that Roman concrete is still curing?)

Turning the pages of a maiden aunt's photo album I come across a tuft of green feathers. It takes me a while to realize they are all the mortal remains of a life's companion, her parrot. Housed alone is hard, but no fate harder surely than alone *and* unhoused. Habilis, almost done with householding, has a roof, has family; Victor, halfway through his householder stage, is alone but housed for now. Dhani's looking worried. His landlady has got herself a new mali. Next thing he'll be out in the cold. He doesn't want to be a burden on his nephew, though the family have asked him to come and live there. They live too far from his few remaining jobs here in Racecourse. He can push the Atlas half a mile, but five miles going and five coming? He's at the start of his Asceticism, alone.

Architecture, *n*. built space in which to do allotted time.

House, hus, etc.
House started out as *hus* in Old English, a place where you were as snug as a bug in a rug. To be *unhoused* was a fate akin to being *unhouseled*, left out of the sacrifice, put out of god's house, in Gothic the *gudhus*. A pagoda is also a *godhouse*, or spirit house, but not always a good spirit's. From the Portuguese *pagode,* via the Persian *butkada*, idol temple, and beyond to Hindustani *bhut ghar,* ghost house, it's the past come back to haunt you. The past tense is *bhut kala*.

—*Rid your house of ghosts, Little Home Science Mother?*
—*The future's more scary than the past, sir.*
—*Banish both, girl. One pinch of asafoetida (bhutari, ghost-fighter) and you're home in hus.*

Timepass
In the annexe behind us (our Nepal, just below Tibet) the young mother dressing her son—named Gyan, knowledge—says 'shoes' and 'socks', her tongue cleansed of the Hindi names of these things. Common nouns succumb daily, and there's an invasion of imponderables too: *problem, loss,* and universally—*death*. Nobody says *maut* (see *mort*) any more, only ever 'death', pronounced *dath,* rendered manageable in this foreign guise.

Tonight I discover a new cracker, *Timepass.* Pure Indian English, completely of its age and class, sweet-and-salt *Timepass* crumbles in the mouth with just the right degree of resistance: next to nothing but, crucially, sparklingly, tellingly, not nothing.

—*The grapevine is not a washline, Bad Husbandman. Such lingerie!*
—*She buys online, Not-yet-Ascetic sir.*
—*Well, hide it. Victor will be here soon.*
—*Red's old hat, sir, but—*
—*The yearnings of bachelors are known only to Google, boy.*

—*If you're going to America there are a couple of things she...*
—*Been prowling my inbox, boy?*

4 November
Invitation from the Asia Society in New York. Taking a leaf out of our book they're inviting a dozen writers from China and India for what they call, a little tweely, the Chindia dialogues.

Suddenly, America. When you have no television they cease to exist: now, after twenty years, Atlantis surfaces.

The red pantry
The unattainable ruled my childhood. The smells from Hindu and Muslim kitchens had you salivating, but what you really craved was what you could only *read* about.

1. **Pastrami:** from hardboiled American crime novels. Something in the sound of the word, a cross-graining in the flesh, rigged this choice; I was sold on it before I ever tried it. Something like it marinated in every Anglo-Indian meatsafe a month before Christmas, beef pickled in saltpetre and grapefruit juice, but how could that compete with New York?
2. **Cheese:** any cheese. So exotic in childhood it was a mystery to me that the Prisoner of Zenda should have it in his dungeon with bread.
3. **Caviar:** a word with so rich an archive in English, when I heard Natasha say *kaver* in Russian it sounded wrong.
4. **Marzipan:** Chaucer's *marchepane* simply compounded the need.
5. **Lobster:** daily fare for James Bond, with the blonde of the day. Some day, you think, at seventeen, some day.
6. **Capers:** from the scene in *Twelfth Night* where Sir Andrew Aguecheek, coward, and Sir Toby Belch, sot, dispute punningly. Later you learn to counterfeit capers with pickled nasturtium buds.
7. **Peking Duck:** bound to disappoint, after its press, and after Canton duck.
8. **Hopping John:** Carson McCullers. Nothing she wrote could

fail, but literary tastes picked up in adulthood don't really count, and this one turned out to be our Anglo *pish-pash*.

Local treats—mustard greens and cornbread when winter is coming on, sugarcane juice at blazing noon in May—can match these dainties; like the call of the koel, they are what sustain you, but the red pantry (see *Red*, a novel of the brush) stocks unattainables. Now, out of the blue, a chance to restock.

I make a shopping list for America.

5 November

Diwali morning, not a cracker at 5:55 AM, but the Hare Krishnas come by beating a tin pot. In Britain today Guy Fawkes meets Goddess Lakshmi. Pilliwinks for the guy, after he signed his confession, Catholic Maeve points out. *Guido* Fawkes, too, foreigner.

Afternoon spent cutting iron. A bloom of rust on the hoard.

Iron work is pleasure, stone drudgery. Iron cuts clean, in a fountain of sparks. Cut stone dry and you release a dust storm trapped in there and raging these ten million years. Cut wet and you spray slurry like a wet dog.

7 November

Dhani squats on the front lawn mowing by hand, nipping just the top inch. Crabwalks as of old, shunts the basket along. Then an altogether new move: shoves back up the pebble-lens red frames that have slid down his nose.

'Intellectual!' Maeve sniffs.

Two kinds of doctors, she reckons: those who make you well, MDs, and those, PhDs, who make you sick.

Dhani, MD.

8 November

Today he swept and swabbed indoors. I glanced up and found him intrigued by the new machine. He would not know a mouse but this new stroking action on the trackpad seemed to intrigue him, linked somehow to the scrolling on the screen. (He tells people I print books in here.) Books he's long accustomed to now; they lie scattered through the house in a manner he must still consider disrespectful. A book belongs on a shelf, in a satin wrap. He would never have been in a library. I think in my time I've shown him two utterly new things: a study and a cemetery.

    Sunset. 5:30. Tea and the failed date-and-raisin cake (just a sunken fontanelle, Maeve points out) at the sunroom seat, the stone still warm.

    'Fanny,' she murmurs. Our fantail flycatcher, a little shy. Its ashy tail flicking from side to side. More timid than the New Zealand fantail, which cuts loops around you as you walk in the bush, making as if to sit on your shoulder. Leaving, it'll flit ahead to the first low branch in your path to lean down and whisper cautions in your ear as you go by.

10 November
Chickpea and rice lunch, the radish greens gritty. Fall into bed exhausted.

    'Railway boy,' I hear Maeve sniff, because I'm wearing a tattered singlet and nothing else. Railway families were poor where she came from in Canterbury. She remembers a swarthy railway family who were not Maori. Anglo immigrants, she wonders. Among the early settlers in Dunedin was a shipload of girls from the orphanage at Kalimpong near Darjeeling.

    But we were police, and I drift off to a bow-and-arrow hunt with another Anglo police boy, Owly Castellas, fifty years ago. Pigeon curry a delicacy of those years; chickpeas show how low we have fallen.

    Returning from the big bin—always overflowing, pigs, dogs, cows, sharing amiably in the spoils, the dogs leaping up into the bin, the ground roundabout trodden into a mire—we see Dhani's garage light on. I think: do I *see* him once he's gone?

GARDEN WORK FOR NOVEMBER
Humus, not cement, under the nails at last. Muscle tissue rejoicing.

    Bedding days for winter plants. A new space has opened up—simply by cropping the mast trees skirts—along the west wall ('Away') where the winter sun now pokes for two hours in the morning. I fetch bricks there two by two, and sand; Dhani brings soil, and compost: for white cosmos interspersed with garlic.

Landscaping a garden you disregard two things: the ultimate futility of the exercise, and the unnerving metaphors in any soil you work. Shakespeare's gardeners know too much; so does my bible, *Sanders' Encyclopaedia*, for that matter. Only Dhani, tied to the ground by duty, seems to get it right. His life is his art. Small *a*.

The small wild goose is on his side. Pagoda of the single glimpse, of the inner eye, it lets things die and lets them live. If you think your life's work is outside you you've swallowed the monumentalist line. You're tied to the great work, to *A*rt. The great pagoda embalms (Mao, Lenin, Tutenkhamen), is the living death of you.

Habilis, who'd love a great wild goose contract, is worried about Victor's bones ever since the marriage fell through. He makes a joke of it, but I can see he's in earnest: who is going to bury Victor if he's left unmarried, without a child?

'So what did he say?' I ask.

Habilis dresses up his shudder as a laugh. He says they were standing on the bridge over the Rispana, the dry riverbed clogged with garbage at the Limekilns.

'*Toss my body in that nullah.*'

Tahkhana

The room I meant all along to build was not in the sky but underground. This pagoda a kind of sidetrack.

From childhood onwards the *tahkhana* intrigued me: a basement for use in hot weather, lit by windows at ground level and ventilated by shafts from above. When India and Pakistan were threatening nuclear war a few years ago, such a room, around since medieval times, took on a new meaning. Dehradun is home to the Indian Military Academy, and it seemed logical that one Pak warhead should be reserved for our Sandhurst. Reasons of morale if nothing else. Another reason for the concealed chamber was civil. In times of ethnic or religious strife a hideaway makes sense. And there's yet another source of anxiety: class.

A stone's throw from the Threenecks is a piece of badland, once the wild ravines below the plateau that formed the racecourse but now squatted on. The squats have been regularized into a slum that extends for kilometres along the path of a sewage canal into which our stormwater drain empties, a warren of half-made houses with leaky roofs, and refuse heaps where gardens should be. If our burglar lives anywhere he's likely there. When my parents were first looking for a plot of land, my mother insisted that it be near the Police Lines. This was partly nostalgia: we knew all the bugle calls that divided up the day, from reveille to retreat to the last roll call. (I still count the hours of night by the striking of the police gong.) But it was also fear that prompted my mother's choice of location. I used to think those fears exaggerated; today I'm not so sure.

Our civil society walks on water. Only the fear of the police and the prison system sustains the charmed existence of middle-class suburbs like Racecourse. When the police force is stretched beyond its limits, there is the army, whose booming guns we hear in rehearsing at the horizon. If these two lines of defence did not exist, this house would be stripped of its chattels within minutes. At such a time it's good to have a mirror you can step through.

Levelling is built into accumulation in the same way as death undoes the lottery of life. Undoing is vital to the larger story. With chattels you can at least start over if you're lucky. We mistake Death when we picture him as the Grim Reaper. He is a living being, virile, unhooded, athletic, the only one alive in his whole kingdom. He simply comes from that far country, holds that passport. He is the vigorous thief of life, the burglar who scaling your boundary wall at night puts an end to your secure existence, your nerve in imagining life could go on forever.

12 November
3 AM Performing a salute-to-the-sun on the Stoneman lawn, full moon directly overhead, when the phone rings long and continuously: Maeve's sister Pauline from Massachusetts, where it's clearly daytime.

Tuesday we went to Haridwar with Wayne, looking for a fort. It's in the manuscript he's translating, the *Shah Jahan Nama,* and he should know, the world's authority on the man who built the Taj Mahal. High above the Ganga we found an old stone foundation, and scouted around a bit, but a modern temple has come up on the site.

Xuan Zang stopped in Haridwar 1300 years ago; I imagine him clambering up that hillside a little short of breath.

China has entered the world of cricket. As a one-sport nation we should blink. They have a sharper sense of the team, but more, an enviable self-discipline. In the Beijing botanical gardens I stumbled on a young man in a black suit at the outermost gate of a restaurant, standing like a statue, his white-gloved hands folded, not a soul to impress in all that empty precinct.

Han, and speaking one language, they're homogeneous in another way: the whole society exists at one broad cut in time. We're at 1497, 1947, 2020, and sometimes 2020 BC. Software, suffrage, field toilets, yoga, all coexist: Vedic and Victorian, medieval and postmodern. The miracle is we cohere at all. But we do.

13 November

Afternoons in November a tenor voice starts up at the nearby ashram, melancholy, otherworldly, pushing out every third note as if life-weary, surrendering to a baritone who spells him seamlessly. Back and forth they go, telling the Ram story, the deep notes sometimes swallowed up but not the tenor's. The same troupe visits the ashram every autumn. For years I've loved this voice and wondered: *he or she?*

Working out a brick lattice for the rear wall of the arch. I see it more clearly down here eyes shut than when I'm up there.

Pagoda of the third eye.

I feel like a piece of fish. At the fishmonger's there's a man, not in rags, scrounging. The young seller will have none of it. The beggar hams it up:

'*I really really felt like a piece of fish today. O lord, what a fate. Never, never be born poor!*'

The seller relents, he gets his bit of tripe.

14 November

Dhani wheels his Atlas onstage, pulls it back onto its stand, looks around blinking as if he would deliver a speech. (His head tilts slightly up, Victor's tilts down. Habilis greets you straight on.) He likes setting up the sweetpea loom so I hand him four of the straightest mulberry branches and the ball of hempen twine.

He turns weaver. I go pack.

17 November

America
The taxi driver from JFK is thirty, Punjabi. He was born the year I was last in New York. He cannot take that decade seriously. The Radisson Lexington cannot take *this* decade seriously (its heyday was the 1920s) but it's close to Central Park and a short hop from the Asia Society. We hardly meet the Chinese at the conference—I exchange bashful smiles with a famous dissident. In the park all the leaves are yellow. I soak in a single wing of the Met, tramp the streets, live on pastrami. But that old crackle in the air is no more; this city cannot take me seriously. The Forest Dweller hops on a bus to Amherst, where Pauline is waiting. She walks with a stick now. The first snow of the year is on the ground. At the Volpe home the sons I last saw aged eleven and twelve are in their forties. Their father Joe walks me through the woods and round a pond that could be one of those ice was harvested from and sent to India in Thoreau's day. The air is crisp and sweet. At night we join hands around a Thanksgiving dinner. Among the smells is a dishwash powder that zings me straight back to Kalamazoo. More time, more time. But my ticket's booked, Dad's already home and waiting. Gina, a family friend, gives me a tub of sourdough starter from a neighbourhood bakery, The Hungry Ghost.

25 November
Back from America.

Dad greets me at the gate, stepping so briskly at eighty-six I take him for a too-long walk.

Is sourdough starter immortal? This batch looks dead. It leaked out into my luggage and left a watermark on my China papers. Millions of dead microbunnies (Gina's word, describing the action of yeast) line my luggage; survivors of the great Halloween snowstorm, they travelled around the world to perish here.

Souvenirs
Why do I keep this now superfluous New York map, and discard scraps full of the sharpest memories? I reach into the wastepaper bin and rescue the following dockets:

1. **Macy's** for 'DRESSY SLPWR' $20.52, for Her-under-the-Quilt, 10% taken off by the Jamaican store clerk even though I didn't have a member coupon (I said I was a foreigner); it cost her a little journey but she went and dug one out for me anyway and ran it under the beam.
2. **Amish Market** 240 E 45th, just blocks from the hotel, $2.49, for 'FRUIT BY EACH' which grammar hides a single punnet of blueberries—the bloom alone worth the price—my ticket into a wonderland of cheeses and meats and exotic fruit laid out with a loving haphazardness nature could only hope to match. Store clerk bored teenage black girl (do whites no longer work tills?)
3. **CVS Pharmacy** 630 Lexington Ave, $5.32, for 1 PILOT G2 PRO FINE gel pen, black, to replace the sketch pen picked up in China, brings back not one but two shopkeepers: this middle-aged black male who lent me his store knife to open a fiendishly sealed product, *and* the placid Shanghai matron who returned my bow with a beautifully calibrated one of her own.

These four souls I would have burnt in the fireplace by the compost heap. I hang my head, feckless inquisitor.

27 November
I use the gift of an iPod touch from the Volpe boys to record Dad on his Indo-China War, then when I try to install an update find myself locked out. The system takes me for a thief because Gina used her computer to show me the ropes. I can either return to factory settings (in which case Dad's memoir is wiped) or stay locked out. I stay locked out.

In New York I read the following passage, written as the pagoda rose:

Some facts about pagodas
1. they are descended from stupas, burial mounds, and like them often contain relics
2. pagodas are not in themselves sacred but may be ceremonial; they are commonly attached to temples but may have their own pundit
3. pagodas are follies of one kind or another
4. pagodas are forms that flock to Wikipedia in 1.08 seconds
5. they do not always have turned-up roofs, but frequently have an odd number of levels, as who should say three, seven, nine, etc
6. the most ancient no longer exist, a category subsumed by pagodas yet to be built, both of which hedge the category of pagodas existent
    a subset of the existent are those with cracks, which let in nonexistence
        a further subset are those not damaged by the great earthquake of 1556 in China
7. other kinds of pagoda include the open-ended (see **skywell**) and the closed;
    of pagodas closed a subset is the invisibly darned
    a further subset are those sutured with iron bands
    a further subset are those sutured with iron bands by monks in a lascivious reverie
    a further subset are closed on Mondays
    7 (a) i. closed blue pagodas
        of these a subset are white, under a blue moon
        a further subset are white under a blue moon of harvest gold
        a further subset are white under a blue moon of harvest gold with a chorus of grey cicadas; the circle of enraptured fieldmice with folded paws is not germane (really)
8. pagodas are first plosive, then palatal, then dental, lastly a fricative sussurus: thus **pa go da zuh**.
9. pagodas are either ideal or real, but seldom both simultaneously, thus the object that bulks behind my eyelid should not be confused with the object that survives when my eye is removed from the scene
    a subset of the unreal is the fruit of a mythical tree, as in the phrase 'to shake the pagoda tree'
10. real pagodas are numerous even where one excludes the many glazed white china caricatures with diminishing curly roofs whose number may

be determined in various pointless ways, for example, counting
a subset of the real is the Portuguese coin called pagoda
a further subset connotes wealth gained by dubious means
a further subset connotes uncounted wealth
a last subset is Egyptian and connotes wealth counted and yet dubious,
for example by Hosni Mubarak: as who should say 'seventy billion
and one US pagoda, seventy billion and two US pagoda, seventy
billion and three...'
11. another way of reckoning is to consider only those pagodas that appear on the base culm of a bamboo standard lamp with a conical shade of reeds resembling a Chinese hat painted in the year 1959 by my father in red, yellow, and black
this number may be taken as the sum of all pagodas that ever existed, namely one
12. the unicum among pagodas has a skywell with a glass chimney (under fabrication and therefore not strictly existent); a tin frieze around the base of the crystal tower shows in silhouette: a galloping horse, a seated dog, a cricket with feelers extended, and a small wild goose
13. when all pagodas on earth have crumbled, the one true pagoda will raise its head

MORAL: *pagodry is a form of punditry; it is inexcusable and all but extinct. It will go the way of all fevers.*

28 November
Two lost weeks. But I have stood back from the pagoda.

THREENECKS
A line of masons and labourers, rustics in flared trousers. Biharis very likely, darker than the olive-skinned Punjabi or the light half-Scythian half-Mongol gold hill folk. The older men look neither right nor left as they walk, rubbing tobacco in their palms; the young men, a step behind, gawp at the mansions of Racecourse (ours the last single storey). In summer all will switch back to cotton pyjamas, worn with the collared shirt from which no self-respecting workman will deviate. The youngest has splashed out on jeans and a pilled hoody

(that has travelled halfway round the world from a Goodwill store in Minneapolis to the parade ground Sunday market). Next Sunday he will buy his first tee shirt, scandalous undress to a mason. Habilis has never worn one yet.

29 November
Mother's death anniversary. The cemetery a tranquil retreat again ever since the boundary wall was rebuilt to keep out the gamblers and lead-pickers and defecators. The earliest tombs mock-Grecian temples from the 1820s: fallen urns like ostrich eggs secreted in thickets of lantana. Dorothy Sealy's inscription already worn. I stand there and interrogate her.

'Are you in some country of ordinary parks and gardens? No human turd underfoot, no evil eye?'

The grave a skywell you drop notes down.

Cloud Ridge Buddha

December

1 December
Dad and Ruth sit on the verandah of the house he built. They lived here once, before retiring to her England. Low winter sunlight bounces off the floor to surprise the scalloped glass lampshades of the living room, milk-white against the Bologna red wall.
    Photographer Akshay calls. In September he emailed to say he had my tombstone ready. He wanted a weathered look for it and thought two months in the ground would do it good. Now it turns out the chowkidar at the cemetery has changed his mind about allowing me in undead. His epitaph project on hold.
    Mulberry in tiny fruit out of season from severe lopping.
    Tail of black cat disappearing through the arch.

The Indo-China War
Locked out of the iPod I write down from memory Dad's now twice-frozen memoir of his '62 posting on the Tibet frontier.
    Deep snow on all sides. One morning clear across the valley, a silver fox. He takes a shot at the fox with his rifle, misses, and the fox sits and stares at him. They make friends. He spends Christmas at 15,000 feet. (The nearest settlement, the temple town of Joshimath, 3,000 feet below, shuts down in midwinter.) One night a flash lights up the northern sky from end to end. Apocalypse! His men, armed with 303s, the World War I rifle, don't know what to expect. Nothing happens: the Indo-China War is already over.
    I remember he took up with him that winter, as a sort of magazine in that wilderness, a newly arrived volume of the *Children's Encyclopaedia* bought on instalments for my sister and me (one volume delivered each month). It was a big purchase, and I recall my parents deliberating over whether to spend the money. In my tenth year, in a town without a library, it was our broadband: a window on the

world. Fifty years on I can feel the onionskin jacket that came with each burgundy-coloured tome, the crackle of it and the smoothness of the glossy pages. This too was left behind when my parents flew to Australia. When I in turn bought a set for Filo as she turned ten, it was pure nostalgia. Arthur Mee's encyclopaedia was already outdated in the '50s, and the marketing drive that persuaded my parents would have been a push to clear old stock. But the pictures in it lodged in my memory for good; dipping into Filo's edition I found I recognized thousands of lost images.

Among the encyclopaedia pictures is a dubious one. I see my father on his last day at home testing the heft of the latest volume (he packs a Bible too), its newness and its scope separate comforts among Himalayan snows he can only guess at. He has never been out of the plains. My mother looks on as he gives it a fresh jacket of newspaper, her man going to war.

It's a false image. Dad says now he left in the month of October. The fact is I would have been away at boarding school.

A pair of fantails has made its home in the cloister, visiting the birdbath morning and evening. They court in the aluminium clotheshorse, flicker in its silver circuitry, flee like lost data.

Dhani raking over the compost heap, a lad again. A crone appears to gather up the raked twigs: she spends an hour snapping and sorting, then fashions them into a vast crow's nest that she carries off on her head. She's one half of a couple that come on a bicycle, she sitting sideways on the carrier behind her white-haired beau. I save the loppings for them every winter. Where is her gallant?

3 December

'Kam-pal-ete,' Dhani says, dusting off his hands at the compost heap as he uses a word I've heard from Habilis too. Complete.

The peach shedding red spearheads, the mulberry yellow hearts. *Another* crone is carrying off the last batch of twigs!

4 December

Waited two hours for the Chief Treasury Officer to appear so Dad could present his life certificate for his pension. No luck.

What good is government? In India very little. We come out onto busy Raja Road where trade takes over right at the gate: a banana seller's cart across from a row of small tool shops (my club hammer and cold chisel wala), a scrap iron dealer loading up a tempo with sheets of iron, three cheap thali eateries, two auto accessories shops, a new hotel, a cybercafé, a tea shop, a garage, an aluminium dealer, an auto parts dealer, a paint shop, an auto electrician, several machine tool workshops, a diesel pump repairer, a travel agent, a real estate office, an ATM, a paint dealer, a sanitaryware dealer, a radiator repairman, a lightshade gallery, many iron merchants, a restaurant, a scooter showroom, a rolling shutter fabricator, on and on. Street of the useful, all at work. Chief Treasurer still out to lunch at a quarter to four.

5 *December*
No sleep. Mosquito lamp empty. Is prallethrin safe anyway?

3 AM Maeve an hour away from Bombay. Gone to meet Filo arriving from NZ.

4 AM Her train will have arrived.

5 AM Two vicious mosquitoes, or the same one twice. Ode to prallethrin.

6 AM Give up, get out of bed. Pension Day.

9 AM Ballcock stem breaks off in roof tank; now a plumber's job.

10 AM Dad dresses for his appearance before the magistrate. The annual November rite. Pensioners must appear to show they are still alive. For the past two years the Chief Treasury Officer has refused to accept the signature of an English Justice of the Peace: the attesting officer must be an officer from this state of Uttarakhand. Pension payments have dried up. Dad's go to the blind school here; I write the cheques.

10:30 We drive to the Treasury, pick up a blank form, my mouth dry from bureauphobia. Aged pensioners, nonagenarian widows converge on the treasury from every side. Dad discovers he doesn't have his Pension Payment Order number. We drive home and fill in the form at the dining table.

11 AM Drive back. The clerk who created the trouble last year is

all smiles: he remembers my connections (cornered, I got the state's chief civil servant, a friend, to vouch for Dad), staples a copy of last year's countersigned form to this year's information and ushers us in to the Chief Treasury Officer. A new man in the seat. He takes one look at last year's form, and jumps up and shakes our hands. Nothing else to do? We're flabbergasted. That's all, he repeats, consider it done. Last year I ran from pillar to post. We walk away stunned.

12 noon Cook chicken biryani.

1 PM Dad realizes he didn't *sign* the form.

2 PM We return to the Treasury. It's as I hoped: the lobby, so crowded this morning, is bare. The Chief Treasury Officer is out to lunch. Dad hesitates at the door, but I know this office well from last year so I push on into the empty room, scan the big man's desk, find the little pile of papers to which we watched our form being added earlier. I go quickly through the forms till I find Dad's familiar handwriting. Set it before him, my own hand shaking from the trespass. He understands the need for haste, but sits down to sign in two places. I replace the paperweight and we flee.

7 December

Dad hospitalized. The day spent getting a range of blood tests. A second shivering fit as we put him to bed, subsiding only when he was given an intravenous antibiotic (two nurses grappling with his wrist, Doc W standing by a little flustered, hands open, fingers apart). Ruth says she managed his first shivering fit, and realized the urgency of the situation. Blood tests narrowed the diagnosis (not malaria, not this, not that) and the high leukocyte count showed a major offensive underway. Spent the night with him at the clinic, sleeping on the window seat of Room 1. The closest I've been to him in fifty years: helping the orderly lift him, massaging the small of his back where he was in pain (kidneys? the infection urinary), rubbing his upper back while he gave the orderly a urine sample, pulling him up into a sitting position when he's tired of lying down, balancing the drip bottle, adding a little hot water to every glass of water he drinks. He has many pills to swallow and has besides to keep up his intake of fluids because of the urinary infection. The urine culture test will tell whether his antibiotics can be orally administered (at home) or whether he must remain hospitalized beyond seventy-two hours.

Today he overbalanced getting out of the high bed and did a crazy tiptoe dance that spun him around and threw him against the bathroom door where I caught him before he fell. The sequence bizarrely comic in the midst of real danger. He recovered at once, dignity unhurt.

Spend the week sleeping at the hospital. Dad recovering well: makes a fist in the air when Doc W asks how he feels. Discharge on Sunday.

GARDEN PLEASURES
House pleasure first: my own bed after a wintry week in a window seat.

Every other passerby tugs at a willow frond, idly takes a leaf. Old as the ages, the drooping habit in the plant, the thieving habit in the animal. I watch Xuan Zang—the only antique body I've truly dwelt in—pluck one in passing through Kashmir.

ROOFTOP PLEASURE
Venus burning like a diamond at six.

11 December

    —*Forest Dweller sir! Forest Dweller sir!*
    —*God in heaven, boy, settle down.*
    —*The sourdough starter is alive!*
    —*You saw it bubble?*
    —*And heard it squeak.*
    —*Good Householder! We are moments from a long slow rise.*

Gina mails instructions from Amherst: mix a half-cup each of flour and water and stir in the starter. Like any other organism it needs feeding. Within minutes, as if starved, the mixture is bubbling over. I empty out the flour bins, finding a cup in the white and two cups in the brown, add salt, and stir in the revived starter. Twelve hours later the lump has doubled, my first sourdough loaf.

The ginkgos continue leafless. Dhani does his thumbnail scratch test on a branch and pronounces it green. I want to believe him but don't dare hope. I think of myself as apprenticed to a bricklayer but this gardener has taught me just as much.

A hornbill lands in the China palm and ogles the dates. With his tin-bird movements and stiff Jurassic flight he's the ginkgo of the bird kingdom.

THREENECKS
A herd of sheep go by the gate, as if on Facebook, then a detachment of wayward goats. *Be a goat!* I want to tell Filo, and know I don't need to. Fresh from occupying New Zealand's Wall Street, she looks askance at the 433. Would I, she asks, sell this place and move to a smaller one to finance housing for the poor? She has been reading the work of a Delhi activist.

Sell up! I'm staggered. We've worked this ground over thirty years. Dhani's here for an hour or two a day. Litre for litre there's as much Sealy sweat in the sod as that of all the hired hands, her poor, put together. Sell up and both were poured out in vain.

12 December
Akhtar Abbas got me here [Dad says, of Dehradun, his last posting] *in 1971. I met him on the hockey field in 1952 when I was about to be posted to Fatehgarh. He said: Sealy, I need you to come here straight away. Can you give up your seven days' leave? So I joined early and got the Police Lines in shape, and he says: Now you can have 14 days. We hit it off. When my transfer orders came for Varanasi he didn't want to let me go. Now Varanasi was one of the five elite cities in the state, and you got a special allowance—of fifty rupees* [we all laugh, but in those days fifty rupees was a lot], *and Abbas said, stay on here in Fatehgarh, Sealy. I said all right, what's fifty rupees. But then he said, No, you'd better go, Varanasi is an important posting. At the farewell party he said in his speech: Sealy was willing to sacrifice his joining leave—even his special allowance—for the good of the district. That was a feather in my cap.*

So I got to Varanasi and there I had two bosses, Superintendent Nigam and Senior Superintendent Tripathi. Both SPs had it in for Anglo-Indians. How were you promoted directly from sergeant to inspector, Sealy? Nigam asked, though he knew the rulebook. *There was a sympathetic ASP, Bajpai, who warned me about these men, so I went to the English DIG* [mouthing the full name with a plummy voice] *Deputy Inspector General William Alan Channing Pearce, and asked to be posted somewhere else. Pearce first said, Why don't you go to England? So many Anglo-Indian officers were emigrating in those days. Eventually he sent me to Jhansi where I met the last of the English SPs,* [mouthing again] *James Mallard Douglas Pollock, who was keen on sport. Once he stripped off his shirt and played basketball bare-chested with the constables. When he heard I was interested in archery he sent me a book with a note, see page so and so. It was an article on making your own arrows. He organized a competition too. On my next posting, to Bareilly, a Muslim carpenter and ironsmith who had joined the force when the Rampur state police was disbanded, made* [he turns to me] *those arrowheads...*

They're in the tool chest, I tell him. I used the arrows as a boy, as Robin Hood. I remember, down to the billowing blue poplin curtain, our clubhouse, The Black Arrow, with its smell of sparrows fried in Vaseline, where only Little John (Owly Castellas) and I were allowed, one at a time, with Maid Marian (Jenny Dee).

Still locked out of the recorder, so I get down Dad's words right away.

13 December
The Fiat holding out, but I'm the only driver. Drive to the clinic for Dad's last injection. Tired beyond belief.

14 December
10 AM 'There's a fine large guava on the tree,' Dhani says, as he leaves, the hornbill tail of his bike-stand scraping Stoneman.

On the sunporch my father is telling Maeve: 'That was the only time I've ever had a shivering fit.'

I take the ladder and climb onto the garage roof to pick the guava. It's a monster. A dozen smaller ones shaping up. I like the way they stagger each other, ripening one by one. When I come down Dad has shut his eyes. I place the guava on the granite table before him and back away, the great yellow moon of it rising in that black mirror.

10 PM Filo rides the Trek, slow-cycling beside us with little tick-tock strokes, as we walk after dinner. Overhead the full moon is working free of a partial eclipse.

Midnight. Trying to imagine the small wild goose, the actual bird, for the glass chimney frieze. First saw a long-necked creature, sedate and elegant, a bit swannish, then something more squat, but still generic. Suddenly I see the neck stretched forward, in classic goose attack, hissing and squawking, the rigid tin goose of legend. *Draw it that way!* Traced onto tin, cut out with tin snips, and Japanned black so it appears in silhouette.

With the addition of the pavilion level the pagoda has met the odd-number requirement of three levels: the kitchen a good domestic foundation; next up the study, food for thought; lastly, under the sky, spirit food.

15 December
Ira drives us to her Katapatthar estate which we plan to rent for a week from Christmas. Our family holiday. Her bachelor great-uncle Prince Shamsher Jung Bahadur Rana of Nepal, hunter and angler, built this lodge on the banks of the Jumna just where it leaves the hills. When we arrive a dozen volunteers from the snakecharmer school, sons of snakecharmers, are waiting for their bus; they have spent the night in the lodge after helping demolish an old clinic to make way for an extension to the village school. When all traces of schoolboy have been erased Ira shows us the rooms in the 1930s house, perched high above a bend in the river. A concrete bench teeters at the edge where the kitchen went down the bank. A great dry rusk of a hill rises four thousand feet on the far bank; at its foot is a famous Asokan rock edict of the third century BCE. The river, fresh and blue and cold from the mountains, murmurs over rocks far below us, eating away at the orchard of litchi and mango and guava trees where we will be free to wander during our week of rustication. A woman will cook and wash up, and her no-good husband will be persuaded to keep his distance. The downstairs bedrooms will be cold in winter, Ira says, and leads us upstairs and down a narrow passage where a sign on the low lintel says: *Here the Vicereine Lady Linlithgow*

slightly knocked her head in the days when the house was young. We have lunch in the warmest room in the house, a dining room hung with postcards from the Great War. Next door in the drawing room framed royals from the Nepal branch of the family pose with the rapt self-absorption of hothouse flowers, ghosts who will sigh through the nights we spend in their company.

17 December
'You're not Irish by any chance?' I ask Maeve Fitzpatrick as she puts on a Celtic tape for the third time. Filo wants Björk.

'Do you know, Filo,' Ruth says, as they sit shelling peas, 'when you first came to us the very first job you did was to sit here with us and help us shell peas.'

The first thing I remember Filo doing was to tie all her belongings into a polythene bag she would not let go of. I was still smarting from being told off by the sidewalk slipper seller.

'You don't know your daughter's foot size?'

I took a stab. That night I watched her three-year-old feet under the deal table of the dining room at St Stephen's Home, Delhi. Size three fit fine. The old cook beaming as he heaped up her first china plate.

I put on *Volta* and leave the four women to it. I want Björk too.

26 December
Treacherous dhadhu, the local simoon, rattles the glass panes all night long in our Katapatthar bungalow room. Wake to the Himalayas, the blue river, and this old frangipani shaking in every digit, naked but for two flowers. Breakfast of porridge and milk from the blond buffalo tethered by the old stone storeroom, eggs from the wandering fowls.

28 December
Following in Maeve's footsteps along an aqueduct, I watch each corduroy shoe pace the narrow way. (A fish etched in the cement path.) I've never known her to stray from the simplest line put out by the Bata Shoe Company. In the gold afternoon light we pick our way down to the fallows.

29 December

Last night. Finish the bottle of Sula red over the Agra double murders of 1903. All this is Indian culture too but don't tell anyone in saffron.

31 December

Stocktaking

Home again. Sit here shut off from the rest, plotting a book called *The Small Wild Goose Pagoda*. The sand running out on the old year.
The almirah door swings open and a hooded figure steps out.
Inquisitor: The problem is you've got out of the way of writing.
Me [*startled, defensive*]: It's this pagoda. It's made a note-taker of me. Scribbling in between building a set of steps and cutting out a tin goose.
Inquisitor: But it's not been all pagoda. You've been ten years building.
Me: Don't remind me.
Inquisitor: All your fifties. In this time you have written a single book, *Red*.
Me: I've saved some trees. And built a house.
Inquisitor: Ah yes, turned master bricklayer.
Me: Habilis has taught me a thing or two.
Inquisitor: The true building was done by your father. He found an architect, locked horns with a contractor, queued for cement in an age when it was rationed, got a water line, an electrical connection, saw the doors in and the paint on.
Me: He spent nights wondering whether the contractor had skinched on cement in the roof concrete (he hadn't, but only because Dad was an ex-cop and living next door), whether the ironmonger had diddled him on the last haul when he was called away from the scales, whether the carpenter had not lagaoed green timber at the bottom end of the doors.
Inquisitor: As he looks back over his life—telling stories you should be recording, by the bye—
Me: Except I'm locked out of the iPod.
Inquisitor:—he must count this house among his small triumphs.

Me: He should. Few Anglos took the plunge in those days. Housing was tenancy with them.

Inquisitor: But, consider, once the house was done your father vowed never to have anything to do with builders again.

Me: So nerve-wracking had been the supervision.

Inquisitor: So exorbitant the demands it made on his spirit.

Me: Yes. He turned with relief to small jobs, a handyman whose box of tools I grew up with. He shook off those nine dark months.

Inquisitor: Fraught term of male gestation.

Me: As my mother paced in the waiting room next door.

Inquisitor: He'd earned a reprieve.

Me: From any job bigger than a picture frame, yes. I sometimes wonder if he looks on amused at my adventures with Habilis.

Inquisitor: Oh, he'd approve of the results. But your building has been mostly rebuilding, until the pagoda.

Me: Don't I know it. All the same, with me there was an opposite tug. After a life of mental work, I was ripe for doing.

Inquisitor: Thanks to him you could do on a small scale.

Me: And work from a secure base: from the house, on the house.

Inquisitor: And thanks to Habilis, you were working piecemeal.

Me: I could call a halt at any time.

Inquisitor: And the satisfactions in the work were palpable.

Me: I was working for myself.

Inquisitor: And they were an inducement to bigger work.

Me: When a job proved less daunting than first appeared.

Inquisitor: Some allure too of physical work in a land where labour is demeaning, no? Where the man who digs for anything but gold is a fool?

Me: Where labour is dignified with a Sanskrit name—*shram*—to ennoble the act.

Inquisitor: And a man sees work as having a separate existence from his true self.

Me: While here I was looking to find myself *in* the work.

Inquisitor: But there was a price to pay.

Me: I didn't reckon with the literary cost.

Inquisitor: You paid it. And still do. Hours you could spend working on a turn of plot, you spend imagining how the concrete hearth should wrap around the frame of that door you want to block off.

Me: The fireplace? There has to be some use for all these falling branches. But it's true, more than time what you are spending is energy.

Inquisitor: Precisely. It's a pouring of self, not concrete.

Me: It began innocently.

Inquisitor: Even worthily. Here was the praxis you dreamed of as a young man.

Me: I was learning, a little late in the day, new skills. If they didn't earn me a living, they could save me money.

Inquisitor: Rot! You were building for pleasure. It was fun.

Me: That much was plain, even to Habilis.

Inquisitor: Himself a jack of all trades.

Me: But the addiction came as a surprise all the same.

Inquisitor: You found that the thrill of a finished pagoda could match that of a finished book?

Me: More than that, at some point the figuring of form in building...

Inquisitor: Had become the stronger magnet. In fact you had already made a choice, turned architect manqué.

Me: Builder-*cum*-architect.

Inquisitor: Manqué. During those ten years you unlearned writership.

Me: Pure strategy. I retreated from books—not ideas—to come closer to things. Then, halfway through that decade I felt my strength begin to fail. I came to realize that any heavy work must be done now or never. I even supplied a cut-off date to support my programme.

Inquisitor: Age sixty. You said to yourself...

Me: 'Self, you are building these unnecessarily beautiful things now against the day when you can no longer lift a hod of mortar. Whereas mental work can stretch far beyond that limit.'

Inquisitor: Meaning, the farther boundary needn't be rigorously patrolled.

Me: Words in my mouth. But with every project stopping became harder, as I juggled books with bricks.

Inquisitor: You *thought* you were juggling.

Me: Because I was accustomed to dealing with books it was easy to assume they were there.

Inquisitor: Flitting from hand to hand even when the eye didn't track them! They were not.

Me: The *idea* of books was, but the materiality had been usurped.

Inquisitor: In the way that power frequently is. One sign of this transfer should have alerted you, the multiplicity of notes to yourself. Like IOUs from a friendly debtor about to abscond.

Me: The way an arrow leaves the bow.

Inquisitor: The way a bow leaves the hand.

Me: But I had always worked from scribblings! They were the way forward from a night's rumination, from random inspirations by day.

Inquisitor: But now they became the work itself.

Me: In juggling, the eye is always a short way beyond the balls. That's what keeps them in circulation. It's on all of them at once.

Inquisitor: In fact it's on none.

Me: All right, it's on the *intention*.

Inquisitor: With which the road to hell is paved. But there's a subtler case with this particular book. Here is, you have decided, a book *about* building. What could be safer than that?

Me: [*silent*]

Inquisitor: And here is a work that comes complete with a set of characters.

Me: I use them the way they use *me*! Because work is sporadic for them, I fall in with their schedule. I'm a casual worker too.

Inquisitor: You can say that again.

Me: Look here, Inquisitor. In the middle of *this very passage* Habilis shows up and says he has three days he can give me. I take him up, put away the book. He works one day and then disappears, taking a loan. Then he sends his sons to explain his disappearance and promises to turn up, but doesn't, of course. I've just settled back in to writing when Victor appears. But he wants an advance, not work, so he's careful to come in the middle of the day. Committed to them, I have to knuckle down.

Inquisitor: So for all the times they've waylaid you in your work here is a small return.

Me: A fitting return for their vagaries: now they *are* the work.
Inquisitor: The work is the action and they necessarily material.
Me: No bad compromise when you consider that here is a way of paying them something more than a wage.
Inquisitor: Ah, I see. A sharing of the royalties?
Me: The best you can hope for.
Inquisitor: Spread the jam.
Me: Six ways.
Inquisitor: And justice, property, natural rights: those bywords of your youth?
Me: There's just your neighbour. Aim higher, and there's blood on the sights.
Inquisitor: Quod erat demonstrandum! Very neat. Do you know, in the Cultural Revolution we hung placards around the necks of such as you, proclaiming your sins, and beat you through the night?

—Is that you in the hooded cape, Good Householder? Why, you vile prankster! Right, just for that the almirah rent goes up tomorrow.
—It's Her-in-kinky-lingerie, Rackrenter sir. Turn a blind eye this once.

[Midnight strikes on the Police Lines gong as fireworks pepper the Racecourse air.]

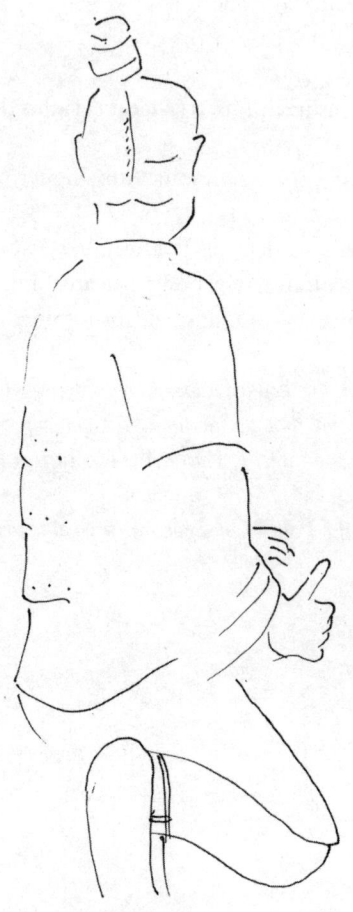

Terracotta archer

January

1 January
Victor turns up on a bicycle. It's his, not borrowed. 'The Wreck of the *Hesperus*,' Maeve, looking out of the window, says. I try out the brakes. Victor unwinds a carry bag from the handlebar. It's stuffed full of food for us from his wedding point job. A packet of deep-fried bhature that go with a packet of chhole and another packet of halwa. Lastly, a large bottle of tamarind sauce. The dog Sairu sniffing the air.

THREENECKS
Up the coral, the pruning saw squeaking in the softwood, leaves spinning into the sullage drain. Dad watching from the verandah over the high wall. Dhani at the foot of the tree, stripping each branch with his machete.
Two birds of passage come by.
'Unnn-day!'
The free-range egg man, said to colour yolks. The eggs in his basket are all brown and the yolks sunset yellow. A Muslim of the khatik caste he dyes his beard orange.
'Shaaa-aid!'
The honey woman, a martyr to purity, swears she mixes in no sugar. 'May-be,' she seems to call, 'maybe.' It is still possible to buy fresh breakfast stores at the gate.

Breakfast
Anglo-Indians invented Indian modernity. Today when every city man wears trousers it's easy to forget those early darks in funny leggings. Now that there's a dining table in every middle-class home we forget those families in Grey Town, Calcutta (or Madras, or a dozen small mofussil stations) pulling up a chair to break risen bread.

'I don't know about y'all,' my mother might say on the seventh day of Christmas, 'I'm having a plain fried egg. But there's mince cutlets and don't know whatall in the doolie.' (I would have liked for once the puri breakfast my Hindu friends claimed to have every day, with hing potatoes rendered down, though for two rashers of bacon I'd have sold them all into Egypt.) This morning everyone is going his own way on the 433, my father and Ruth stirring a vat of oats, Maeve brewing tea in her Quetta pot, slow-cooked shank-meat from the Inamullah building re-simmering for me, while a vegan Tochter soldiers on with last night's beans. The Byzantine (and largely legendary) Raj breakfast, with its fish and chicken and devilled kidneys lives on at the Old Victoria Hotel in Madras but nowhere else on earth.

GARDEN PLEASURES
Planting out late larkspur, undoing the little bundles wrapped in leaves and tied with hemp string, you glance ahead to March and the seedling in your hands glows midnight blue.

—*And this liquid crystal glow in your lap at the swing seat, Forest Dweller sir?*
—*Broadband in the garden, boy. Fringe radio, fifty newspapers, four online quacks, three mailbags, two alarm clocks.*
—*No partridge in the pear tree, sir.*
—*The boondocks redeemed all the same, Rootless Cosmopolitan! Scoff all you like. And it works in the new study too.*
—*I saw you up there last night, Forest Dweller sir, your face bathed in light.*

BROADBAND

Sealys
Epiphanic, the new speed. A metropolitan cannot *begin* to imagine the thrill of liberation on the 433. Tonight I google just for the heck of it, while the family are sitting at the dining table: *Sealy+Calcutta+image* and the machine throws up a picture, the first I've ever seen, of one

Charles Sealy, registrar of the Calcutta High Court in the 1790s. Even with his two-centuries-gone collar and coat and what could be a little pigtail, this man looks like Dad. I cast a little more and come up with an image even more astonishing, this one a full-length oil portrait by the painter Tilly Kettle (who appeared, in the first eyeglasses seen in India, in my Lucknow novel, *The Trotter-nama,* at the court of the Nawab of Oudh). The painting, which hangs in the Cortauld Gallery in London, with the title *Portrait of Charles and Captain John Sealy,* shows the same Charles Sealy as a young man posing in a red coat with his sea-captain brother John in an oriental setting. It was done in Calcutta in 1773.

—*Google* Tilly Kettle+Sealy, *boy.*
—*She-who-lives-online already has, sir. Is smitten with John.*

Dad has always maintained we're a Calcutta family even though he himself only visited there. There's a tradition in the family of the oldest brother being named Charles. Dad's oldest brother, Charles Arundel Sealy, was born there in 1913, and their father Charles Arundel Sealy was born there in 1875. That's as far back as Dad knows (his father died when he was five). Until now. Googling, we discover (through a Calcutta bankruptcy notice in the *London Gazette* of 1881), their *grand*father: Charles Arundel Sealy, insolvent, born in Calcutta in 1835. *His* father, again a Charles Arundel Sealy, born in Calcutta in 1798 to a John Sealy, bachelor, and Isabella Rebello spinster, his wife. This John was also born in Calcutta. Just when the young Charles and John Sealy are buttoning their frogs to pose for Tilly Kettle. Listen to the painting.

'I don't see why not the red,' Charles is saying to John, who feels grey or fawn are better for formal wear nowadays.

'A bit sixties, don't you think?' John thinks. 'Nabobs and that. Ah well, we'll have him throw in a palm tree. Then all is forgiven.'

A daughter, Ann, is shown as having been born to Tilly Kettle by his Indian mistress in 1773, the year of the painting; the same lady bore him another daughter, the following year. Might either of his sitters here have fathered such a child? There is a Charles from the previous year, no father given, 'son of Julia, a slave', but we're looking for a John. And there the trail goes cold.

Dad goes to bed with the expression of a man who has learnt something about himself late in life. I must have a glow on my face too. Thirty years ago I tracked the Sealy line on microfilm in London, cranking the old machine in the India Office Library, but lost my way in a forest of pencillings. Broadband does it in seconds.

It's like Dad's water mains pipe. We're close, but it'll take another dig.

I keep the Tilly Kettle painting on my hard disk. The resemblance to Dad is too strong to wipe.

Besides, it's a fine oil.

6 January

Snow on the hills, mist in the valley. The rain that's been in storage these many months fell all night, with great sheets of crackling thunder that penetrated my dreams. Woke to a garden washed clean of its ancient coat of dust.

15 January

Dad and Ruth leave; Tochter with us for another two weeks.

17 January

Habilis turns up, limping. He was riding his brother's Enfield and skidded and broke his leg, he says.

'Here, and here, and here.'

'No old women killed?' I'm thinking of his last accident. He sold off the motorcycle I gave him, Dad's old Kinetic, and said the cops took it off him when he ran down an old woman.

'This was in the fields, just outside the village. We were riding along a bund.'

I know the place, went there for his daughter's wedding. A dry crust of a hamlet with unpaved lanes and a pond where buffaloes bathe. Brick houses with baked earth courtyards and electricity for four hours in the day.

'It's healed now: I just can't climb ladders.'

'You could build me a gate,' I say. 'Like they have in China.'

19 January

White wedding
'*Cat thief!*' Maeve is babbling. '*Slinky dog!*'
Her brain wants to say 'cat burglar', like the slippery black-shorts walas who grease themselves when they come into your bedroom at night. She's upset because I slipped out of bed in the middle of the night and took the car in. And was back in bed asleep when she woke up. She can't believe she slept through it all.

Only in the middle of a winter's night do I find the courage to drive without brakes.

3 AM Hour of villainy. (When you are most likely to find a stranger by your bed in the dark.)

Snow on the hills. Silence so deep you can hear the weevils tunnel through chickpeas in a glass jar.

I dress quietly, start up the Fiat. The phlegmy adenoidal ignition, that heavenly smell of petrol and old rexine, how I'll miss them! I slip into the power train, her gearing butter-soft as ever, and inch down the empty road. Encouraged, I allow her a little speed, till I remember the crossroads. Nobody there. A cop car at the hospital corner, its red and blue lights revolving, so I slow right down. The cops take the jail road turn and when they're gone I creep along the empty Haridwar road, sipping petrol like a miser. Swing up at last onto the verge at Inam's garage. As I park a chowkidar appears. I use Inam's name. OK, he says, but the cops don't like to see a car on the side of the road. I get back in and start her up and nose slowly into to the rutted grease-black lane.

3:30 AM Walking home. Not a soul abroad. A pi-dog trots along behind a wary pig, an odd couple. The dog yawns, a squeal at the centre of his yawn: he'd like to skirmish, snap at a trotter, but his heart is not in it. The pig wouldn't mind being chased.

I walk down the very centre of Racecourse Road. Marking the hour, of course, but also a milestone. Something tells me that was my last ride with old lady. Twenty years I drove her; Dad drove her ten before me, and before that Uncle Terry for twenty from new in 1959. I'll miss the looks: hers, and those she got.

3 PM Prashant delivers the white VW Polo. One week after Dad. He would have liked to see me buy my first car. It seems a little late, a white wedding at sixty. But what a beauty! How must the old lady feel?

I want to commemorate the event with a planting, a white rose. But which rose? I'd like a climber. *Eleanor Roosevelt*? ('Hopeless in bed,' she claimed, 'but fine up against a wall.')

28 January
Habilis appears looking sallow and shotten. It's a raw morning and he's hatted and mufflered. Today he makes an inner gate to shut out the busy world.

First to Manjeet Hardware to get us a pivot (a 'peen'), then to the welder. A new quipping Mohan, spraying rapid-fire questions he answered himself with immense assurance, on his way up in the world, not the man who sat waiting for custom under his rolling shutter in an empty, poorly lit shop. New disc cutter, no more hammer and tongs, said it all.

Unwell, Habilis is laconic, withdrawn. At his coolest when he set the pivot in concrete, graciously taking on board (long slow nod) my suggestion that he add a scoop of shingle for the mortar bed. Sat himself down before the half post he'd just built, seized my 1-kilo club hammer, like a man arming himself, aimed and casually took out a couple of old bricks with the long chisel. Then tapped the space beside the hole with the tip of his trowel. Without looking up.

'Here.'

Gaffer set down the heavy pan on the spot and began a story about his son.

'Shut up,' Habilis said.

'What?' the old man said, taken aback, but shut up.

In silence Habilis whips the mortar into a flan. 'Beat it better next time.' (To the air beside his mouth.)

One scoop dropped into the bed to hold the pin steady. Three readings with the new plumb line (I bought it for myself but he commandeers it) one down each available side of the pin, delicate readings, pushing once with a little finger against a perceptible lean in it. It could be the axis mundi. Satisfied, he fills the grave. Pats the quick grey mass with the tip of the trowel so it quakes at his touch.

29 January
Wayne is dead. Maeve brought her hands to her cheeks when I broke the news. I thought at once of our ride back from the nursery with the golden bottlebrush roped to the roof of the Maruti 800. No more hill climbs hunting for Mughal forts. What will happen to the Shah Jahan chronicle? To his vast library? To his special knowledge? That Wikipaedic brain, that whole private history that began in Kentucky, stopped short. His application for Indian citizenship now come to a halt in some government file.

At the ironmonger's yesterday when buying the pin, a dilemma: a regular iron bolt or axle-grade steel at twice the price? I consider for the briefest moment and realize it's not the price that's determining the choice but my mortality: how many years do I have left? I go for the regular bolt.

30 January
To Rishikesh by the foothills road (purling canal, landslips, upland villages, the Polo handling beautifully, sucking in the miles). Lunch at the green bow in the Ganga, on the left bank. They have a no-cheese pizza for our vegan. Her last week with us. I'm getting used to a modern car, its supersensitive moods. Twenty years I clunked and wrestled, loving the cut and thrust of old-world driving. This creature has airbags, central locking, and a rear window defogger; it even has a rain sensor for the wipers. But I think only:
'THE BRAKES WORK!'
Home in time to vote at the Racecourse booth. I press the button with the elephant, symbol of the Dalits, in many villages still untouchable.

February

1 February
When the house is built, Death comes. There's a savage irony in the saying, almost too cynical for words. Has Death been watching all along? Or is folk wisdom simply merciless? So of course you don't stop building. Let him wait. Wayne built himself a modern Mughal garden here. Dhani rolls up, scoffs when he sees new work in progress. Under his shell, the old tortoise, carrying his house wherever he goes. He's always working on it, even when only walking it.

The new gate will frame the pagoda, the way the old gate, with its six seasons, prefaces the 433. Dhani should be pleased with the added security, and Maeve already likes drawing the latch at night. I like drawing it by day, though it offends the postman. (When did we last see him, since broadband?) People don't know what to make of an inner gate, but an Arab merchant in a souk would feel he'd come home. In China certain hutongs have such a passage, and some old Russian mews. Swung open, its iron door does double duty as a garage lock-up.

For the pagoda itself, I need a set of double doors, at the study: glass to let the light in, wood to keep the noise out. The Xian pagoda of the Small Wild Goose was a tranquil place. I go looking.

3 February
The old rag and bone market used to be opposite the Protestant church. I bought countless books and half our Raj furniture there. Then a lady mayor decided to shift the ragmen, squatters all, out of town. The new kabari bazaar is off the bypass road, opposite a foul stream on whose right bank perch wooden hutches full of ragged kabari children. Behind the pukka shops on a stretch of open ground are the squatter's squatters, still lower down, low caste doms in crouch huts built of wattle and plastic sheeting. A line of trespass there too.

No wooden doors, but I buy four flyblown books from the only bookseller in the row. He's happy to make a sale, I know, but how on earth did Lady Ottoline Morrell find her way here? Jonathan Raban, I can understand; travellers end up in the oddest places, but *Lady Ottoline's* memoir? Stepping around great lumps of broken concrete that obstruct the pedestrian and jut into the street, I think: God, this is why people leave.

But they overstate the hardships.

5 February

Talker
Before she leaves Tochter produces a must-see DVD, *Stalker,* a movie I'd not heard of. We watch it together in the drawing room, or Maeve and I watch it and she watches us. I think she sees me as the figure in it called simply Writer, someone who comes off poorly against the hero, Stalker. I remember an identical situation, only audio, in this room thirty years ago: a younger me looking to educate my woefully ignorant parents, listening together to some piece of classical music, except I'm too busy watching them to listen. The showing's a pain, an exquisite phantom pain. The film is ravishing, verbose, late: a sphinx that chats. It should be called *Talker.* (It can *come* late; it needn't *be* late, but late-phase culture is more concerned to consume ideas than to live by them.) It's late by the time we finish too, and she's gone the next day. I want to tell her I liked the only Tarkovsky film I ever saw, *Mirror,* (which moves by stealth, a true stalker) but it's too late for that too. I also want to tell her I love a daughter who can drop out of university ten seconds away from a degree and do what she really likes.

10 February
Power steering makes play of driving. Astonishing pick-up: now I see why those Japanese cars have been zipping around me on the road these twenty years. But *GERMANY,* says the engine, meaning: *enough said.* Italy was fine by me, land of the Ducati, but there were no parts for the old Fiat. Long hot afternoons I scoured the last repositories in the medieval lanes of Old Delhi. Today it stands under the camel-hoof,

on public ground but under a shroud, a fitted cover I'm surprised to find in place every morning, not stolen to mend a dom roof. (I check the tyres for signs of sag.) The new car is half dream, half video game. The song of a thousand bees in your blood is adrenaline, but it enters by the soles of your feet. Countless the number lured to that black rock in the middle of the highway, draped with luscious sirens.

12 February

Sunday morning bicycle ride across the Rispana Bridge (built by the New Zealand women's league) along a puddled dirt road behind the Raphael Homes I find the forest retreat of one Osman Khan, a moss-black manse behind a locked gate. I see his ghost pacing the avenue of peacock macrocarpa with an unsent letter. The Dalanwala rich: that whole generation dying off, their children all abroad. The mansions on Rajpur Road are no different, but Racecourse with its bizarre gates and tiered wedding-cakes, teems with the new rich, their sons sulking behind cash registers—but here. Ten years on they'll be inured, and breeding, and richer still. When we bought the 433, any middle-class punter could make a bid; today, the cost per square foot risen a hundredfold, only businessmen can buy here.

The Pingyao gate

The town of Pingyao in Shanxi province is an almost perfectly preserved Ming artefact. Within the city wall it is full of brick lanes and courtyards and gateways covered in brick latticework. I was drawing one of those brick lace entablatures in a back street when the four schoolgirls from Wuhan found me. It was a working sketch, each brick outlined in place, meant as a guide: I must have known I would want to replicate the lacework at home.

That time has come. At dusk I dismantle the formwork at the beam across the inner gate. The gate is in use already: it just lacks a crown. I whip up a batch of mortar, with gravel and cement at 2:1, the mix so rich it's choux pastry. Before she left Tochter helped me select clean-faced bricks for the design. This is her gate. A brick is twice as long as it is wide, the width again almost (but with us not quite) twice the depth. The proportion then is 1:2:3, stretcher, header, edger, as perfect an arrangement of things as can be hoped for in an imperfect world. I choose three bits of wood as measures so I don't have to use the tape measure at every turn: they answer to gap, margin, and overlap, so the intervals are regular and the pattern, when it emerges, in harmony.

But things go wrong in the half dark.

—*Best not start brickwork at dusk, Good Householder.*
—*And never when it is spitting rain, sir?*

I miss the chalked centre mark, which washed away when I wet down the slab, or in the rain, so the pattern starts a little further left than it should. It makes a complete bar of music all the same, one minim out of true. Four chords, alternately inverted: stretcher-under-header-under-edger; edger-under-header-under-stretcher, twice. The simplest Pingyao pattern. Darkness has fallen when I wash my hands. The Pingyao gate is in place.

14 February
Dhani brings in the Bethlehem lily from the verge where its glory was wasted on the pigs. It occurs to me as I dig up corky bits of the old bitter wild drumstick, that this axle shaft *is* the closest I'll get to that grail, the dig-down spade of the East. Under Tochter's bedroom window, this lily will spill its scent after dark. For a single night it rules the garden, by morning a dead white rat.

16 February
Reading Mrs Gaskell's *Life of Charlotte Bronte*, in battered kabari paperback. The great fascination of the *Life* is that it's of a fellow provincial; my heart goes out to Charlotte as it never could to a Londoner. When I read the account of the narrow bedroom at Cowan Bridge, I see Maeve's dormitory at Villa Maria, its canvas awning flapping in winter. I also run a grateful eye over Tochter's room, half bedroom, half bakery, where I'm parked: panning from the restored almirah to her framed black-and-white 1969 Beatles enlargement, to its little companion piece, the four Clement sisters with their pudding-bowl haircuts of 1930 (my mother would be George), to

the Shorter Oxford, to the oven.

Why did I pick up the *Life* just now?

Because a pink toothbrush lying across the paperback masked just Charlotte's eyes, making of this forthright woman a coquette.

17 February

This vignette from a teenage Charlotte at Haworth: *While I write this I am in the kitchen of the parsonage; Tabby the servant is washing up the breakfast things, and Anne, my youngest sister, is kneeling on a chair, looking at some cakes which Tabby has been baking for us. Emily is in the parlour, brushing the carpet. Papa and Branwell are gone to Keighley.*

Even the absent men brought to vivid life by the present continuous: *while I write this*. Art can't hope—not even Bronte art—to match the absolute truth of this voice. You wonder, as you read, at the legend of Bronte privation: they led far from impoverished lives. The moors, bleak but beautiful, were their capital, and the parsonage was better appointed than the average Haworth home. Blessed with imaginations far beyond the ordinary (their servants, loving and protective, were in awe of their little charges) they led inner lives of great plenty, and despite the lack of creature comforts, they were gentle folk, gentry. Books surround them. Household duties come naturally: home from a second failed attempt at boarding school Emily takes on, at ten, the family's ironing (irons would have been coal irons, heavy) and bakes their bread, her German book propped before her as she kneads the dough. Their maligned father is severe and aloof but that is par for the course, and he is neither cruel nor parsimonious, taking a measured interest in his children's education, proud of their achievements. How resolutely the sisters try and try to make a go of things! Fresh out of school themselves, they decide to run an establishment for young ladies, (as well as linen each student is expected to provide 'a Dessert and Tea-spoon') but there are no takers. They don't fret excessively; hapless they are not. Death, in the graveyard ten paces from the door, is a good tutor.

—*And for company, Good Householder, the sky:*

'more than any inanimate object on earth—more than the moors themselves.'

18 February

A single violet has got away. It flowers by itself beyond the swung wall, the violets' violet.

Xiao Yan Ta

The Xian pagoda of the Small Wild Goose got away.

The Great Wild Goose Pagoda stands clear for all to see, the pagoda of the fair, high way.

The Small Wild Goose Pagoda is the pagoda of the pinched way. You enter ours at a dogleg, where the old portico all but met the boundary wall, and climb up the iron stair to the rain room. At one time anybody could go straight through to the backyard; when we walled in the portico for the kitchen there was still this gap at its hind pillar, where the property line angles sharply in (the lion-mouth effect) creating a Venturi tunnel. You could squeeze through there, though it made more sense to go around the other way. In the beginning Dhani would sometimes forget and curse because going back out his weeding basket couldn't fit through without tipping over. Today even that option is closed: the iron stair blocks your way. Only the wind has free passage.

It must be the narrowest pagoda entrance in the world. It could be the Needle's Eye, the strait gate in Jerusalem's city wall that was every caravan's undoing. (Easier for a camel to pass through there, Jesus warned his listeners, than for a rich man to enter into heaven.) Wall-to-wall the entrance is less than two spans across: only a child could pass straight through. You can't front up full on.

Just outside the old dogleg hangs a rusted sign in heavy sheet iron. It reads:

Xiao Yan Ta. Small Wild-goose Pagoda. Its Mandarin characters were cut and shaped and welded by a bemused Mohan in half-inch rod. It used up all the leftover 3" bits from the iron pillar of '98. Six-inch pieces for the three long strokes, a brushstroke curve tapped into two of those; lots of 1" tiddlers. If you look closely, the ideogram *Ta*, pagoda, actually has a curved roof at its heart. A watching schoolboy turned to me: 'Is this some code, Uncle?' In a way it is. It says: *All Face Abandon Ye Who Enter Here*. But turn even half-civilly to face the wall and you slip through. The price of admission is that sideways turn.

20 February
Habilis turns up looking for work so I have him build a forward parapet for the little patio up on the portico. This rain room patio, shared with the giraffe-neck of the overhanging rosewood tree, will take a single armchair, so we add a bench seat to the parapet. The bottom step in the hairpin stair up to the main roof terrace will make an additional seat.

Bricks arrive by rickshaw. (No, they don't: Bhim pedals them here, stacks them, drops gravel, lugs a sack of cement.) We chain: the Afghan chucks straight up from Stoneman lawn, Habilis catches, I stack.

A brick is a tome, you think, handling it, is law. It has the solemnity, the gravity. But really, it's more like a loaf (though a loaf should not be a brick). Struck with another brick it rings like a bell. It's a note, you think, stacking mechanically, the very first note. Monad, atom, phoneme; fundamental, sufficient, something to live by. A brick is a word. Stacking, you pinch your fingertip: it's just a brick.

There's a gesture in bricklaying when the mason is filling in the gap between two bricks and needs to stop the mortar from spilling out. It's made with the back of two fingers, sometimes just one. It's a preemptive gesture, a closing off that's half philosophical (at that moment the universe is divided between that gap and everything else) half aesthetic (ballerinas use it). It's a gesture of great beauty, and I've seen Habilis make it in a reverie. You can't do it yourself; it has to be witnessed side-on. Perhaps the only time a dancer sees it is when she is beside herself.

Half a day to build, a day to plaster.
Bit by bit the pagoda rises.
Progress is not the J-curve of economists: it's the object shifted

by degrees towards its destination. Six moves bring the tall ladder around to the back, each shift incidental to the journey, made with small awareness of event, on the way to somewhere else, and some other task, so the dedicated journey becomes the exception. Or you tire. It's teamwork, except you're the whole team. The spill allowed to evaporate, the loaf baked inchmeal, not all at once—or how would the wash fare? Staging posts multiply: a little at a time is the least taxing of regimes, harsh only on haste, lost to a century of deadlines. Writing, too, you obey wayside prompts; stagger, and the shortest way turns out to be a crooked line.

The way of the small wild goose.

21 February
Watered the parapet, then stood in the pagoda as night fell. Suddenly saw the black granite piece as a desktop framed with the pale wood from our dead willow sawn up and waiting these ten years.

22 February
Dhani at the harp seat. He's tucking his broom and basket under the seat (a straightforward action for someone bent in half) when he turns and sees the peach tree in full bloom. He goes to look fully at that massed pink, can't unbend, and overbalances, a C toppling backwards into a U, so he must sit where he falls, luckily on the seat, and steady himself. As a young man he once hiked across the fields to Ram's birthplace, Ayodhya. I see him on the run that bright, vanished morning, rooting up green chickpeas with one hand and hooting at the adventure of it. Yesterday when I asked about our washerwoman's son from my mother's time, the same hand went to his neck.

'Lallan? He hanged himself!'

The little boy who one day when this house was new sprang back and shouted '*Snake!*' as black lightning streaked out under the old gate. The last marijuana thicket cut down, the watchman's dry brick hut dismantled: where could a cobra hide?

'The mother threw herself under a train,' he goes on. Sapna of the spinach vine, who pressed shirts back to factory-new.

He's seen them out, Old Dhani. His bike goes crawling off around

Sri Lanka to his other job, where DP's wife serves him lunch. Then he hirples home and his tattered shoes come off. Evenings, he turns in early, this votary of the starlit pagoda.

The Great Wild Goose Pagoda

Da Yan Ta. The Great Wild Goose Pagoda is the pagoda of the full moon.

The pagoda of high, triumphalist art, pagoda of arriving, of Xuan Zang's own arrival at the centre, home from India to the metropolis of Chang-an in 645. A hundred years later, the original rammed earth structure collapsed and a ten-storey pagoda came up. Du Fu climbed the new pagoda and wrote an anguished poem. The new pagoda lost its top three stories to the great earthquake of 1556. (The Small Wild Goose Pagoda was not touched.)

Pagoda of the panoptic, the Great Wild Goose Pagoda would strut if it could. Pagoda of the *jinshi*, the successful examinee (Du Fu had failed), it values rank above worth, speech above silence, expediency above experiment; it is the pagoda of the careerist. Colophon for grand titles, scholarly and journalistic: *Chinese Imperium, India's Century, Asia Unbound*. Cadenzas to the absolute, Nietzche warmed over. Pagoda of promises and proclamations, of the Great Leap Forward, the Five-Year-Plan. A Han pagoda, a Hindutva pagoda, pagoda of pagodas.

23 February

A package of *New Yorker*s arrives from Pauline in Massachusetts, one or two almost new. That 'almost new' recalls the pathos of the New Zealand poster I once saw for a rock band 'direct from New York!'

'I feel as if we were all buried here,' Charlotte writes to a friend, but then a bundle of French newspapers arrives and she wallows. She has Paris, *and* her moors.

Where are our moors? A single moor would do today.

On the same day, direct from Australia, grated Parmesan. From opposite hemispheres our older sisters watch over us still.

25 February
Random nature turns orderly in this nursery of caterpillars on the juvenile pear tree. Tiny glass-green hairy creatures suspended in cobweb drifts, their appearance mysteriously linked to a grid of white dots on a terminal twig. The markings on smooth pearwood as deliberate as perforations on a motherboard, here given a cellophane varnish that gloves the stippled twig with the sheen of godly engineering. Five rows of four dots each made by a robotic arm or tube, twenty floutings of the garden's rule of chaos! First inklings of a remote future when machines mount Mother Nature and from the tumid bolus of matter breed a hybrid plastic tree, with larvae so gorged on new leaves they shepherd into being crystalline pears lighter than air. So your enjoyment of each goodly thing may increase.

26 February
Coffee berries ready on the tree, holly red and sweetish, so I can imagine sucking on them in dotage, stripping them of their flesh before roasting the beans in the Beijing wok.

    Fetch out the Petersburg cups, Fair Hostess, while I get my mother's appliquéd napkins.
    Should one beware of house pride, Forest Dweller sir?
    Arabica, imported, deserves the best cup in the house, girl.

Besides, if not lace now, when? At sixty you find (what in past centuries was found at forty) yourself suddenly running out of time. You begin to use things once salted away. This napkin—she would have said *serviette*—has traces of a vanished mother who sat hours over it with her needle. I owe her this usage.

    —*The coffee already!*
    —*Tea, sir, but hot.*
    —*In a plastic bag, with a rubber band?*
    —*From Him-at-the-corner, sir.*
    —*Tea, girl, is a drink taken in leap years, in extremis, at gunpoint, in the Thar Desert, in deepest Rajasthan, and then only when the Northy chaiwali at some wild crossroads shows real confusion at the word 'coffee'.*
    —*The Almanack thinks Mr Forest Dweller is being a little choosy, sir.*

—*[pause] Fair enough, my lovely, fetch out the Japan set.*

A hundred-year-old white porcelain, so lovely I was shaking when the kabari took it off the shelf. One cup missing, so he was reasonable. Three hundred rupees! I would have given three thousand. The crudest Bengal pottery tea sets sell for a thousand.

A local dentist comes to enquire about the Fiat he sees up on bricks every time he goes to his surgery. Glances up at the pagoda over my shoulder. He knows his cars, has more than one classic, but makes a Bengal pottery offer for the Millicento.

28 February

Maeve in Delhi to get her PIO booklet. Person of Indian Origin. Which she is not, of course, but being married to one she is somehow entitled to become. It makes life easier with officialdom.

BROADBAND

Tonight on YouTube, 'Sympathy for the Devil' from a concert attended only forty years late. Light from dead stars, but it sparked something of the insane craving that kept a seventeen-year-old ear jammed up against the Murphy radio in darkest Saharanpur. So my parents could sleep through the shortwave-shredded late-night broadcast. Strangely, I never felt I missed the real thing.

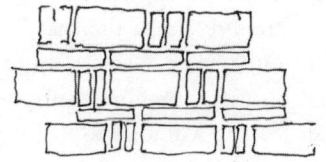

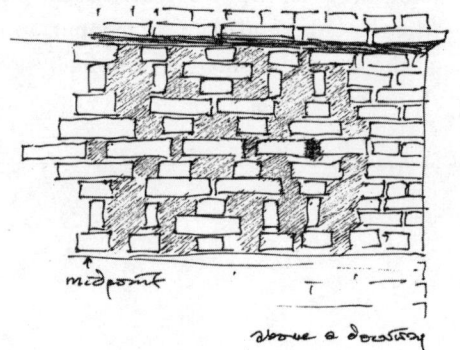

midpoint

above a doorway

Brick lace, Pingyao

March

ROOFTOP PLEASURES
Raindrops out of a clear blue sky. High wind up there.
    Creamy tinge to the hills. When the Fiat was younger we took it regularly into the forest in March. Seen from above, a sal forest in flower is a buttermilk sea. Seen from below, a society of dervishes: a topwind will set each tall sal swaying to its own individual rhythm.
    The cell phone tower now almost hidden by the avocado. Once every tree is grown there'll be only sky to see up here.
    The sunbird looks each way along the bare length of the wire from pole to pole: '*All mine!*' he shrieks like a child. His call pierces every corner of the Threenecks, good microwave.

THREENECKS
The camphor is shooting up, and the ficus has almost caught up with the Mexican silk cotton. The little forest outside, once a littered verge, is now an aviary. As a rule the visitors, hornbills, coppersmiths, drongos, parakeets, larger birds mostly, stick to the greenbelt, while the smaller residents, sunbirds, tailorbirds, bulbuls, robins (strictly the only ones that count in a history of the 433), prefer the sanctuary within. Up above, a local power line neatly divides the one zone from the other, but the wire is more meeting place than frontier.
    Two springs ago a curious thing happened. Around sunset a couple of plains mynahs, the dark brown kind, unusual in these parts, came and perched on the wire. As I watched they were joined by a pair of grey hill mynahs. This was odd; the two don't flock together. They were joined by a huddle of seven sisters, clubbers apart if ever there were. When a pair of bulbuls joined them and sat very still facing the same way, I called out to Maeve.
    A solitary drongo now appeared on the wire alongside the company, slightly apart but facing south like all the rest. Then, out

of nowhere, the sunbird. I'm always happy to see this bird, the little lord of the garden, if not the universe, but this evening I just watched. He streaked in, took possession of the Mexican silk cotton, twitching on the topmost twig in his restless way, flying straight up into the air once, looping the loop and landing back where he began, facing south. (Mostly he faces the lion-mouth, a resident.) Every bird was agitated, and they were all facing the same way, like gulls on a beach staring downwind. Their nervousness communicated itself to me.

'A storm.'

'It's always still like this before an earthquake,' Maeve said.

But it passed, the birds dispersed and darkness fell. Well, birds do gather at sunset for one last look at the day.

The next day, in the other hemisphere, was the Christchurch earthquake. The city was destroyed. It was a week before Maeve learnt her house was still standing.

A shiver in the magma, a shockwave running up the globe? A tiny wobble in the axis? A century ago the whole idea of continental drift was a madman's fancy.

In the only earthquake I've felt, I was up late at this desk around midnight when there was an uproar among the crows high up in the Police Lines eucalyptus trees. I looked out into the dark. Seconds later the tremor struck. I heard the rocks grind under my feet, this house shook like a railway platform, and there was a sound like an express train passing.

1 March

Habilis turns up with the old Afghan to make a screen. This will at long last enclose the garage, and add another Pingyao motif on the way to the pagoda. Today I broke his (and my) rule about good rubbish and chucked out two or three wire coathangers among the cans and bottles when the kabari wala came by. Sure enough when we come to lay the rod we're short of ribs for the backbone. (The Pingyao gate beam swallowed up all sorts of scrap: bent hasps, old shelf brackets, hooks, even a rusted dog's chain once used to fasten a suitcase to a bunk on an overnight train.)

I supervise the pillars, then leave him to it. The Afghan scrapes ivy root off the fibreglass sheet, I cut rod. When I return Habilis has built a level platform out of nothing. I had forgotten his talent for bricolage. His scaffolding spans an uneven floor occupied at one end by bricks and shingle, but he has found footings even on that unpromising surface. Out of sawn-off tree trunks and branches, bits of ply, and an old ironing board, he builds to a true level top. He spreads a plastic sheet, then a bed of wet sand he smoothes off with his short float. Last, he lays a row of containing bricks, endstopped. In this bed we lay the iron rod, lace the cross-stays (minus the coathangers, halfway across town on the kabari's bicycle) and pour the beam.

Now limewash the pagoda.

2 March

Shivratri, and the women of Racecourse go to the temple with their hair down. Dhani will be at his do. One of his days off.

Sun shining through the tender new rosebush stem so the young thorns are points of incandescent red. New leaves on every tree, except the ginkgos.

Looking up limewash: the walls need first to be dampened. One coat a day to allow time for carbonation. When the paint dries, says Wiki, initially it is uncured and has almost no strength. Brush against it with your shoulder and it comes off on your clothes. Whitewash cures through a reaction with carbon dioxide in the atmosphere. Bathed in sunlight millions of calcite crystals catch the falling rays and bend them slightly so the whole wall glows.

Acrylic can't do that, and gives you headaches besides. Limewash is cheap and versatile. One has every poison known to man, the other has none: take your pick. Pigs' blood was mixed in as a colourant in Europe; the delicate yellow in our bedroom is turmeric.

This time I'd like to use eggwhite, imagining a better bond and a smoother finish, but am afraid Victor would disapprove. He would rather eat the eggs. Come to think of it, so would I.

Yesterday made cape gooseberry jam, best of jams.

3 March

3 PM So quiet you can hear whole passages of magpie robin coloratura.

9 PM Block D parochial. On nights when our walk strays into Racecourse Block A I begin to feel the lack of a visa.

8 March

Old Master

Tabby cat in the kitchen just now, some door left open. The marinade lid fell off with a crash. Jumped up, chased it from room to room. Last ditch skid spun her out to skulk under the Fiat. Its classic fish-shaped indicator lamps not good enough for her. Reminded, I make a note: RESCUE OLD MASTER.

When the car was repainted a few years ago I took off the rear license plate and found a painting concealed on the reverse. I did it myself as a teenager. In the language riots of 1967 the anti-English walas were stopping every car that came their way with the Roman alphabet on its plates and smashing its windows. My urgent commission from Uncle Terry: to change the letters and numbers **USK 4104** to the Devanagari script. He would have turned the plates back to 'English' when the troubles blew over, and the work went into hiding for forty years till the car was painted.

15 March

Designing the new study window (four narrow upright casements, with a crosswise pair at the top) even as I try to frame the narrative. World has caught up with story, hinges and latches trip up months and years. The point of the book is to write out the building of the pagoda, so I should be glad, but I resent the conflict.

Hardware woes compound the problem: every part here must be fabricated and got right: with iron work once the thing is delivered you're high and dry. I lie awake groping for some way of combining knob and latch that would have been worked out a hundred years ago and patented and beautifully machined in Germany. Yesterday I returned the heavy amalgam knobs that wouldn't take a weld, but could not find a single iron replacement. (Found the season's last gooseberries though.) So went back in shamefaced today and rebought the returned knobs.

Bolt them on! Every kind of machine screw waiting these fifty years in Terry's Macropolo tobacco tins. Our welder's drill jerks like St Vitus, so I measure and cut eight iron latch strips for the machinist by the courts. Without taking his hand off the controls of a space-age drill, he calls his assistant who turns the old '60s machine on.

16 March
Bit by bit the pagoda rises. Windows delivered this morning, by rickshaw. Victor and I carried them up onto the roof. At the U-turn by the foot of the stair he jockeyed to go up first: the leader steers, the follower is the donkey. Unsteady tonight after that haul: at the top there was a moment when he let go the hundredweight to open the roof door.

Cocky young welder—no goggles—works fast and intuitively, thinking many moves ahead, sometimes just hunched over a weld, puzzling so intently you worry he'll burn out before he goes blind.

19 March
Female sunbird stealing the tiniest straws from the soft broom and streaking over the back wall to No-man's-land.

That narrow neck was created when the northwest neighbour (our Afghanistan) insisted on taking back a strip on our side of the boundary. It was his by right: the man who sold us this plot, already fenced, had simply followed an established practice and taken an extra bite. In those early days, the racecourse was wide open.

I stood and watched our back wall knocked down and rebuilt. Did we start out with 455 square feet, then? Today it's a neck the sun never reaches. I toss my apple cores over the wall there and my orange pips, without result, and sometimes place fish scrag on the coping, a walkway for the alley cat.

At the height of the Great Game, Britain created just such a neck to stop the southward drive of Tsarist Russia. But for that Afghan corridor, so piddling on the map, so terrifyingly snow-bound in the satellite photo (Xuan Zang sensibly came round through the Khyber Pass, by way of the bright new Bamiyan Buddhas), India and Old Russia would have had a common border.

Something did come out of the northwest rebuild: the projecting redstone seat where the circle of the back lawn touches the new boundary. Habilis knocked out three bricks in the wall (something he couldn't have done on the old boundary without pushing through into their garage) inserted some iron rods and built a concrete shelf we topped with Agra stone. Winters I lean back there on the warm bricks of a south-facing wall, a squadron of black dragonflies my palace guard. On this spring day the sunbirds go about their hidden business three inches away.

22 March
—*Forest Dweller sir! Forest Dweller sir!*
—*Calm down, boy. Decorum hurt nobody. Now, what is it?*
—*New leaves on the ginkgo, sir.*
—*JESUSMARYANDJOSEPH—what are you standing there for!*

24 March
Still celebrating.
A tree beloved in China, the *Ginkgo biloba*. When I lingered under a branch at our Beijing hotel a passing guest raised a finger.
'Biloba.'
'Bil-*o*-ba?' I rubbed the leaf.
'Biloba—' he nodded, tapping the cleft in it.
'Biloba-ah...' I showed appreciation.
'Biloba,' he bowed by way of leave-taking.
'Biloba,' I bowed deeper by way of thanks.
'Biloba!' we waved, in perfect agreement.
My Chinese improving daily.
Maeve reading out loud *The Brothers Karamazov* in the Constance Garnett translation. The sound of a book in the ear. Sometimes when I miss a word I hunt for it on the page and there it is like a foreign thing, in *writing*.
Twenty-five years since she read out *War and Peace* at Gore Bay, Maeve is still our TV. (One more thing Filo missed out on.) But walking on the roof this evening I tell her how I suddenly remembered, thumbing through Dickens at the Racecourse fair's

battered book tables (located between the stoles of the 'nonviolent silk' stall and the potted crotons of the brotherhood of reformed crims), that *Great Expectations,* not *War and Peace,* was her first reading out loud for us. Back in '78, so long ago we had both forgotten and now 'began' with Tolstoy.

Wemmick again, the lawyer's clerk. When he invites Pip home he shares their conversation with his stone-deaf father: *Isn't that so, Aged Parent?*—a title he shortens convivially to *Aged P*— and the old man glows. It became a refrain with us. We'd say '*Aged P*' and laugh out loud. This afternoon I spotted it on the page and it all came back.

28 March
New use for the Xian sable paintbrush: pollinating the lemon. In the old days they used a rabbit tail.

SPRING RITES
Woollies to mothball, rugs to cane. My dressing gown: every year it comes out of the trunk, every year it goes back twigged and unworn, too small, a skinny seventeen-year-old's Christmas gift from Uncle Terry. Also his trout net, and his English football scarf from 1932.

31 March

Writing
Dhani and Habilis can't write. I write for a living.

All Anglos were writers once, in the old sense of clerks, when they were not soldiers or bandsmen. And on my mother's father's side we were of a writer caste too, Kayasths who trace their ancestry to a scribe god. My mother's grandfather, Umed Rai, converted to Christianity and took the name Uriah Clement. There is a photograph of him, with a bushy white beard and speaking eyes, seated with his four spinster daughters and only son. A sermonizer, I think, flinching under that gaze, and recall coming across pious postcards to his daughters, graduates in an era when women, their own mother, for example, were scarcely able to read. I want to ask this man (oh, he would tell and tell) about his journey and I feel he would understand mine. I've gone from being a potential lawyer's clerk, a Wemmick, to roughly the rank of lawyer, stepping out of the lower into the upper middle classes. I imagine this pragmatic man lecturing his headstrong son (who has married his landlady, a widow with six children) in the vein of Crusoe's father trying to persuade Robinson of the advantages of 'the middle station', and eventually making an academic of him, the way my mother would have liked to do with me.

My own father, a thoughtful man who had not been to college, never lectured me. A sportsman with a steady eye, good with an artist's pencil, he once peered through a library window and remembers wondering what happened in there. He followed his brothers into early employment, chose the uniform—and the motorcycle, he remembers—of the police, though there was an older brother who went to university and prospered. It was my mother who went to college and got ideas, a little above her station. Writing was always a tool of social mobility (the whole class of Kayasths used it for advancement); in my case it was almost an evasion of responsibility, the pursuit of a muse. Among writers too I would find a division between the adventurers (the Sternes) and the stay-at-homes (the Dr Johnsons). I went the wayward Sterne way, though I've sometimes wished for the grounding in journalism Defoe gave himself, taking the elder Crusoe's counsel, a devotion to fact that turned him into the extraordinarily rooted writer he remained throughout his life.

Pingyao city wall

April

THREENECKS
Ice candy man rings his row of bottles, six on each side: *tring-quang-tring-quang,* half a gamelan orchestra. He shaves ice off a block with a jack-plane and packs the shavings into a cup that he douses for you lime green, madder, pineapple yellow, or gentian blue. Other colours too, darker and more virulent, in his xylophone. The most popular flavours (the lowest levels) ring the highest notes.

Our fenced off Threenecks frontage is now secure. The city has twice sent bulldozers to Racecourse to discourage such appropriations. The last time a great hulking machine turned up at dusk with its floodlight blazing we meekly dismantled our fence. (Only the sessions judge kept hers, and who would tangle with her? The rest of us at Threenecks waited a few months, then replaced ours.) If the fence were torn down now the tree trunks of the greenbelt could hold their own against pigs and buffaloes. Protected by state law besides. You may not cut down *any* tree, not even on your own land.

1 April
Weighed down to the ground with fruit, the mulberry is full of birds, the crested bulbul singing rare raiding songs, as if delight did matter in birdcalls.

The sunbird tries to force entry into a yellow hibiscus bud, gives up after the second try. When he's gone, the bud opens wide, for the sun.

7 April
In Delhi for a week for the Padma award. As we sit in the Durbar Hall of the President's palace on Raisina Hill awaiting the little lady, my eyes wander across the Persian ceiling. Scenes from a nama: lovers disport in a pavilion, a bent old woman clutches the robe of a mounted

knight. I see the carpet of mulberries under the tree in the cloister, the bowl of curds forming in the fridge at home, when a fanfare breaks in. All rise. The President's bodyguard escorts her to the chief seat; the Home Secretary begs her permission to let the ceremony begin. She bows. Sixty medals, less than a minute for each one! What vanity makes you nervous for so short a space?

We return to jungle.

The curds in the bowl have not set—how could they in a fridge? Maeve finds some mulberries the birds spared, makes jam. Dhani has his own ideas.

'A pinch of salt, a pinch of chilli, *then* they're worth the trouble!'

ROOF TOP PLEASURES
Back from the big city we stand on the roof staring at Tibet, the empty house behind us.

'Buy it, knock it down,' I say to Maeve. 'And turn our back on the traffic.'

She looks drily at me.

In no time at all I've bought and knocked down Afghanistan as well.

24 April
Peach days.

I find a set of glass-paned deodar doors at the Limekiln salvage market. Habilis, who lives next door, his ear to the ground, chances by. Gets three days' paint stripping.

'Ever since kerosene vanished from ration shops,' he says, brushing on the chemical that turns the paint all bubbly in a minute, 'turps have disappeared from hardware stores. People have to cook on something.'

He works in the shade of the peach tree.

'Government shops are finished. Good for nothing, their rice not fit for pigeons.'

He spurns the bucket of soapy water I set down beside him for dipping his hands in: the burn tells you when to dip. I make three trips to the hardware store for stripper as the grey topcoat yields to green. Green yields to pink Himalayan cedar heartwood. These doors are a hundred years old. Habilis's fingertips stripped too, to peach flesh.

Maeve sees what happened.

'His fingers are so calloused he wouldn't have felt the sting until it was too late.'

The doors lie face down on the lawn. Peaches rain on them, splat and shrivel to brass bosses.

In the last flowerbed the petunias just keep flowering and getting stalkier. Long after the cornflowers have gone to hell and even the nasturtiums are looky ratty, the petunias are putting out new white flags.

'If I could press a button and be in Delhi,' Maeve says.

I marvel at the patience that makes her unlike the women of the Raj: 'All right power, you can come on now,' she'll say. (Meanwhile I've strung up the lineman and lit a small fire under his feet.) And she's frugal, to a degree I think pathological: a half teaspoon of sugar at the bottom of the bin, just in case.

One corner of this foreign field she's colonized: that square foot of the 433 where the compost bin stands in the kitchen. Or why would we all call it the *chooks' bucket*?

27 April

Hungering for slowness, some return to the pace of the past; visitors just sitting quietly between remarks, speaking only when moved to. I long to read an ancient diary. A hundred Indic calendars, and we have to depend on a foreigner, Xuan Zang, for our knowledge of the seventh century.

Out of the blue I find we had a modern Xuan Zang. Rahul Sankrityayan, a self-taught scholar and polyglot of my grandparents' generation, travelled widely through Europe and Asia (including China) in the '20s and '30s. Brought back from Tibet twenty muleloads of sacred manuscripts sent there in an age of zealous sultans for safekeeping in monasteries. Taught at Moscow University, married a Russian woman and got him a son, but neither was allowed to travel abroad. Back home, he married again and wrote up his journeys in a brisk unvarnished Hindi. His daughter still alive in our town.

Along with the deodar doors a freak find at the Limekilns:

another mapmaker's desk! Exact duplicate of the one I found years ago straddling the municipal drain in the old kabari bazaar. Both from the Survey of India, Raj office furniture, identical slat-work understorey for housing rolled-up maps, the teak worn but sound. Countless Anglo surveyors tramped the length and breadth of the country with their chain links, making those maps. The first desk cost 1,800 rupees; ten years on I pay a thousand: bizarre luck, not deflation. Awaiting the axe beside a pile of firewood.

28 April
Surprise guest at the peach-tree banquet.

All the usual birds: a lone parrot (where's the flock?), a solitary squirrel (who prefers the rindy scavenged bits), a butterfly (malingering in a yellow gully), sundry worms.

And then at dusk this flibbertigibbet bat. Not the great fruit bat we see ploughing his lonely furrow in the evening sky, but the little flickering pipistrelle.

He flips low over the roof and Maeve ducks and claps her hands to her ears. In India every child knows bats latch onto your earlobes, but where on earth did Maeve learn that?

—*Monkeys sniff out a menstruating woman, Sir,* Her-in-the-housecoat says.

—*And you too no doubt, poor simian.*

29 April
Big bang from the Threenecks transformer plunges us in darkness. After dinner Maeve reads by candlelight on the front verandah (one candle on the windowsill, one on her armrest) the astounding scene that ends with Father Zossima falling at Dmitry's feet. At the end of the chapter we're left staring into the darkness. When the power doesn't come back on at midnight I trim the wicks. It stays off all night so the fridge defrosts.

Wake in the dark to the magpie robin. The only bird I know that sings in the middle of a rainstorm, but this is still black night. I know he's our first bird up, but I'm curious to see *how* early. Go out onto the lawn and strain to see my watch face but can't. Strike a match. 3:30 AM!

Does he sleep at all, our nightingale?

Housing (3)

Reading Dostoyevsky you think: do we have *any* novels in English? A surprise contender steps up: *Robinson Crusoe*. Defoe addresses a hard question *The Brothers Karamazov* considers (and *War and Peace* ducks), the question of shelter. Housing as a cloak for a naked thing or man, the hide (not the skin, though that fits too) of barefoot man. Not the big question of God, the small question of solitude: nakedness as bound up with aloneness, the question the Forest Dweller begins hesitantly to ask, and the Ascetic confronts directly. What do you do with your singularity, that unique shelter, in a world you will shortly vacate? The answer is almost mathematically precise: self and shelter are inversely related. The more you put on, the more naked you're left. At issue is not the nature of the beyond (dubious metaphysics) but how you face it in the world. It's like the impress a dentist takes before making a plate. The point being not the vanished tooth, marker of all that is daily disappearing in you, but the bridge that will see you through. Not soul but soul-making.

The brass tacks of Crusoe's existence on the island can all too easily shift the novel's focus to economics ('Defoe and the rise of Capitalism', etc.) but the paraphernalia of his camp are minutely rendered so as to make his predicament the more piquant, so that when at the end of that material innings he goes for a walk along the beach, complacently, in full tat, almost a gentleman, he gets the shock of his life.

A footprint in the sand!

For sheer drama it's a moment without equal in English novelling, but the fright of it is complex and must include the danger not just to himself but to *his* self, to that accursed aloneness (in the middle of painfully secured comforts) that he is suddenly called upon to surrender. The Farther Adventures actually begin right there, and the whole train of events that drag him back to society and the world and eventually his own country. It's as if Defoe backs off from a more enthralling but less viable engagement, because he senses that the novel form he is busy inventing has a default social setting (the Russians simply use that setting, like no one else) but also because he has reached a logical impasse, where you can have your delicious solitude and rue it too. It's the zero point of the novel (in building terms, its angle of repose) but for that reason the point of maximum potential, the point at which the novel ceases to be Crusoe's and in fact becomes Friday's (the French novelist Michel Tournier realized this and made a fresh bid with his spirited *Friday, or the Other Island*), the point of defeat in victory which every novelist dreads and yet lives for, the downhill moment, the way a lover secretly dreads achieving what he looked for when he began to woo.

You neither write to live nor live to write: you write as you live; two illiterate men have taught me this. Crusoe's engines and devices are not diminished by their ultimate pointlessness. This garden and pagoda are a kind of island, a hide. Quit this place, gift it to the poor? My self is being asked to throw away its docket (what I've done with my time), to surrender its preliminary reading of unbeing taken in the workplace that is only the (if not the only) visible cage of the 'real' me. It can't be done.

30 April

The cell phone tower's signals may penetrate the cloister, but the cloister's field extends some way beyond. The nothing at its heart was always a powerful idea, enabler of everything. Or why do you cherish the smile that comes up from the dark after hours of dredging? *Laugh you, laugh you.* And then you make a note to patch the roof. Trust in God, the Tuareg say, but don't forget to tie up your camel. Du Shun, philosopher of the small wild goose, spoke of a return to the phenomenal after the negations he found at the heart of the great tradition. The affirmations of nature in Chinese landscape painting are part of this return. The painter dips his brush in the lake.

Walling in is an indulgence, if a strategic one. Breaking out has its own allure. The sheer intoxication of a way knocked through: bright light pouring in through a gap where blank wall stood just now! No sound like the first blow of the big hammer so the whole house trembles and something inside you sits up. Maeve, who comes from a land of wooden houses (and no car horns, and no fireworks), rolls her eyes when Habilis and Victor appear, and takes to the hills, away from the dust and the shrieking cutter.

Send peace in our time, O Lord. The prayer rises unbidden every time you read of war. The cloister is a place of quietude, not isolation. Bound up with that strife beyond the gate, the war of the classes, the war of the worlds, the war on nature. Victor's eyes soften at its gate, Dhani goes *erhu, erhu,* Habilis has a half-throttled refrain from some old song that sneaks out: 'Look-ee here!'

'What's happening with the widow, Dhani?' I ask as he leaves.

'Plants-wants I still water. Dog-wog's gone, but I still do for her now and then. She said the other day: "you do me odd job and you can stay on."'

'Dhani!'

He allows himself a tentative weary trusting skeptical smile.

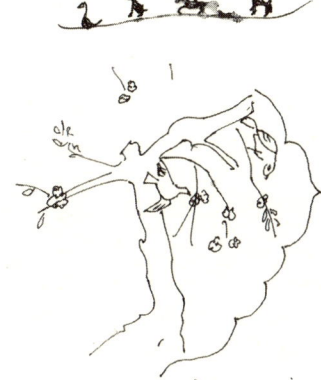

damaged bas relief on mosque
outer wall

Chance on the mosque while looking for an internet cafe.

Afterwards find it's on my street! Youyi Hotel stone end of a sand road with old doorways of it opposite the mosque well. Behind the mosque a bakery selling yesterday's discus too hot to handle (straight off the stainless tabletop sized griddle) Smiling concierge gives me a fresh flask of hot water for Nescafe sachet

Munir the benefactor must be home by now: set out on his Silk route the day we left for Shanghai

Ancient stone block on the paved approach to the Small Wild Goose Pagoda (Monk Du Shun's) in Sifu Village Changan Dist. Dharma Master Du Shun 557-640 AD

Du Shun on a mule

May

How would I describe this book to Dhani? If I called it a **Shastra** he might begin to understand me. For the Chinese poets I'd have to call it an **Analects**, although if I said a **Farmers' almanack** they'd nod: their whole tradition of propitious days and hours, good and bad places in the house and on the land, consorts well with ours, though individually we favour palmistry over face-mole reading. Habilis? 'It's a **Workbook**, a **Handbook** of the left hand' (he bridles at that: the unclean hand); 'a **Chapbook**, in the old sense of cheap and colourful' (Victor's happy there). Tochter would twig right off when I said: the **Anatomy** of the 433 square yards; and Maeve would understand if I said it was a **Meditation**, on housing, the sort of book where you could include both a recipe and reflections on a septic tank.

I learnt the word *long drop* from Maeve. (Also *malingering* and *umbrage*.) In the early fifties she grew up with an outdoor toilet on the farm, a place where stoats and cobwebs could terrify a four-year-old on a moonless night. Our toilets on the 433 are indoors, but they're on the Bengal side—no good to me in a study on the portico, Pak side—so I have lately begun to look down prospectively on Away. Pretty much where the phantom pisser struck. I google **New Zealand+long drop+septic tank** and the first sentence my eye lights on reads: *A simple 'long drop' (pit latrine) may be all that is required for a church hall.* Used occasionally, that is, in emergencies, and one Dhani would be comfortable with. Something one foot square, where you simply send the water Away, and 432 square feet remain.

But first the pagoda.

1 May
At lunch today Victor comes by looking sick as a dog. (Sairu, at his heels, the picture of health.) Habilis has sent him to say he'll come Monday (and loves peaches). He fills a bag—at the end of a good harvest I still think, *God, he got the best ones!*—and takes a leak in the

stormwater drain outside as I dream of the toilet he'll help me build.

—*The* pagoda, *Forest Dweller sir.*
—*Yes, keep reminding me, Good Householder.*

Outside toilet

The one thing that holds me back is making the join with the old sewage pipes: just that. I don't want to disturb a system functioning perfectly well. The tricky bit would be introducing the new pipe to the inspection pit, a shallow covered cesspool to which all gross solids are conducted before travelling down the ceramic sewage pipes. A join would require the breaking of the brick surround and certainly the pit wall and possibly the pit roof—which would mean a complete rebuild.

Habilis put in the present roof. The day, a sheet anchor for the chronology of the 433, is set in stone. Clara and Riccardo, fresh from Ravenna and translating the compost novel, scratched their names and the date while the cement was fresh: *20/11/2001*. On this day Habilis and I were squatting amiably on either side of the pit.

The inspection pit always has an inch of water, clean flushed water, at the bottom, but because it links directly with the two toilets, by two primary pipes entering it at their peculiar angles from the two bathrooms, it can have a turd floating in it. Today there's just a tiny fragment drifting idly. Both of us are aware of it, and look everywhere but there. As Habilis works, a morsel falls from his trowel and lands in the clear, but compromised, water. Obedient to some law of physics a droplet splashes up from the pool.

It settles on Habilis's chin.

Here is a terrible moment, an *egregious* moment. It is also a comic book moment, and a historic moment, the closing of a paradigm. Heisenberg should be there.

'But I am,' says a voice.

I see the droplet land, Habilis feels it and knows I've seen. I want to say something but there's nothing to say. The situation is too complex for words. All the social distance between us, which I have tried to ignore by squatting down companionably beside him to watch him roofing over my shit, is reduced to that void between the surface of the water and his chin. Eternity is in that clear but tainted droplet.

Habilis doesn't blink. Lightly, and with great delicacy, he brings his shirt cuff to the offending drop, and dabs it dry, accurate as ever, giving it the precise measure of attention it deserves, not too much because that would demean him, but not too little because that would exonerate me. He goes on working unruffled, as if to say: *these things happen,* and *all in a day's work,* but also *such is life,* and *such is the world.*

2 May
Tailorbird, sunbird, bulbul and robin, small birds all, have built their nests for the year on this plot. The doves at the birdbath dither; middling birds, they build sometimes on the 433, sometimes in the green belt outside.

One bird won't demean himself with any kind of building.

Koel (*Eudynamys scolopaceus*) *2: summer*
He's Jack Nicholson; no, he's the Joker.

No, he's his own bird. And nobody else comes close. Because *he* knows he's nothing, nobody. Which nobody else—somebodies, Jokers, Jacks—seems to realize.

He's the cuckoo. No. He's The Cuckoo. Koel.

Koel is the first bird you know, anybody knows. There when you first go to bed alone, there when you first wake up at dawn. And in between, when you learn sleeplessness, all night long. All night long his iamb:

I am, I am alone aware
I am, I am, don't sleep, don't care.

Compare the bulbul, going *whack your beetroot, whack your beetroot.* Nesting, bless his fuddy-duddy heart.

Koel sleeps by day, while you wear yourself out with your hundred games. Then when you've had your glass of warm milk and can't keep your eyes open any longer, he laughs. And how he laughs. *Ke ke ke ke ke ke ke!* Just as you're dropping off.

Keh keh keh kekeh! Last thing you hear.

Reaching upwards in the middle of the night, his sublime negations: *No, no, no.* All the summer night. Lhude sing cuckoo, respect no damn curfew. King Cuckoldry, would cuckold himself if he could. Knows his own, daysleepers, odd men out. Ragpickers, thieves, vagabonds, beggars, bogeymen. *Some in rags and some in robes and some in velvet gowns.*

His is black, with green and blue lights, and his eye is red.

He knows he's in your head, knows he what he means to you: Bird. And what do you mean to him? *Nothing*—but with a small n—*n*othing. So listen well in your cot, son. He was Nothing—that terrifying thing—before you were born. And he's the reason you'll never leave this land. Who can live without Bird? Go away and you come to the land of merebird, of nightingale and whippoorwill and kookaburra, and whatsisface. Tomtits, nothings.

Koel's the first bird up, not the magpie robin. The magpie robin is just the early bird. Koel hates early birds, stays up, last up, first up. Hates thrift, industry. Hides his face like God. Sulker, skulker, glimpsed, not seen, heard but hid, so you see the tree he's in, the burning bush, but never Him. If you do, you take him for a crow. Crows think they're smart. Leave your eggs in a crow's nest and the crows—they're smart, right?—crows hatch them for you. And feed the young for free!

I fly at rooftop level, Nothing Bird. Skim trees, parapets, roofs (watch your head), never seen against the sky. Sky I hate. Sky's for merebirds. Stuck to duty, nest eggs, desk jobs, keeping their butts warm, coddling the kiddies. Housing? Wipe my ass. Love? Cuddly henshit, stuff you wake from with your pocket picked, ass bare. Look who warned you: Nobird.

Swift chitter way up there. Swifts! The one bird—well, never mind. Chitter birds. *I don't chitter, don't chuck, don't snigger, won't suck. Jeer? Don't care enough to. Congeners? Would keep a cat for a pet, nice puss, for my old age, for when I'm done with other men's wives. A fat cat sat—but where's the mat? No mat, no door. No lap either, so I won't do that dream, goodbye cat, goodbye boy, goodbye little cuckoos, may the crows keep you well, hello night, hello no pillow, no roof, no sky, hello Nothing, it's me.*

Nobody.

3 May

Pay water bill for trickle from the mains. Thrilling head massage with haircut at A.N. John, cappuccino at Barista, where *Red* opens. Skim their *Economic Times*.

Going home, my sandal split and I spoilt the rate for every bourgeois in town. Paid 170/- for a half-sole job at the Clock Tower, three times the actual rate. Forever forgetting to fix a price in advance. My mother had a strict code about spoiling the rate. That was what you did when you paid a rickshaw man too much. But what's the true service rate? A family will eat well tonight. It just hurts because the bastard saw me coming. Dignity the only way out. I handed over a big note without a word and the man went looking for change as the whole shoeshine row waited, sternly suppressing their smiles.

Victor owes me two thousand, Habilis sixteen hundred. (Current account, earlier debts written off.) I don't want this money back, I want their labour. And debt is my leverage to get them here. Unless there's work in progress they come at their convenience, not when I need them. My fault: their standing instructions are to come when they can't find other work. Mostly when it's gone nine I think: 'Good, that job can wait.' A wild sense of relief as I sit down at this desk. Then they'll turn up, late, in the middle of a page and wipe out a day. As far as they can see, with writing there's no urgency, whereas they have immediate needs.

They live close to the edge, but money sets each of them apart. Each has his own way of receiving it: Victor will fold it into his fist to hide the embarrassment of it, Habilis will tuck it casually into his shirt pocket, Dhani takes the notes in one seamless action like the flick of a lizard's tongue, and always—a refinement in him—has a sentence ready to deflect attention from the transfer. Habilis keeps close track, always comes out ahead; he has a family to support. He spends as much as he can of other people's money. With Dhani I'm never quite sure: his needs have dwindled, but money has for him a dharmic valence; he uses it prudently, for rituals or relatives, and possibly hoards it. Victor likes what money buys, turns it loose on food and clothes and drink. Dhani no longer borrows; Habilis's loans I forgive, Victor's I forget.

4 May
The rights to my two best-known novels, my bread and butter, have passed out of my control. The publisher has gone very quiet. My emails vanish into a black hole. And the galling part is I didn't sell him the books in the first place. I signed them to two friends who turned around and sold their young company to the present guy.

Sold down the line, I begin to doubt the whole tribe. *Trust?* Suddenly I'm on the side of the shoeshine men.

Well, the cheques were pathetic anyway. More material is a supply-side drought, the simple lack of books in this town. Something tells me I'm worse off for reading (if not reference) than when the whole digital revolution began. I expected by now to have access to any book in the world.

Still, Forest Dwellers *re*read.

'You OK?'

Maeve looks in the door, sees tears running down my cheeks. I'm laughing helplessly as George Borrow, scholar gypsy, fights the Flaming Tinman for Belle. One by one the bumpkin magi file up my iron stair: Narayan, Brautigan, Giono, Han Xiaogong.

The door in the lawn
These double doors, in their hardwood frame, lying face-down on the lawn. Opening into grass and stones and earth, doorway into land. The old iron latch is drawn, barring yet inviting entry. Stripped of a hundred years' paint in a few seconds under the high speed wirebrush, it shines like it didn't when it was new, the studs black diamonds. You bend over the knocker next, riding the whiplash of the power tool, peering through the fogged panes, forehead dripping sweat onto clouded glass. Bolt after bolt comes up shining: every hasp and boss and rivet called out, rubbed to a depth beyond time. Suppose the door opened to let you in? You braille your way down into black earth. Antique warehouse whose ancient keeper winks from his rocking chair set in the ceiling. The bat boomerangs in there, a barn owl stares, salvage shop mascot; your way blocked at every turn by tectonic bric-a-brac till you step through the last pier glass into another world, remade, gyroscope and pipistrelle and man.

When we lift the doors after two weeks, their imprint stays on the bleached grass like a reminder of this afternoon's vistas. It says: *all that is still here,* buried in the 433.

6 May
A little small for tennis, the roof is just right for badminton. The net would be strung between the iron doorway and my projecting steps up to the pagoda terrace; spectators up there, just this side of the old opera box.

Or the pagoda terrace could be a stage, complete with skywell-trapdoor (the hell-jaws in a miracle play), the audience on the main roof. (Do *The Cherry Orchard* or *The Good Woman of Szechuan.* Provincials, watching a bunch of provincials.) Lately I've been thinking of painting the willow pattern on the stage apron, that chest-high parapet that challenged Old Gaffer.

I come up after a day at the desk, cloud mapmaker, walk twenty brisk times up and down the roof before slowing. This sacrosanct terrace, never to be built over. Look down the rosewood terrace steps one last time at the naked room on the portico before the wooden doors go in. (If Habilis and Victor show up.)

7 May
A peach first thing in the morning.

Eating in the dark a taboo as old as man, like daylight lovemaking.

8 May
The doors up. Hoisted in their heavy sal frame up a ladder off Stoneman lawn, rung by rung to the fourth rung: then the whole ladder simply tilted up. Next lifted over the new parapet. Lastly manoeuvred under the giraffe trunk of the leaning rosewood and stood under the jut of the roof slab. Habilis's plumbline a pendulum, pushing time back; I have my hundred-year-old doors.

9 May
I dip bricks in the bucket and hand them one by one to Habilis building a lattice beside the double door.

Victor asleep on his feet this afternoon. Actually nods off once, right where he stands, while passing down to me, two by two, bricks he's carried up the Bangla staircase. He drinks all night, Habilis tells me, and sleeps any old where. Eats with whoever'll feed him, doesn't bother cooking. I don't know how much of this is true and how much stock 'Christian' behaviour. Bollywood Victors always have a bottle in their hands; Hindus are upright, chaste, and steady.

We stop the lattice halfway up: it's our only entry into the new room now the double doors are boarded and bolted from the inside while the brickwork cures. The new wall not quite firm, so we quit work on that face and dress the parapet bench with grey stone. There's now a bench seat facing the study door. We top the six steps up to the roof too with grey stone. The heat torches, rains dry malice. Habilis tired and irritable. He needed four more bricks for the bench but sent for eight. Rather than make two trips Victor put them in a sack and fetched them in one go. (Five at a time is usual, though yesterday I watched a boy do nine.)

All find a second wind in the day's last job: water. Flushing the sluice drain before we top it with slabs of stone, we all get wet. Habilis sending a jet from the hose all the way down to the boundary.

'Long strokes, *long* strokes!' he cajoles Victor, his impatience forgotten. Going, he surprises me: takes just a hundred and wipes three off his debt.

They head off, yelling out to Sairu, who pretends he'd rather stay in the greenbelt; when they're out of sight he jumps up. It's a forty-minute walk and both have lost their wheels, Victor his bicycle, and Habilis his motorcycle. My third shower of the day spoilt (just a little) by the thought that they're still on the road. Victor shares a tap, Habilis and family will have their own above the fish shop; the smell of that fish in summer must cling to their ablutions.

11 May

Quack: *If I didn't know your angiogram I'd say this wasn't your ECG. You've had a natural bypass. The collaterals simply took over.* He doesn't say: *By rights you should be dead.* I tell Maeve, waiting in the car. She unfolds the ECG accordion, the crests in it leap like Hokusai waves.

We go looking for rose-coloured floor tiles.

SUMMER RITES
Changing the desert cooler bats. Filling the birdbath—for the squirrel, dainty drinker, for the seven sisters, slobs. Pickling mangoes, so many fallen green this year. Lopping the peach for mosquito-net poles. Setting up a folding bed on the lawn after dark: wake to green leaves on the poles.

13 May
Sting of paint stripper where the glove got wet.
   One door ready for sanding. Inching closer. Rescue a tiny red spider, twice, from a blue paint pot. Climb in over the unfinished lattice, prise off the crossplank with the axle shaft, and unbolt the doors. Sit in the rain room imagining it tiled, the rescued mapmaker's desk brought up and installed, cooler blowing.

15 May
Dhani in his red headscarf, bent right over sweeping leaf by leaf. Yesterday on the Stoneman lawn I was impatient of his every-last-twig approach.
   'It *looks* poor,' he said gently.
   Victor comes and spends a day burning off old loppings, stripping paint. Less secure than Dhani, freer than Habilis, he's more refined—not just citified—than either, though all three started out in villages. He doesn't see himself as poor, just unlucky. At teatime when I take him a fruit bun with his tea I find he is still bashful about being served, this occasional waiter. When he's alone I sometimes widen the menu, knowing how he likes his small pleasures. He once asked about a series of empty mackerel cans in the workshop. 'Not for your sort,' Habilis scoffed, and it's true neither would have ever used a can-opener. Habilis would dismiss such things as beyond him. Not because he doesn't care what he eats, though he doesn't especially, but because he's the more pragmatic. Victor does care; he would never scorn dainties. If wishes were horses Victor would ride, in silks, with a mandolin, sucking sugared almonds.

Last tea-break Habilis ribbed him for lushing his tea and Victor turned his head round a long way to hide a sheepish smile. What would he do if Habilis were to mention the older woman he frequents? His head would twist right off. (Not that Habilis would; he has his own sins to guard. But I suspect Victor's the more sensual. Habilis takes his pleasures; Victor gives in to his.) He would eat with gusto at the weddings he jobs—he brings me the choicest dishes—one of the perks of waitering. His nattiness, his very choice of waitering (if Habilis had another chance he'd be a machinist, never a waiter) his gifts of food, suggest indulgence. Knocking off, Habilis simply tucks his work clothes under the workshop bench; Victor folds his and slips them in a plastic bag. Habilis is fussy about work, Victor would fuss with play. I see him resisting the next drink, and the next, with a wry little smile, until all his money's gone.

16 May
Victor respects the order he finds here, unlike the chaos he returns to. How to tell him the master plan intends a letting go? Order, before you step aside. *Do* things simplify into concord? It's an old dream, the withering away of control, going from holder to lightly held. Maeve, getting ready to go home after two years, says she would not give up the 433 if I disappeared, that it has become a way of being. I think: *The chaos outside too?* And I think the answer is: Yes, that too. She's at home in that now.

19 May
Forest Dwelling, a time of small doing, when little is expected of one.
　　The Ascetic, of whom nothing is expected, sits at the brink, clapping with one hand.

22 May
Back to the lime-kilns this white-hot afternoon: the doors lack a threshold! Find a heavy five-foot sal beam among the salvage timbers, weathered, grimed over; it shouts *threshold* to anyone who grew up in an old bungalow. Sal wood lasts centuries.
　　Strip it, dovetail the ends to tuck into the door frame. Chisel,

saw, plane away stock, till the doors fit snug. A piece of my childhood to step over.

One in every old Chinese temple, a caesura, at the chief door.

26 May
Victor comes to borrow money. He's been sick, vomiting. He's moved house, now lives in an upstairs room for which he pays a thousand, the going rate. His job with Habilis is on hold for want of a plumber. Habilis has trouble keeping labourers because he has a way of forgetting to pay them. I ask Victor if his brother knows he's sick.

'He cycles down on Sundays, sometimes.'

This brother, who he says must be sixty, has done well. He has a tea shop, which also serves chowmein and snacks; his son has just passed his BA. Their father Yesu Prem had land—the grandfather was a formidable farmer in his day—but got swindled by a relative.

'The case went as far as the Meerut high court,' Victor says.

The oldest brother was swept away in a flash flood when crossing the Jumna with a friend; another brother, last in the line of four men who formed a chain to cross that night, was saved. But a year after that he too died.

'He had drunk too much one Holi and lay in bed sick. I had to go to Simla on work. I had hardly reached there when I fell strangely ill myself and wondered what it was. Then I knew. I asked God for forgiveness for leaving my little brother alone and turned back at once, but on the road I met a neighbour who told me he was dead.'

He tells me this in the lowered voice of a man sharing a secret. The boy is buried in the Christian cemetery here, where his mother also lies. Now there are just two brothers left. The wedding season begins on the fourteenth, when the moon is right; then there'll be waitering work. For now he needs money.

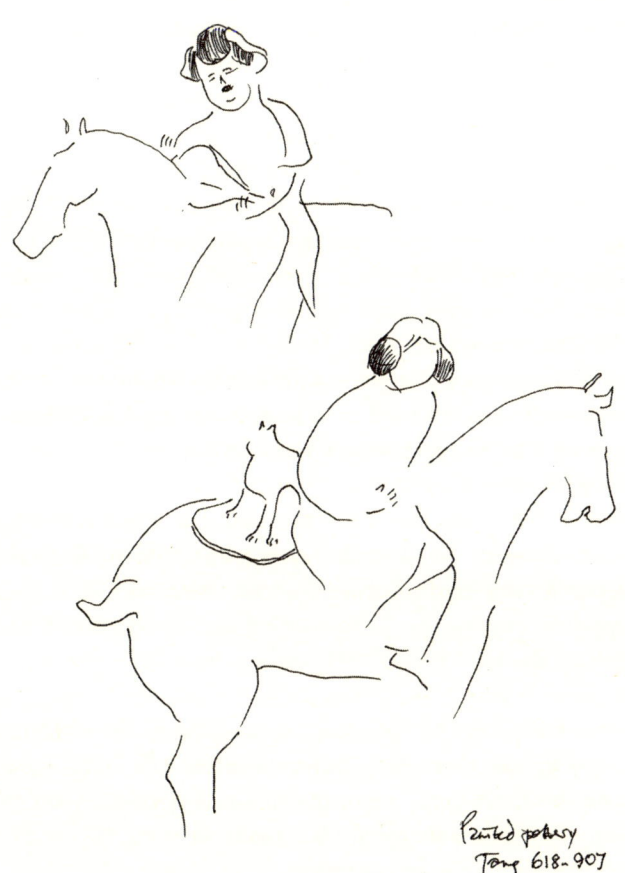

Painted pottery
T'ang 618-907

June

Solstice month.
A midsummer's day deadline for the pagoda?
Yes! It can be done.
You look to the heavens for markers if not signs. But I need skilled workmen: marblers for the terrace, tilers for the rain room. Habilis can lay stone while I cut; either of us can tile at a pinch. But this job I want done well.

4 June

ROOFTOP FEARS
Litchi season, mango season. Hordes of parrots flocking to the groves, screeching as they go. A scout will land in the coral and eyeball the prize tree on the 433, our rose-scented litchi.

The koel is merely malignant, but the parrot is evil. No wonder he takes up with man, talks. The only bird that flies backwards.

Watch this one hover with rose-scented fruit in its beak and, slowly, *reverse,* landing further back on the same branch.

Diabolus.

7 June
Ever since the threshold went in, like a bridge in the wilderness, it has shown up the floor. The spaces on either side of it, room and tiny forecourt, have begun to ache for tiles.

Once the floor is in, the pagoda is all but done. All bar the glass chimney. Longing now for the *finis.*

9 June

Tilers
After weeks of hunting I go to our original tile shop in Dilaram

Bazar and find not only vitreous tiles, but a tiler. Pushed by the dealer, he accompanies me home and inspects the three pagoda sites (rain room, and its little patio, for tiling, terrace above for marbling) and makes his quote. I make the feeblest attempt at bargaining, then we shake hands at his pot belly. This morning I'm up at five, last quarter moon hanging in the sky, wondering whether the tiles need soaking. We soaked the kitchen tiles overnight I remember, but these are two foot square. Where to find a tub that big?

10 June
The rain room is finally tiled. Old rose, with a centred square in ivory below the skywell. Its glass finish gives it the look of an indoor pool. Your bare feet on its mirror feel wet, appear refracted. The little rosewood court beyond the threshold is not vitreous but matte: buff, with a mosque green inset. Habilis will love it.

The potbelly turned out to be a contractor. The young men he supplied, tiler and assistant, worked against the clock. Before leaving at six, after a long day's work, they decided to shift a bit of gravel for tomorrow, looking ahead at the big haul of marble. The tiler has an elfin face and lean muscular arms with two or three small tattooes, done without any special art, one a heart with initials and one a Shiva trident. He cleans up with as much care as he lays. Bent over, at the end of a hard day, a way of lifting the soft polishing cloth and peering under it that says: *you beauty!*

'The colour pales the minute you open the box,' he says, noting my initial reservations about the tone.

His word is insipid, the pheeka stronger in its weakness than the English pale. No remedy unless you choose granite, brought to a heavenly finish in some polisher's hell. I see a dust choked closet somewhere and am satisfied with this luke-crimson.

11:30 AM Waiting on the gravel.

Meanwhile the stone-setters establish the level with water and hose and mark it off all round the pagoda terrace; once the gravel is spread, the slope to the corner drain will be achieved with string held taut over little marble dolmens set at intervals across the floor.

The elf, a former mechanic who has worked ten years at this trade, cuts and shapes the marble slabs on the roof. He makes precise arrows on tile and marble with his graphite battery stick, takes no shortcuts. Yesterday he thought the single-mattress-sized slabs would have to be halved to be carried upstairs; today he hunched over them for a long time making up his mind again in silence while his assistant and I stood by, so long that I was inclined to break the silence but didn't. Then he turned to me and said:

'We'll take them up whole.'

The gravel arrives. Bhim, the flatbed rickshaw driver is thirty. Ten years he's delivered here: gravel, shingle, bricks, cement, his intense boyish face now frowning, now beaming. A Bihari, like the tilers—a stream of Biharis has worked on the 433—his parents landless sharecroppers, now living in the pukka house he's built them.

'I've had it with Dehradun', he says.

'Back home, then?'

'There's no work there. But there are rice mills in Andhra where a man can make 600/- a day. I'd go tomorrow, but I owe the Sardarji five thousand.'

Marblers

Very soon the pagoda terrace will be a sheet of white marble. On that beach the rosewood in full leaf will break like green foam. For now it's all pebbly screed, the marble sheets seemingly back to front. The tiler-turned-marbler stands under the arch noting the ins and outs at pillar and pilaster; he marks the marble page, then cuts. Where his ins and outs will fit baffles me every time till just before the slab slots in because it's all mirror thinking. Tiling, he let the apprentice learn with simple corner cuts; the marble sheets he does himself. The boy hauls and fetches: gravel, cement, water, twine, hose, bricks, the inchitape. (Biharis, they use the Hindustani *pheeta*, not 'inchitape'.)

The marble they hauled together, with hurried steps, the mistri taking the main weight at the back. After the first four he sat down to rest, the youngster, Chhotu, scoffing: 'and just *four* down?'

The two men who delivered made short work of the twelve sheets, but they had just ten steps in from the truck. Today's haul was all the way round the Bengal side of the house, a U-turn where Victor and I jockeyed the window, up the external stair (at a trot), through the iron gate, and across the roof. Cutting done on a bed of gravel, so they don't score the roof: each slab trimmed of a half-inch all round. I imagined they would cut and lay pieces as they went, working around the skywell, but the way is to picture the whole surface as a single sheet and clad it all, every inch, in a dry run. Each slab laid on gravel, eight sheets of marble laid whole, side by side, four and four, covering over the skywell completely. The skywell hole cut out of that. The far end where the boundary angles in (the old opera box, I have to remind myself) is done piecemeal.

Gravel and cement mixed and spread dry for each slab. The actual fixing in the wet comes right at the end, with a dredging of pure cement, handfuls broadcast like seed in the shadow of a slab that has been dry set—and lifted back up. Water fanned off the surface of the trowel, marble flapped like a bedsheet, then the slab is lowered one last time—*'Mind your fingers!'* Now the mistri stands on it, knocking all over with the chump end of a plank, working by sound.

Dusk as the last slabs went in, the grouting done at nightfall. Ribs to flange the skywell cut at the last minute. The cleanup, as on slab day, done in haste, in the dark. Bar the pouring of the slab, this was the longest day of work on the pagoda.

My legs destroyed. I need two days' rest after, but get one.

11 June
4:23 AM Doors banging, trees bending, dust blitzing this keyboard.

Up since three. Useful hour up on the pagoda terrace before the storm, drawn up there by the weird tug of the dying moon. White marble of the new terrace steeped in that wan light. Puddles of purged moonlight in the rosewood shadows; black rosewood hole at the cicatrice where the tree lost its chief branch to the terrace slab. Graveyard-shift stars: head-over-heels Cassiopeia, not seen for months, the Plough handle just visible, the share dug into the earth, a whole range of unknowns overhead.

Stood the wrecked table, its top long gone, on one end to do a mock-up of the glass chimney. It fit the mouth exactly, and was four feet high. Pure chance, and just standing it there told me the chimney could be done.

3:00 AM Always a good hour, the last roisterer in bed. Only a cop on a bicycle giving directions to a walker in a great hurry. When they're gone, just the slipper moon. My shadow cast down the skywell through the topless table frame, I go and stand below looking up through the well mouth at the slipper. An hour later as dawn floods the white bougainvillea from the east, the doomed slipper light persists like dew from above.

In just two days the works have been turned around: the study transformed, the little court tiled, the terrace marbled. *We are very close.* Now the glass chimney looks doable, the 21st of June's a distinct possibility.

I go over a guest list, start to think of a menu.

12 June

Night-table page
The *Red* page proofs have been scratch paper for the present book. The last book always backs onto the next in this way, its verso blanks on the night-table, riddled with pencil scrawl. The longer you leave working out the scrawl, left-hand jottings, arrows shot off in the dark, the harder they are to make sense of. This page, miraculously, has no overwriting:

<u>China King</u>:
dim sum parcels
spring rolls   *cut and dry PALM FANS*
wonton?
    finger food

                KABARI:
                iron rod for the frieze stand
                tin sheet for the frieze
    at the ceremony:
                EXPLAIN <u>skywell</u>

15 June

Nightmare at 3:30 AM: spidery threads of blood on a face bending slowly over me. I lunge out and find myself clutching a chairback. Get out of bed, unlatch the gate, and walk up and down the empty Racecourse road, trembling. It's a wonder ghouls haunt a man, when all the violence he need ever fear will come from a man or a machine.

I stop in my tracks. On the crest of a black hill straight ahead, a point of yellow light has appeared. As I stand there the point begins to rise, like the tip of a pickaxe. Always that Trotskyish prickle of scalp under the icepick.

A crescent moon setting is the crescent moon we mostly see, just after sunset. To watch a crescent moon *rise* you have to be up at half past three in the morning. It's a chastened moon, quite unlike the stripling of yore. It peers out with a watchfulness the Forest Dweller will recognize, sombre but undaunted, looking down with dispassion on a sleeping world. You watch it come up and know your days are numbered. And weirdly, warily, you rejoice. This was one rising you had to see, and it happened quite by chance.

Pagoda of the remnant.

It's the hour when the trees breathe easiest, farthest each way from the busy world. For this half-hour until four the whole road is theirs, and yours. Then the mullahs begin to bray and the milk truck goes by and the first of the fitness crowd begin their hawking and striding and arm-swinging. No gap this precious in the almanack, Tuesday acolyte, not in the whole benighted country, a moment of oneness with the crickets and the smallest stars.

Pagoda of the unseen.

—*Every man asleep, Forest Dweller sir?*
—*Or pulling on his sport socks, boy. So the trees breathe evenly, at peace.*
—*And the last particle of carbon from the Polo has settled, sir?*

NOON GARDEN CHORE FOR JUNE
- *Sow drills of radishes and spinach.*
- *Watch them drown in July.*

19 June

Unbearable heat. Yesterday we slid open the hatch above the bathtub, mangoes peering in.

Last night when the fan died I slipped into the cold tub.

'Building and writing converge,' I explain to the stars, steering two fingertips towards each other, 'and meet on the 21st June.'

[The fingertips miss and cross over, ships passing in the night.]

Rise dripping, cool for the next hour. Maeve sleeps on through the power failure.

20 June

In the countdown to the solstice rite Habilis and Victor let me down. They were supposed to come yesterday to help install the glass chimney. Today, again, they failed to appear. Tomorrow is the ceremony.

I needn't have pitied the marblers: each 12 mm glass pane is karmically half the weight of a marble sheet. I take up two sheets before dinner with a rest stop in between, then two at bedtime. During the haul I tell myself neither Habilis nor Victor is to blame: I didn't tell them about the solstice bash. Partly I wasn't sure we'd make the deadline, and so left the invitations to the very end.

Twenty guests coming.

THE ALMANACK PREDICTS

—*Rain tomorrow at a quarter past four, Good Householder.*
—*The Rain Dance will be a success, sir?*
—*Judge for yourself, boy.*

21 June

The Sino-Indian Eclectic Circus

6:45 PM Guests, each required to bring a flask of ice, led to the rooftop carrying palm fans. A ring of upturned clay waterpots, prize-pumpkin size, up there: at the centre of the roof, where the badminton net might be. In one court a black tar barrel, in the other a white drinks trolley. Hottest year of the century, hottest day of the year, so naturally we have a bonfire on the roof. Ritually we burn in the tar barrel loose page proofs from *Red* on which each guest has sky-written his or her sin of the year: champion sinners get to fan the leaping flames. Then the fans are burnt: a dry palm frond, with fifty points to every leaf, burns spectacularly. An excitable sinner races about with hers (an architect) as others cower. The ice flasks find their first use as the flames are ceremonially quenched.

The second use for ice: the High Priest reads a passage from *The Small Wild Goose Pagoda* heckled at any pause and ritually stoned with ice cubes at every fullstop.

Towering over us all, the iceberg of the glass chimney, set in white marble under a silver arch.

7:21 PM The penance undergone, the High Priest in kimono mounts the steps to the marble terrace. At Dehradun sunset, we chant the sun into the ground. 7:22 PM! A large earthen pot flies through the air. It falls in the ring of pots with a bang. Maeve who slipped away to set out the food down below wonders at the explosion.

Lastly, High Priest whips a cloth off the tea trolley to reveal a punchbowl. He pours vodka, soda, pomegranate juice, on the rocks. (Third ice use.)

'Good vodka down the drain.'

'I'll have plain soda.'

'No ginger?'

The day that began with glass ends with glass: the glassware washed, every last wineglass gathered up from the random corners where the party spread; one perched on a ledge by the swing seat. (Who was that?) Dump food remains in the compost and walk the bagged rubbish to the bin. Lights out at ten.

22 June
Ashes scattered over the roof. Wind but no rain last night.

Sweep up, carry the tar barrel down, then slip into the bathtub. Dhani crouched outside, so I make not a splash. A bathtub he considers decadent, if not perverted. Read half a page, then just lie there and stare at the mangoes. The sun, now one day past the solstice, edging up on me. At noon the shadow of the gnomon slices me in half, to fall in with a line on the wall drawn the year the sunroom was first constructed.

The day rings hollow after yesterday's high drama. At noon I find Maeve sitting quietly on the swing seat, rocking. A host of ants on the white plate she put down. When I blow on them they freeze, toes dug in, skaters on a Dutch pond.

I email:
```
dan
we celebrated the solstice here as a kind of fullstop
to the pagoda and therefore the pagoda book
twenty people on the roof each with a flask of ice
ice used in three ways
1. to quench the flames of a bonfire just before sunset
(our worst summer in a half century)
the fire in a tar barrel set at one end of the roof
and lit with sins written on the back of loose
sheets of red
fanned with palmyra fans by the four worst sinners
(the fans then also burnt, quite spectacular that
with their frilly ends)
2. to stone the reader of a short passage from **the
small wild goose pagoda** (me)
3. to ice a ceremonial punch on a trolley set at
the opposite end of the roof
large ghara (clay pot) exploded at the climax of
the ceremony 7.22 local time, sunset
hurled from the newly (white) marbled terrace of the
pagoda by the high priest (who else)
into a ring of gharas at the centre aligned with
the new glass chimney
(at the skywell of the new study)
etc
```

Cc John, and friends across the seas. I feel this need to report the proceedings, to sign a quietus to the whole pagoda progress. Besides, these are the friends I write for.

4 PM The storm comes a day late. In the true monsoon, rain turns on like a tap from a grey sky, but pre-monsoon showers have a sense of theatre: sand seethes in the ear as trees groan and sway, *barukh habba, barukh habba*. Mangoes flail, the avocado tree is bent right over. A leaf

will sail up into the sky as clouds of dust chase through the yard and pour in any open window. Then the first drops splat like suicides. Rain of four different kinds falls over an hour, the last a fine temperate spray that puts a glow on all that the downpour washed clean. The aluminium sheet arch shining like the future.

The phone ringing as guests call from four parts of the city.

'The ritual worked,' they shout. 'It's *RAINING!*'

'Did you doubt me?' I ask.

The roof washed down for the first time in months. The first ten minutes the gush from the downpipes ran ochre. Nip up to the rain room to find puddles on the floor under the skywell. But they're from trickles *under* the chimney, can be stopped with sealant. The glass is secure: at the height of the wind, rain lashing the roof at a vicious slant, there was just the barest clacking as the geometry of the overlap went to work.

The glass chimney

The geometry happened quite by chance, so the tube of silicon and the applicator gun weren't needed.

The night of the glass hoist I had a dizzy spell. I had meant to work in the cool of the morning, but got up late after that turn, the sun a bright band of bane at the workplace. I washed and dried each pane in that orange glare on a rubber car mat. Then lifted each in turn up onto the marble terrace, great fat sweat drops splashing on the newly dried glass. (A rug spread on the tiles in the rain room below, in case a pane fell through the skywell: the very first one almost did). The hole of the skywell fenced off all round in iron, using a desert cooler stand whose cubic dimensions match the gap perfectly. One by one the panes were lowered into place in its frame. Coming directly on the marble, the bottom edge of the first pane spalled, so I cut the Fiat car mat into narrow cushioning strips.

I'm installing the third sheet when the cowbell rings.

'Her-at-the-stove had a right royal stomach ache,' Habilis explains. Victor looking sheepish.

'I have twenty guests coming this evening,' I say, barring their way. But step aside. Lots of little jobs waiting, and the guests not expected till six. I put a lump of putty in Habilis's hands and the cobweb brush in Victor's and go back to glazing. I know Habilis is dying to see the skywell (though evidently not enough to come to work on the past two days) so what better task for him than to replace the cracked windowpane in the living room. Besides, I work better without his hectoring.

When I get back upstairs I find the third sheet of glass simply balanced there without a stay: the slightest wind could have toppled it. I call Maeve up. She holds the sheets steady while the last one is slid into place.

A thing of great beauty, bevelled plateglass. I polish it again with my singlet, tribute, and then we stand admiring the finished chimney. A crystal mountain under the solstice sun.

'How's the glass chimney?' Habilis asks when I come down.

'Go have a look,' I say. 'Memsahib finished it,' I call after him. That'll gall.

The overlap? Every standing sheet projects an inch beyond the one it meets at the corner, a stay. Each a check on the next, and the next, and the next. The pattern of infinite interlock a gift of chance: the sheets simply slid into place that way, and the strongest of winds doesn't rattle them.

23 June

Still moving in a sleepwalk. Fit only for zombie work. The drumstick harvest sorted into crooked and straight, the crooked for the kitchen, the straight for giving away. Lunch of leftovers, the corn-filled dumplings from China King best of the lot.

A feeling there's just one corner to turn. Now the last days of the build must be written up.

I need a cut-out of the small wild goose for the frieze of animals around the glass chimney. Also cut-outs of a galloping horse, a seated dog, a cricket with feelers extended. I picked up a sheet of tin at the kabari's but my tin snips are not up to the job. No hurry now the ceremony is over. I can take my time with the adornments. In September, when our China group meets for the last time, I want to bring back from Yellow Mountain a windchime to hang over the skywell. I see it already, suspended there, stirring with every current that rises from the rain room below.

24 June
I go up to the rain room in the afternoon and am drawn to sit in the armchair at the window where a gentle crosscurrent makes the afternoon heat bearable. My slippers are at the door: the large glassy tiles demand this respect and reward you with a mirror finish. A monk of ancient times would be entranced. The floor inverts the rosewood tree, every last leaf and zigzag stem trapped in ivory. I look at the tiles, at the window, the deodar doors, and say out loud:

'Sahi bana!' Pleased at once to have used Hindi by instinct. Well made.

I tilt my head back. The skywell looks right too. It breathes out air, breathes in light. A grey cloud drifts into view, spreading like a stain. Its ragged edges offset a series of crisp yet random chevrons: the forward corner of the well, the corresponding angle in the iron stand above it, and a still higher V in the arch frame, all made at different times and for different purposes. A hawk glides by and slips away.

25 June
Installed at last! This morning brought up lamp, table, and cooler to the rose study. Now sit typing under the skywell, its glass chimney a kaleidoscope that twins every real angle with reflections in plate glass. A right angle becomes a blanched Maltese cross, the silver girders under the great sail of the arch become the receding ribs of an old flying machine. Even where the sky is not visible, in the Pak direction, where that house hides it, it appears reflected in plateglass, a smoke-blue skin. Phantom swifts bank and vanish there, colliding with a flock in the square of real sky. Below, the limewash walls return you to yourself. Installed at your mapmaker's desk, you must deliberately turn your head to see the world: the rosewood patio one way, and the back garden the other.

The thing is done. Nothing for it now but to finish the book of the thing.

The gooseneck

Hauling the tar barrel downstairs the day after the circus, I drag it through the brick arch to its home on the gooseneck behind the swung wall. This corner of the garden is the nearest thing we have to a wilderness: it's where a small wild goose might choose to nest. It lacks a water body, but when the monsoon makes a water butt of the tar barrel it'll have that too. The high wall and the arched entranceway festooned with wisteria give it an air of sequestered sovereignty, a republic unto itself. (The swell of the goose chest comes at the arch then narrows to a long neck behind the mulberry; there's even a head and beak tucked behind the swing seat alcove.) It's a hide like the ones sought out in childhood, full of dappled shade and fallen leaves. A lanky Persian lilac overshadows an African podocarpus with needle-like leaves, a silver oak bides its time in the far corner where the goose's eye would be. Three papayas, too young to fruit, lean away from Tibet. This is the one space Dhani doesn't bother with.

This hot afternoon I restack some bricks to make a seat, disturbing two frogs in green fatigues. Like the Venturi alley, the gooseneck has its own induced draught. Bright yellow switches fallen from the young papaya trees litter the crazy paved path that curves from the archway into the far corner. All broken things come here. A white crust like snow marks the spot where the tilers heaped the marble tailings. Marble offcuts, half-tiles, broken panes of glass lean in corners. Upturned flowerpots are stacked among potsherds and brickbats, stone chips berm a soil that's spongy by July. The shattered gourd pot of the solstice ceremony had a band of leaves in low relief around the shoulder. A terracotta leaf from that explosion glitters among real leaf fall, wisteria, star jasmine, Persian lilac. Black leaf shadows play over them, cast by a sun whose gold lies scattered on the ground. When a breeze runs through the treetops the whole floor jitters, a stock exchange.

27 June

I walk up on the roof in sketchy rain and think of the monsoon morning when the idea of a tower first dawned. The pagoda stands there, an idea magicked into fact.

Magic? Hardly. Some part of Victor is still up on the slab, huddled in the corner with the hired mistri, cement slurry lapping at his feet, Habilis heckling from below. I see Beauty spelling one of the two old men, feel my own crippling tiredness at the end of that day. The solstice ritual *was* a piece of magic, with flaming tar barrels and exploding pots and cloths whipped off gleaming punch bowls, but even there the props wanted carrying up and down.

28 June

Magick
When I was a young man writing my first novel in Lucknow, a man used to sit on the pavement outside our apartment with a tiny motorized wirebrush. He polished watchstraps. There was always a knot of people standing around at that corner of Hazratganj. I think it was the pleasure of watching work simplified, or speeded up, that did the trick. Work made magic. (It also showed—a burnished watchstrap—how easily we were pleased.) I hope the man got rich. Further back, at childhood fairs, stood the man with the magic vegetable slicer: it was cranked of course, but it too let you diddle drudgery, and it drew a crowd as big as the one for the boy with two heads. Wizards of efficiency, the men were also deliverers from labour. But their machines were the inventions of a practical race; when the same task can be simply handed to a drudge, as with us, the spur to invent falls away. Habitual delegating of practical tasks enfeebles; it also dents the standard of material production. This other magicking, the evading of labour, and its attendant disregard for workmanship, explains why our goods are shoddy, why our hardware lags behind our software. It shows in the state of our trades and trade schools, and our top-heavy education, where learning has outstripped knowledge.

At college in Delhi I ran into another magick set, their watchword, *er-who bothers*, spoken with an Indo-Oxford drawl, their favourite novelist P.G. Wodehouse. I used to wonder at the appeal of this man from another age and climate but I didn't see that it was less the humour than the class calling; the appeal lay in the delicious idleness and the pranks of that vanished Edwardian moment. (A member of the college Wooster Society knocks off a policeman's 'helmet', gets caught and thrashed: hilarious. His parents get him off the hook). Princelings, industrialists' sons, the flower of their class, they were there to fill in time, and did. This was the function too of all novel-reading up to Defoe. Until *Robinson Crusoe* the novel looked to make leisure interesting, with chivalry or romance or simply sword-fights. The trick dies hard: every illusionist is inclined to leave out the sweat (but not the blood, James Bond) the sweat (but not the tears, Mills and Boon). The novel of ideas sweats to give you the impression of labour, of working things out. Even poetry leaves out all marks of work, then indentures you forever. *Il miglior fabbro*, remains a two-edged compliment, the magician's nod; the finer craftsman must bite his lip, poor sod.

29 June

Samarkand
I slap the laptop shut and run down the iron staircase to the gooseneck. When work becomes a fetish contemplation calls the worldling apart.

There's such a thing as overwork. Out of the depths of your fatigue you want to scream. You begin to dream of another place, of simple distraction there, of days of idle looking. This dream place looks familiar—from books, from vanished childhood photographs—but it is virginal. Yet it's not novelty calling: I have never visited those chocolate-box castles on the Rhine, nor have I ever wished to: there's a whole arc north of the Alps that I happily take on faith. So what is this land I've been dreaming of lately?

Only a handful of places on earth left calling. Most are clustered not so far from here as the goose flies. I've dwelt on them all my life. One December when I was seventeen we stood all night up to our knees in icy water just beyond those hills to the south, waiting for the geese to land. The hours went slowly, my feet were numb, my father and his shooting friend got drunk, my mother scolded, but we got our birds for the Christmas table. The flock were winter visitors, Siberian geese that had just flown over the Himalayas. Today I want to turn goose, to do their journey. I plot a route for them, see them settle on various lakes and marshes on their way south. Many of the sites on this route are wildly off course for a goose, but the radar of this flock is all askew: its charts take in the Uzbek cities of Bukhara and Samarkand. The route is of course not for the geese at all: it's an excuse for me to sit in some courtyard in Shiraz, to dawdle in the Fergana valley, to stand in the atrium of the Bibi Khanum Mosque and frown at some detail in the vaulting lit by those fabled alabaster skylights. The temple architecture of China failed to stir me, some slight discontent, as in Europe, always intervening. Some similar lack, or excess, in Hindu and Buddhist and Mayan temples (or again in me) nags at one, and the gamut seems run through.

Then the simplest Muslim gesture in stone—from Morocco to Tajikistan, it could be nothing more than a heap of rubble in the desert—redeems the race. The Islamic dome still unsurpassed. A lifetime's looking, much less a Forest Dweller's span, would just scratch the surface of that unparalleled half millennium of building. (Can it be that it takes a desert to wring the truest urge? No monument in India to match the stupa at Sanchi, on a hillock rising out of a stony plain.) Sitting in the gooseneck I plot a pilgrimage to Transoxiana, to monuments that were not yet built when Xuan Zang came by.

I grew up on the flat Gangetic plain. We never understood perspective or prospects. Courtyards were our comfort, high walls our delight. A view was something you held, or aired, strongly. (A caravanserai would have been too much to ask for.) The gooseneck is the cloister's cloister: you sit on a makeshift seat, your back up against the curve of the swung wall, the true boundary hardly three feet away. Brick walls of great character surround you, mossed and bearded, crusted in places with a shaggy grey-green scale, plaited with maidenhair fern and pocked with slag holes. In a dungeon this size you'd be apoplectic, but this cut is open to the sky. Wildings apart, you have for company the juvenile papayas, the patient podocarpus (a Gondwanaland survivor), the upstart Persian lilac, the Australian silver oak. There are edifying ruins to contemplate, the wreckage of the civilization beyond the swung wall (a house with a pagoda attached). A crust of bread will see you through the afternoon, now the punchbowl's empty, and Beauty (Khayyam's Thou) fled. The book of verse is in your head, and the days are getting shorter.

The gooseneck is too narrow for labour. You can't swing a mattock here; at best you could raise chickens. (A dovecote would take building.) It was always a glorified potting shed, and could still be a toolshed, but tools would violate its neutrality. Once the trees have grown proper trunks, the Mongolian hammock can be slung here. A hammock is a hyphen: hanging here, among the empty flowerpots and marble tailings, it'll mock ambition and preserve this corner as a refuge.

—*All Work Abandon Ye Who Enter Here, sir?*
—*Well, maybe cross out* Work *and put in* Action.
—*Done, sir.*
—*Better still: All* Thought *of Action. No, wait, make that: All Thought of the* Fruit *of Action.*
—*Meditate on it, sir?*
—*Yes, never mind. Wash the brush, though.*

The cloister gives pause, but this small wilderness is time's undoing.

In the ornate lobby of the Regency waiting for my train to ~~Datong~~. Mongol kitsch or Mongol taste:

Gengiz Khan today

July

1 July
Furnishing the new study. One at a time, pencils, cushions, books, go up the iron stair. The smart little cooler, China-made, already up and running.

Last week's chance find: a mottled pink-and-black granite offcut, of shelf width and eight feet long, longer than the room. Trim it to fit and go looking for someone who'll round off the fore-edge. A stone polisher turns up and thinks the job not worth his while, so I bevel it myself with the angle grinder. Suddenly a bookshelf worthy of the room.

Hot. This afternoon I pushed a tempo driver who almost ran me down. He saw me crossing but nosed in so I all but fell. First went up close and whispered menacingly in his ear he should respect pedestrians, then before I knew it pushed his head—not hard, just jogged it like a country barber—and walked away. He kept calling after me—for what? a fight, an explanation, a finger?—but I refused to turn. This summer has been hideous, tempers lost up and down town.

2 July
Cool after this morning's shower. Can rest, even think. Yes, the gooseneck slights the tower, but the tower's a beauty. Every time I open the iron door onto the roof I marvel at it. Geometry of arch and canopy and skywell, but equally the materials: silvered aluminium, plate glass, and wrought iron, the whole ensemble floating on a sheet of white marble.

Down below, you see the tower from the street, a silver pavilion rising above the rosewood tree. Or from the cloister, from its entrance at the redstone patio: the old iron arch there, covered in red quisqualis, now rhymes with a silver arch above.

When we brought the iron arch home from the welder seven

years ago it had to be hoisted over the front wall (the way the burglar came) because it wouldn't fit through any gate. The pagoda arch came over the same way, the two segments, each a complete arch, ferried home from the welder's one by one on the Fiat roof like tiaras. Next they were hauled up onto the house roof—the Bengal-side corridor not nearly wide enough—with Terry's rope from God-knows-when (it would have pulled the Fiat out of some jungle waterhole in its day). The pagoda arches remained up there, bolted together on the roof; the iron arch let down again, lowered with the same rope into the cloister.

Last night during the power failure I put up a mosquito net on the lawn. Woke at dawn head to head with Stoneman, and lay there wondering: is my repeated pushing out of house walls simply a doomed effort to recreate the mosquito nets of childhood? Only the poor sleep out any more; the middle class is afraid to. Every night during the hot summer months we slept under the sky. Nothing so comforting as those gauzy enclosures, airy yet protective, at once communal and private, each bed a ship or tent you learnt to slip into without letting in the enemy, mosquito or gremlin, while leaning out for one last glimpse of the stars.

4 July
The Pingyao gate, a few steps in from the outer gate, and a few more from the front verandah, is our real gate now, an iron door that swings shut to lock out the world. Dhani has learnt to draw the new door shut behind him on his way out. He doesn't put the bike back on its stand but simply turns and crooks a finger round the door and pulls it to. It swings silently and as it does he begins to wheel the bike again so the mudguard isn't knocked, then just when it's aligned with the pillar he stops it with the same crooked finger and goes on his way.

The wicket gate at the front wall (with bars anybody could look through) is a now token gate, some nights not even shut. The little vestibule between the two gates, an enclosed section of the old brick path, is festooned with harp-seat passion fruit and hedged with bamboo; white bougainvillea spills from the garage roof. A visitor can compose himself there before ringing the cowbell. Today's courier gave it a little tinkle while I signed, and smiled.

The young squirrels that live in the hollow garage pillar are testing their teeth. They've twice gnawed through the cowbell rope and Maeve is looking for a length of wire to hang it by.

5 July
I carry Dan's early Victorian edition of *Selborne* up the iron stair. Juliet's oakleaf hydrangea is dead, killed by the monsoon, last of that fragrant Scottish cargo.

Victor brings gulab jamuns, the spoils of a wedding job. He takes out a big note and hands it to me, returning the last loan. I tell him I want his work, not his money, but take the sweets. Just *one* more, he murmurs, the gracious host, and rolls out two from a polythene bag that has further to go. Stolen sweets are sweetest.

Tomorrow I must shave, after a week ('Hezbollah,' Maeve mutters every time we pass), and go get Dhani a set of wheels. His rims are warped and his tyres flat and worn.

'If you let them go flat that kills the tubes, Dhani, even without riding.'

These tyres are bald and not even a pair, definitely not the tyres bought when we last remade his bike.

'The bike wala did some jiggery-pokery.'

'Now I have a pump we'll fill the tyres here.'

I want to show him how much easier it is to wheel a bike with inflated tyres. Pushing, he's forgotten, and seems not to care, but it would lighten his daily round.

7 July
Yesterday, up the twelve-foot ladder, clinging with one hand to green willow wands as I lopped the branches that stuck into the power lines, I felt for the first time in danger of falling.

The body begins to fail. Tree-lopping is work for a younger man. Even Victor, holding the ladder, has grey in his sideburns.

—Sick of this *householding*, boy.
—Forest Dwelling is not forestry, Aged Forest Dweller.

—*Nor orchardry? Today Maeve spotted the first avocado.*
—*Worth seven years watching over the tree, sir?*
—*With avocadoes, worth every slice. With a squeeze of lime, and two turns of the pepper mill.*
—*Her-at-the-binoculars spotted the first sparrow in years, sir. An albino hen.*

Sitting in the new study, I x-ray the pagoda. These old deodar doors hung a hundred years in some bungalow, keeping out the winds of another century. The threshold lay in some neighbouring house, worn down by generations of feet. The iron frame overhead is twice reincarnated: a desert cooler stand on castors that became a marble table, it's now a glass-chimney brace. There the recycling ends. Plateglass and marble are new, and the vitreous tile. I run an eye over the floor: it's a limpid pool of old rose with one step down in the middle where you dip your feet in ivory. The limewash walls will presently match that shade. I have my ivory tower. But for the opera box none of this would exist. The roof of the portico was a leafy nest and would have stayed that way. Yet now it's done there's a rightness, an inevitability to it. Writing up here, after a series of interruptions below, the seclusion fits.

Since the rains broke the air is washed clean, a little chill. A fine spray of monsoon mist comes down the skywell prickling the skin and dusting the laptop screen with tiny beads that take on the colour of the pixel band behind, red or green or blue; larger droplets show all three with a leadlight line of black in between like stained-glass.

The cowbell rings. I go all the way down the iron stair, across the redstone patio, through the kitchen, and out the front to see who it is, and find it's a young squirrel from the garage family. But there's a sadhu in saffron passing by on the road, with trident and bowl and matted locks, and it's worth the trek just to see him walk.

Maeve, my barometer, says after hearing me out the other night (I told her for the first time about the student and the householder and the Forest Dweller, and how they are used in the tale) that really the Ascetic stage is the least convincing in the classical schema.

'If the Ascetic has to wander, that stage should come at fifty when he still has his legs.'

'Better still forty,' I say. 'That's when I did the Yukon.'

But the two last stages *are* entangled. Unless what was meant was a distinction between the onset of old age and the twilight of your last years.

'Is Dad the Ascetic?'

He's been mailing lately, happy with the computer he distrusted just last year, getting me to disburse his pension: today I must write out one of his blank cheques to the Clara Swain Hospital, started by an American in the mid-nineteenth century. The missionaries who ran the hospital were among our good friends in Bareilly fifty years ago, sunny Californians with spring mattresses and 3-D slide viewers and baroque Jello moulds.

8 July

Steve Alter buys the old Fiat, gets it going and drives back up the hill. Virginia, the VW, watches them go with ill-disguised relief.

—*He'll teach her new positions, sir. Her-in-the-back-seat reckons the old lady needed a change.*

—*Ah yes, boy, the American is full of exotic tricks. He'll bring a new urgency to her twilit years.*

On the same day Arvind turns up in his shiny yellow Nano, its teardrop shape and 600 cc engine a perpetual reproach to all guzzlers.

—*Good Householder, what's that green card in your pocket?*

—*[Hesitantly] New York calling, sir. Her-with-the-reins has been to the American embassy.*

—*[Pause] Why am I not surprised, boy, inside my surprise.*

—*Dog-walking's a pain, sir.*

—*Well, go be the pet.*

—*We leave on Monday, sir.*

—*Go peddle spice like all the rest. Tradesmen's entrance for you, boy.*

— *She has a job lined up.*

—*Oh, all right! Go well. Put down roots. Be that thing. For god's sake don't live there and spout India.*

—*I'll look after the boy for a bit, sir.*

—*Good man. Drive a taxi, stay free. Keep clear of that brown-nose expatriate crowd. Fall in with them and India becomes a topic: 433 trillion square yards of handy topos. Stuck there, licking ass (they'll say kicking), playing the bent old India card.*

10 July

THREENECKS
The schools are open again after the summer break. Once again a thousand children go past the gate in their various uniforms. They are noisier on the way home, Maeve remarks, than on the way to school. I watch an older cousin drag a little boy in tartan shorts: the boy allows himself to be led with the constrained air of an animal; he has trouble keeping up, and his solemn concentration and slow stretched gait as he steps carefully along suggest an old man. The cousin, unshaven and possibly unemployed, carries the boy's bulging school bag and clearly can't wait to get home; in fact their ways parted long ago.

—*Forest Dweller sir, that almirah you lent us…*
—*Tipped over? Don't tell me!*
—*No, no, nothing like that. It's fine, but Her-with-the-home-science shipped it ahead to New York. She couldn't live without it, sir. Nor could I. Every time she steps out of it my heart…*
—*Mail me, boy.*

Shi Jun

In the museum beside the Small Wild Goose Pagoda in Xian I found a richly carved sarcophagus with scenes from a man's life. It had only just been unearthed, after a thousand years, the resting place of a Sogdian from the far end of the Silk Route. The man was Shi Jun, or Wirkak to use his Turkic name, a caravan leader who died in 579, some twenty years before Xuan Zang was born. A prosperous merchant, he was the leader of the Sogdians settled in Chang-an. I stood by his sarcophagus a long time, so long my legs ached, then drew a single scene from one of the lesser panels. It shows a forest hut that could be anywhere, perhaps in the land Wirkak left behind with its forests of spruce and walnut and wild apples. In the doorway of the hut sits a turbaned man, perhaps a hermit, drinking from a cup. Outside sits a well-dressed man on a rug, also drinking; they appear to be smiling. It's a convivial scene, unlike the stern encounter you see in countless miniature paintings where a king has come with his retinue to call on an ascetic. Less exalted callers sit nearby among the shrubs that ring the hut, and a dog, also apparently smiling, stretched out beside the rich man. It's hard to say whose dog he is, or who's richer, or happier, the hermit or the merchant (or the dog) but in this moment of stone, as a brace of wild geese fly over the roof of the hut (where a vine has burst into flower) it's anybody's guess. It's only when I look again at my sketch I see that no one there is speaking. It's the silence of deep contentment. Not disease, not war, not calamity—all of which will come—not time itself, can touch this moment.

Visits and visitors should be rare, or you risk the vulgarizing of character Charlotte dreaded at Haworth. You long for company and then you long for solitude. The telephone rings and sometimes you answer. One should be free to talk or not. The best callers, birds, make no demands. Without a word the Sogdians drink at the door of the forest hut, without a sound the small wild geese pass over the forest skywell.

16 July
Letter from Home Ministry to Foreigners' Registration Office (copy) says no objection to Maeve's being issued a PIO. She is now officially a Person of Indian Origin! But won't believe till the booklet is in her hands.

Reading out the word 'sojourn' in *Karamazov*, she puts the emphasis on the second syllable.

'You're not a Person of Indian Origin by any chance?' I ask her. 'PIO' a catchword now, like *'Aged P'*.

Day by day my speech approximates hers, and hers mine. I say 'frudge' for fridge; she says 'conwent' for convent.

THREENECKS

A death by cancer, a young man in the house under the cell phone tower. The drum kit at the top of the tower has been growing lately. Our emissions are ten times international levels.

20 July

The iron stair screened at last. Habilis and Victor gone till autumn. Both took their full wage (Habilis requires, Victor asks: I admire the nerve of the one, the nervousness of the other), both left owing money, roughly the cost of the fibreglass and iron. Shouldn't materials and labour be on par anyway? Leaving, Victor turns full face and smiles 'Namaste.' Habilis strides off flinging a hearty 'Namaskar' over his shoulder. It's a long walk at the end of a hard day. Sairu hauls himself up off the garage floor where he's slept the day away, and goes trotting after.

I'm in the shower before they turn the Dhobi Corner. The last few days have been harder on me than on them: such days I don't have sympathy to spare.

21 July

Fall back into bed after tea. Sleep fitfully till seven, dreaming of a dark flower. Plod upstairs in the failing light, open the roof door onto a lemon sky.

'You missed a sunset,' says Maeve, already up there.

As she speaks a faint shaving of ice appears in the faded pink, forming not melting. A new moon.

We watch it into the trees. A month since the midsummer pagoda rite, so that was a new moon night too. *Pagoda of the sliver.*

22 July

After a year of wondering where to put the Chinese orange I carry the pot upstairs and set it on the landing of the stage steps. It fits, all but sucked into place. *Pagoda of waiting.*

23 July

Insomnia. *Stop* it, I tell myself. Sleep. And stop right here at Forest

Dwelling. The Ascetic is another story.

4 PM Habilis turns up, looking more drawn and anxious than I've ever seen him. His brother has killed a man. It happened in his village, point blank, and in the melee he disappeared. Now he's on the run. The day Habilis left here in a hurry he was going to his village to tell the family to tell the brother, one of four, to keep clear of his house here. Too late. The police came by to question him. Warned, he and his family left by the back way, ran along the riverbed, and went to stay with friends outside town. The police have put a lock on his door so he can't get back in. No one can. His younger son left half naked and all his clothes, everybody's clothes, are locked in. They were eating dinner at the time so the food is right where they left it. I look at him. I've never seen him so twitchy, his body less his. He draws one leg up behind him where he stands and rests the foot in a flowerpot, crushing the plant. I give him a thousand. He wants more, three. I say not now, tomorrow, and just two. He nods. He won't come at this time, he says, he'll come in the evening. He thinks a tempo driver may have recognized him. There's a watch being kept on his house: one of the murdered man's cousins is sitting there with a cop in his pay. The villagers have sacked the family house in the village and all the brothers have fled.

So that's all I need: accessory to an accessory to murder.

24 July

Dhani turns up late today, Tuesday. It rained all morning yesterday so he didn't come, and three days without him is a gap. But my first glance is not at him: I look straight at the bike. It looks new. *He's changed the wheels!* Brand new tyres, shiny new rims. The spokes twinkle. The whole bike grins.

25 July

Victor just left.

He brought a large white envelope with an x-ray seemingly of a child's chest. It's his own. Also a smaller envelope with a doctor's scrawl in which the word *metastasis* appears. He says he's had trouble swallowing lately, neither food nor water goes down. The doctor has referred him to a hospital in Chandigarh where they'll run a series of tests on him. The lump in his throat could be anything. His voice breaks when he leaves, but he controls himself.

Victor! And I've been looking at Dhani. He speaks the dread word cancer without blinking, half innocent, half old hand. Last time he just had this cough. He's got a friend who'll take him to Chandigarh, whose wife went through the ordeal at the same hospital. His brother has lent him more than half the money, and he's here, though he politely refrains from asking until I make the offer, to make up the rest. I'm happy to, but I'm concerned to preserve the fiction that he's indestructible.

When he's gone I consider that in the circumstances he should get his share up front, the share I proposed to the Inquisitor. (But what will the book earn? My track record is pure woe. In ten years of building I've pushed such thoughts aside.) Better simply to meet his expenses. What troubles me is how readily I assent to his mortality. Just yesterday he was one of us, the living. Today I'm prepared to pay him off.

The thief

If death is a thief, is the thief death? Either way you'd like to give this guy the fright of his life. Hours I've waited up for him, dark monsoon nights, not even starlit, the dogs quiet. (Animal dread or poisoned meat? In presence of a tiger a dog's whole body will quake.) You sit tight behind the mesh waiting as he tries each door; you're trembling but you have a special word ready to breathe in his ear that will drive him crazy. Is it a tangle you're after—a brush with Old Bladderwrack—that'll teach him never to come back? Or do you simply want to go down fighting?

You *do* want, that much is certain, to hear him drop lightly on the lawn out of that jump from the wall, you want to hear the gravel crunch under his sandals, the clink of tines as they spill from the ruined padlock onto the verandah, time running out, on him, on you. He's your ticket of leave, but you'll send him packing. And then he reaches your door. Through the mesh you see his ruined face. The crack in his forehead is the new day; he's late today (the late Thief

Death) and anyway it's time you were about your business. Why not just leave him to what he does best? So you climb the iron stair, let him clean out the house. You sit down at the desk under the skywell, the pagoda lovelier at dawn than by moonlight, and in the first light that sifts down the chimney you start to write.

A little past midnight...

Stone Slab of
Shijun's Tomb

Northern Zhou
557-81

Waking dream this morning of a weird opera stage, young people getting ahead, some old Forest Dweller fear of being left behind. Victor in there shifting furniture, real furniture not props, in his head-down way while the prima donnas, one actually in a blonde wig, a Garhwali beauty, preen and carry on. Some link with a video watched just before shutdown last night.

BROADBAND
'Princess of China.' It's a seductive video, built on the original Coldplay song. Like a pagoda on a portico, but built on wrong. The song meant this fragile love thing (china, the material, not the country) broken, but the little drama quickly escalates, the blond hero striding along the Mongolian grassland, *show us how to walk,* mouthing his lines for Rihanna locked up in her castle, all China a stage on which black and white strut. Black and white, that have become colours for the world, colours to the world, are soon flying through the air, in the Chinese martial arts way, occupying the Chinese air, the Chinese on the ground props, palace servants, background. *Show us where to go from here.* Asia a stage for the West to figure on, still. Even a record company should not have got China so wrong. *Show us how to walk* was simply courtesy.

I switch on power and router, then lamp and laptop.

Something calls me out. I unbolt the mesh door, step onto the back verandah, into the garden. There's some glass on the lawn, from a broken window upstairs in Pak. Was the thief trying to get in there? Did he mistake the gate? Maeve told me about it last night, their servant's little son chucking the fallen pieces over our wall, till she clapped her hands and he stopped. Now she's asleep. I left her there at first light, her head on the pillow, breathing softly. This head that has made room for itself here.

THREENECKS

I unbolt the front door, swing open the Pingyao gate, unlatch the wicket gate and stand looking out at Threenecks. I'm up late. They're all already there, the morning walkers, the striders too, each one meditating on some enormous advantage. Make a morning video, I think, for the Palmyra Gallery: the Threenecks coming to life, just that. The dry-cleaner, no, start with the white-haired semaphorist in the half dark up on the Sri Lanka traffic island, then the palsied dry-cleaner, Orion baker with his swagger stick, the left-arm-swinger with murder in his eye, the dhobi's dudey sons, these three Garhwali grannies in saris, the with-it bania couple in their designer tracksuits, the Seven Sisters (a noisy group of middle-aged males with canes and umbrellas) early schoolgirls in their pale blue-and-white salwar kameezes coming over the rise at Dhobi Corner, the dog-walker with his Dalmatians, the retired accounts clerk with dyed ginger beard, the pig-girl, the tubby surd Maeve calls Justin Trotter, the crazy radio-tuner, five cops on magnificent Arabian horses walking clop-clop, the gent with one blue eye.

This is how we walk.

Dhani walks his bike, his bike walks him. His eye is on a future just beyond the mudguard of his front wheel. Nowadays that's far enough ahead. But who am I to say what's on his mind?

Housing (4)
Hard soap, as ALL who purchased the Last Issue know, is made of Wood ash, Lime, Water, Tallow, and Salt. Hard cheese, is much fimpler. Take one Garage (on rent, say) and live in it till it begins to fmell like home. A Hard-Hearted Widow of the Rentier class is not altogether necessary to the workings of this or any other recipe, or known world, but Hard Cheese is made when she changes her mind repeatedly about whether the Tenant is worthy of his hire, in cash or labour. Too Bad, Hard Cheese, Stiff Bikkie. Unlike Certain Other Almanacks, Poor Dhani's (formerly *Old Hornbill's EPHEMERRATA*, already the most widely used Almanack in **Post-Vedick Astrophysick**) minces no words. Go to the other for

amusement, but for wisdom and a certain cure come to Old Dhani. My Master who will in good time discover that the best pencil makes the worst dibblestick, and whose Quarterly visit to Doc W. has turned Half-yearly, WOULD DO WELL TO give that Quack the slip altogether and ATTEND instead *(D.R.) Hornbill's Clinic* here in his own front yard under the sign of the China Palm. **THE ALMANACK HAZARDS**: If every Houfeholder waited 24 hours before running to the Quack, the health of the world would not be greatly affected (indeed it might improve) *and* the entire Medical Industry would be reorganized upon the *Best* Post-Vedick *Principles.* As for the unholy *Inventions* currently taking shape in the new **PAGODA**, the leff said about them the Better, though I have it from the Koel that the first is almost ready, his Reverse Osmosis *Gurgitator.* Once the hinge on the flap that fits over the mouth is perfected it will return to your tongue all the wounding remarks you could never hold back. I say keep your counsel in the first place, put off the Widow's importunities, and let the cheese harden of its own accord. A hole in the Roof is a hole in the Roof, I say. Why call it a Skywell? And even if it does let in the Sky, well why has the Widow not attended to the one in this Garage? Never mind peeping Toms, there is the Monsoon to consider. Just as the (surely no-longer-young) *Sahib* does nothing but fieve ftarlight for Sorcery, this One sits Twiddling her Thums, especially now with the Dog gone, while the Deferving toil and fweat and return to a leaking Room. What if I am excessive Poor? This Almanack thinks the Widow is excessive Stingey and will publish it for all to know. MORAL: *If it ain't broke don't fix it* (Warren S____ll of K____zoo county, Michigan, pray forgive Poor Hornbill) but, hei Ram, there is a further maxim:*When it gapes it POURS.* **Let this interminable monsoon once pass and we will find another Garage for the Office of Old Dhani's Almanack.**

Irwin Allan Sealy

The monsoon does pass, and with it an era.
In September the phone rings one night and we learn that Ruth has died. Dad is stricken, but it turns my life upside down too. All October the ordeal of applying for a UK visa from India. You hate them for presuming you want to disappear there, and you hate your countrymen who disappear there. November I fly out to England to bring Dad home. But we must first get his papers in order, and he must complete a course of medication that lasts into January.

Day by day we wind down the little semi-detached house that's been his home for eighteen years. He's grown old. His heart is holding out with the new stents, but his step is unsteady as he approaches ninety, and his hearing poor. Everything must be said twice. He is also accustomed to having things done for him. The cooking I enjoy, the errands I do not. He feels his memory playing tricks and would like to hand over his affairs to me by power of attorney. Some days I find him rooted to the spot, staring into space. His wife had taken to doing the things that mattered; she carried the money, remembered his bus pass, set out his pills. Alone, he's grown confused. He sleeps poorly, has fallen in the bathroom, and feels the suppleness has gone out of his limbs. A clot in his shoulder has occasioned the warfarin programme that continues for another month. He has spells of clarity, then a phase when he forgets what happened this morning. At bedtime he'll come with a lowered head and say, 'There's no milk.' 'What's wrong with powdered milk?' I ask. Lighter to carry when there's no car. But he holds with fresh. He needs a night light, won't be left alone. My trip to Scotland is off. One night I wake to his voice on the phone calling 111 because he's having trouble breathing. When the ambulance arrives he describes his symptoms so clinically the paramedic sees at once there's no emergency. 'What am I doing here?' he asks good-humouredly, 'at 3 a.m. in the middle of a rainstorm.' At 3 a.m. too he'll come into my room and fire a series of questions into the dark. The lights go on and off all night. I feel helpless and put upon. In the middle of all this I am trying to inhabit Calcutta in 1773. I need to wrap up the book. I'm grinding my teeth. Maeve, left behind in India, flightless kiwi, emails daily. Well-wishers pour in. I'll shoot the next well-wisher.

The New Year brings hope. Little by little we have sorted out Dad's money, assembled his papers, got him a PIO card, and arranged for the shipment of his furniture to Dehradun. During all this time he has been at the medical centre every other day, the National Health system evolving. Our first set to, a shouting match I'm ashamed of, clears the air: he discovers he can do many of the things that were done for him by Ruth. Sitting in the next room I hear him phoning one by one the gas company and the electricity company and the water board to arrange the shutting off of our various supplies before we leave. He chats with the clerks at the other end, bellows meter readings. The instructions he takes down carefully do him more good than any prescription; he brightens almost immediately. He is sleeping better. Every day I watch him digging himself out.

21st January
The container is gone. We are camping in the empty house, my father and I. Now he's heading home to the 433 square yards, his wife dead, his goods on the high seas. My Aged P. I am Wemmick after all! I didn't know it, but when Maeve read Great Expectations *out loud and I first met Wemmick and his father all those years ago, half a lifetime, a course was set that has led by twists and turns to this moment. It's a fulfilment of sorts. Or will be: we have still (my heart skips a beat) to get to Heathrow, to get on the Air India flight to Delhi (by wheelchair), to get from Delhi to Dehradun, to reach the Kalidasa gate of seasons in Racecourse, to enter by the wicket gate. Then we are home. All of these hurdles, routine in themselves, represent for the Aged P a steeplechase.*

23rd
Three months I've waited for the warfarin programme to run its course. Just when my room with its Parker Knoll chair was starting to look cosy, the container. Thanks to the shippers packing has been simpler, without the usual tormenting choices. Now we're down to suitcases, for the flight. Since we're not coming back, anything left behind is left for good. His life with us will be made easier by the new orthopaedic bed, delivered last week, by his recliner chair, a rocker, by familiar things: pictures, china, clocks. One whole steel trunk, picked up from a high street recycler, is filled with photograph

albums (another, a veteran of Indian campaigns, holds things I have chosen, such as garden tools; at last I have my dig-down spade). There will even be familiar tea towels.

So we are both starting a new life in India. My life has changed so completely I feel as adrift as he must. The solitude I imagined once this book was done is now put away. Dad's life here could have gone on (John next door is ninety-five and alone) but he has declared he can't manage. Besides, he needs a change of scene. We take slow walks around the neighbourhood on which I assure him that India will cure his ailments: a warm climate will unstiffen his knees, a largely vegetarian diet thin his blood, and we'll get him the new nano hearing aids that work twice as well as the clunky National Health ones he forgets to put on now. This endless string of surgery appointments will be history; with a wallet in his pocket and no bus pass to misplace, he'll be on his way to self-sufficiency.

24th

We turn on the TV that's been sitting there black and mute since November. A big flat screen that Val next door gave them when she got a still bigger one. Just as we're leaving, this bright window. For ten weeks the supermarket, the streets around Clive Road, and my rambles in Hinton Wood, have been England. Suddenly cabinet ministers, scenery, drama. Ten minutes and we've had enough. Broadband is better, with its painless bytes, obedient if not always reliable. Last evening we checked with the BBC before walking out, and were rained on. But the trains run on time and the post comes through the door, torrents of appeals to charity and greed. They go straight in the green bin now.

25th

Grey light of morning through the curtains, small bird noises through the double-glazing. Walk to the supermarket, for their lost leader, four litres of milk. Just that. With my kind they'd go bankrupt. Home (home!) to bake an onion seed loaf with the last of the self-raising flour and the last sachet of yeast. All the garlic can go in. He won't have to worry about how he smells now.

26th

Last day but one. I check our passports ten times, the PIO card a hundred. Dad's on the back lawn crumbling fat for the blue tits. This is goodbye, blue tits. There's a sunbird plundering the guava tree this minute, in midwinter!

27th

Sub-zero out there. Frost on the grass, seagulls crying down the chimney, and we're in slippers. Hot showers, pizza, red wine. Crusoe we're not. The container left us with carpeting, with a Tibetan rug, with remaindered pictures glowering on the walls, and faint rectangles of unfaded paint where the chosen ones hung. Hurt pride emanates from the rejects, and also a bitter urge to share their relegation, if only for one more night; this is how the fallen angels felt. I go prospecting on Google Earth, but the sweep of that cunning software again conjures Lucifer cast out, cast down, as we streak across the shining planet with one last meteoric flare, swooning down upon its beauty, tumbling at breakneck speed into our valley, homing in on Racecourse and the 433.

Maeve is on the roof, crossing the badminton court in real time. She glances up at the sky where an angel's falling, then leans over the parapet, more concerned that she forgot to draw the bolt on the Pingyao gate for Dhani. Because there he is, wheeling his bike past the pollard willow, early. Habilis is late as usual. Or is he in jail? I heard his wife hauled him up before a magistrate after he tried to strangle her. And is that Victor stepping in shiny new boots along the road from Antarctica? He's spending my medical money as he thinks fit. Still a lump in his throat, but dressed to kill. And he has a message from Beauty: she's going to kill Habilis when she finds him. So he's better off on the run.

Monster winter guavas ripening on the garage rooftree. *Hide the ladder from Dad!* I shout to Maeve, forgetting we're not there yet.

God, the tamarind has shot up while I've been away!

But who's this at the gate of seasons? A half-naked sadhu all smeared in ash.

—*Good Ascetic at the Gate, how will these legs fare in twenty years?*
—*Mine are skinnier, Forest Dweller.*
—*You flatter me, friend.*
—*Flattery? What is that?*

He goes off. And suddenly, as he goes, I see what's eluded me ever since I came on the theory of the Four Stages of Life: the difference between the Forest Dweller and the Ascetic. The Forest Dweller still has room in his heart for beauty. All the beauty he has ever known, as Student and Householder, and held onto in his declining years. Every fair home science student he ever flung his waning heart at.

The Ascetic could have taught me one last lesson—only he's gone. *How to walk away.*

Even from, especially from, a pagoda.

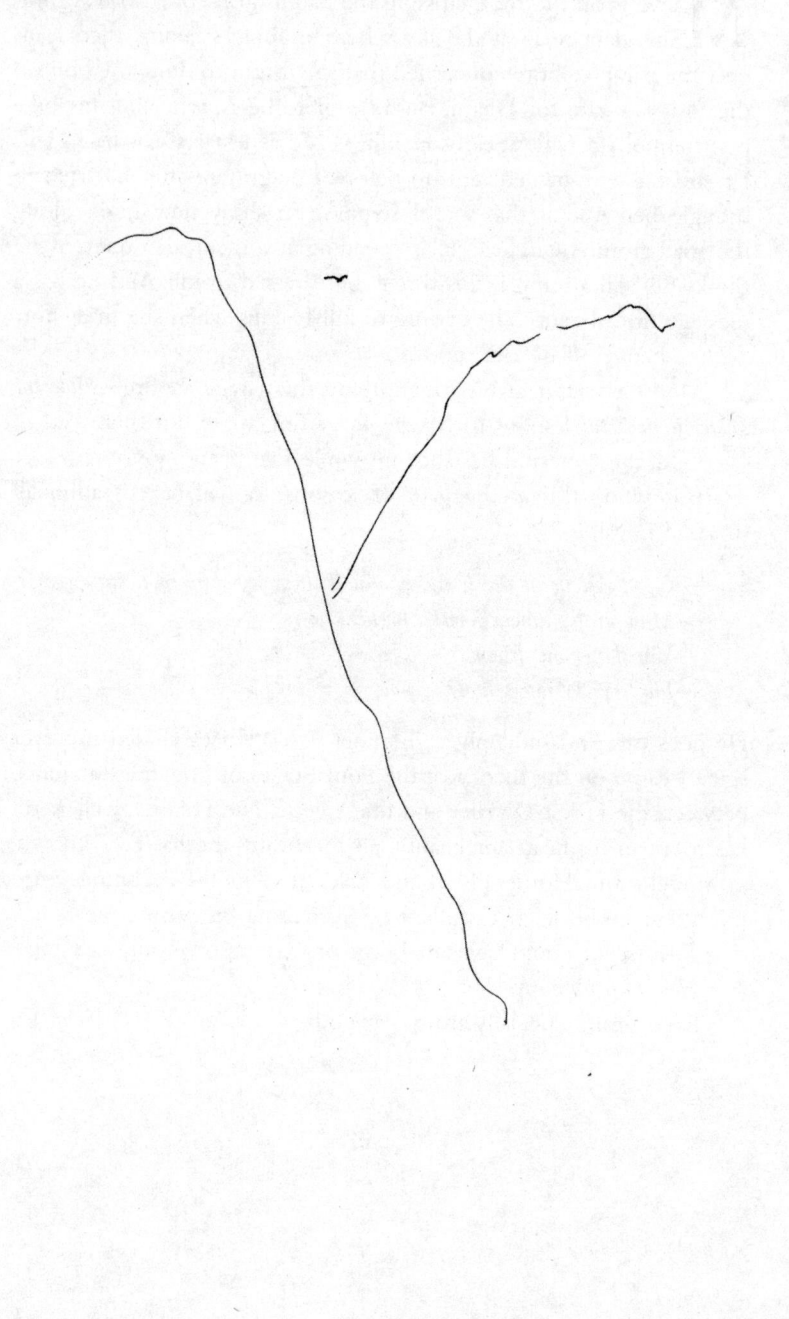

Walter ('Victor') Masih
1963?-2014